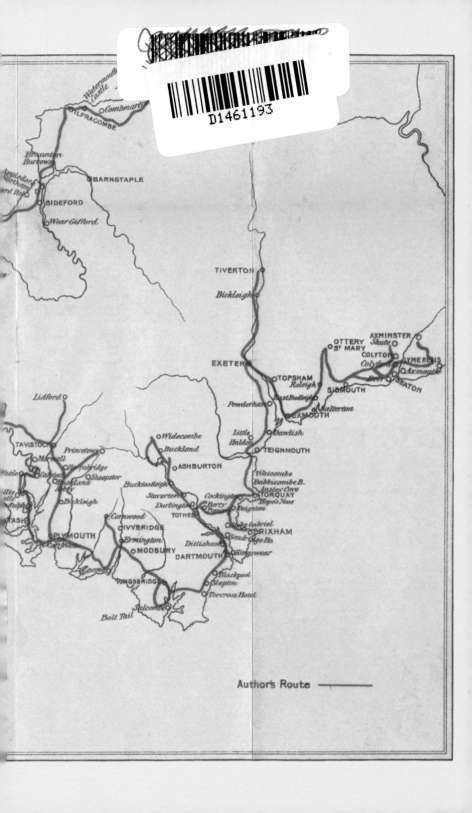

Watermouth
Castle
ILFRACOMBE   ○Combmartin
Braunton
Burrows
Appledore
Northam
ard Ho   ○BARNSTAPLE
BIDEFORD
○Wear Gifford

○Lidford

TAVISTOCK
Morwell
thele   Calstock
            Horrabridge
Buckland   Sheepstor
Abbey
Bickleigh

TASH

PLYMOUTH
Caterate
thcoud

TIVERTON○

Bickleigh○

                    OTTERY   AXMINSTER○
                    ST MARY   Shute○
                    COLYTON○
EXETER○   Colyfor○LYMEREGIS○
        ○Topsham   Beer○ ○Axmouth
        Raleigh   ○SEATON
East Budleigh   SIDMOUTH○
○Powderham   ○Salterton
            EXMOUTH○
    Little   ○Dawlish
    Haldon
○Widecombe   ○TEIGNMOUTH
○Buckland
    ○ASHBURTON
                Watcombe○
                Babbicombe B.
                Anstey Cove
Buckfastleigh   TORQUAY
    Staverton   Cockington○Hope's Nose
    Dartington   Berry   ○Paignton
        TOTNES   Pomroy
○Cornwood   ○Holy Gabriel
IVYBRIDGE   ○BRIXHAM
○Ermington   Sandridge Ho.
○MODBURY   Dittisham○Kingswear
            DARTMOUTH
thcoud
            ○Blackpool
KINGSBRIDGE   Slapton
            ○Torcross Hotel
    Salcombe○
Bolt Tail

Author's Route ───────

THE
HIGHWAYS
AND BYWAYS
OF BRITAIN

THE
HIGHWAYS
AND BYWAYS
OF BRITAIN

EDITED BY
DAVID MILNER

MACMILLAN

First published 2008 by Macmillan
an imprint of Pan Macmillan Ltd
Pan Macmillan, 20 New Wharf Road, London N1 9RR
Basingstoke and Oxford
Associated companies throughout the world
www.panmacmillan.com

ISBN 978-0-230-70692-7

1 3 5 7 9 8 6 4 2

A CIP catalogue record for this book is available from
the British Library.

Typeset by Intype Libra Ltd
Printed and bound in the UK by
CPI Mackays, Chatham ME5 8TD

For
Patrick D. R. Milner
1941–2007

Contents

Introduction

The *Highways and Byways* series was a publishing enterprise of great scope and ambition, running from 1897 to 1948. In all some thirty-six volumes were published, in several editions, many of which were revised and updated. The guiding principle at Macmillan was simple: to publish a series of lavishly illustrated guides to the counties (or historically distinct areas) of Britain, giving free rein to the authors to approach the project as they saw fit.

This book is a selection from each of these thirty-six volumes. That there is a wide variety in the way individual counties are written about is no surprise given that the fifty years covered by the series were a time of immense change in Britain, and that a large number of authors contributed to the project (only seven authors wrote more than one volume, and none more than a total of three books). Some authors, especially those in the late Victorian and Edwardian eras, write with a patrician high seriousness and an unshakeable belief that not only will the reader share their fascination with vernacular ecclesiastical architecture, but also that the reader will be as familiar with its technical lexicon as they are. Some of the volumes written in the interwar years show a sense that the rate of change – social, economic, technological, cultural – is increasing, and are imbued with a nostalgia, even a sadness, that is absent in many of the volumes written before the First World War.

While some authors are most comfortable in their role as an objective guide to landscape, buildings and history, others are happiest telling shaggy-dog stories or writing about people and habits known only within their locale. In this sense, the series doesn't confine itself to the *physical* highways and byways of the country – some authors take the view that the best way to represent their territory is to write about its inhabitants, past and present, famous and obscure. In a spirit of objectivity, some authors try to absent themselves as much as possible, while for others the actual journey they take in order to write the book forms the basis of their narrative, leading to much more personal, impressionistic, lyrical, opinionated, or sometimes comedic, volumes.

What is the portrait of Britain that we find here? In so many ways it is an unrecognisable place, where trams and cars are new beasts (almost all of the writers assume that the tourist will travel either on foot, by bicycle or by train). Rural traditions are still highly visible and important (though disappearing fast). It is a portrait of a country which is for the most part strong, energetic, independent, comfortable with itself and proud (in competition with continental Europe and the wider world, comparable aspects of British life and landscape repeatedly come out on top). For many authors, Ruskin is a revered figure of great authority, an icon to whose words they repeatedly turn. All of the authors subscribe to a theory of the 'picturesque' which seems from another age to our eyes. There is a sense that modern (i.e. Victorian and Edwardian) 'improvements' have weakened the fabric of a national architecture. (Whereas today people spend much time and effort trying to save what we now see as desirable, culturally valuable period buildings erected by the Victorians and Edwardians, in these volumes they are often viewed as distasteful, disrespectful, sometimes even as the work of arrogant vandals.) The Civil War, fishing and fox hunting are topics that come up time and again. (In the Gloucestershire piece, written in 1932, the author tells us that 'fox-hunting, they say, with England, is on its last legs', and there is a repeated sense in many volumes that hunting and the state of the country are somehow linked.)

The twin facts that hunting survived until only very recently, however, and that there are still plenty of doomsayers around to tell us that the country is on its last legs, perhaps indicate that in some ways there is not such a gulf between Britain now and Britain then. And there is indeed much we can recognise in these pages too; many issues recur which remain vitally important today. Environmental concerns – particularly as they relate to the health of rivers and fish stocks, and the impact of mass tourism on the landscape – are repeatedly voiced, as are worries about the consequences of urbanisation, industrialisation and the associated decline of a rural, agricultural economy. Even the parlous state of our general level of fitness is discussed (it is suggested that one of the benefits of new developments in rural towns which bring people out of cities is that they might stop the 'physical degeneration of our people of which we hear on all sides'). Property developers are generally viewed as rapacious. Many authors complain about the creeping, invidious influence of government, whose instruments are destroying old practices and curtailing individual freedoms, bemoaning new laws which are turning Britain into a 'kindergarten'. All these things may strike a chord with readers now. Every era sees its past as a Golden Age, never to be recaptured; in this sense the authors of this series are no different to us.

Of course in the end the truth is that the Britain we see in these pages is simultaneously very different from and very similar to the country today. The seventy-plus years that divide us from the time when these books were written are either an abyss or a mere stepping stone, depending on the point of view.

'Britishness' and how to define it are much in the news today, and while the world has moved on in so many ways, I hope that this selection, by giving us a feeling for what a relatively recent incarnation of our culture deemed important, and on the grounds that we can only know who we are if we know where we came from, might go some small way to clarifying one or two elements of this foggy question. Ultimately, though, my hope is that this selection is simply enjoyed for what it is – a period piece.

Restrictions of space are such that there is a doubly reductive prism at work – these snapshots are selections from books which were themselves necessarily selective, and I have been able to select a total of only eight or ten pages from each volume, most of which are at least 350 pages long. I have tried to make selections that, when viewed as a whole, deal with a range of aspects of Britain and British life of the period – the people, history, landscape, literature, class, local traditions, markets and fairs, sports and games, food and drink, architecture, and so on. There are a few sections on historical matters which inevitably tell us things we already know, the facts of which are not altered by the passage of time – I'd venture that the interest here lies more in the way that our 'objective' history is presented to us by people writing out of a particular time and place. Similarly, I have included pieces focusing on landscapes which, for the most part, have not changed at all, and again the interest lies in seeing anew a familiar and timeless natural world redrawn through different eyes.

One contributor to the series who gives it such a rich flavour, and who to my mind deserves special mention, is the artist Frederick Griggs (1876–1938), who was commissioned to illustrate thirteen of the volumes. Well known and greatly admired in his day, Griggs has recently been the subject of extensive reassessment through the publication of a biography (*F. L. Griggs: The Architecture of Dreams*, Jerrold Northrop Moore,

OUP, 1999) and several exhibitions, including those at the Ashmolean in Oxford and at the Fine Art Society in 2007. Griggs brought a purpose to bear on his work, wanting to capture the fast-vanishing Britain that he felt was on the point of obliteration during and after the First World War, and whose loss haunted him. Beyond his technical brilliance, there is significant emotional weight to many of his drawings, which adds a great deal to the volumes he illustrated.

Unless specifically stated that they appear in the original volumes, all the footnotes are my own, as are any errors within them, of course. Dates of publication refer to first editions, unless noted otherwise. I would like to thank Georgina Morley and her colleagues at Macmillan for their hard work, support and patience.

David Milner, February 2008

I

BERKSHIRE

James Edmund Vincent, 1906

The Berkshire Forest District

If, taking a map of Berkshire, a line be drawn due north and south through Sunningdale, it will bisect Virginia Water and it will form the eastern boundary of so much of the 'Forest District' as lies within our subject; and the River Loddon, entering the county from Hampshire, near Strathfield Saye, and discharging itself into the Thames a short mile above Wargrave, may be taken for a western limit; while the Blackwater may serve for the southern line, as the Thames does for the northern. Within this very irregular polyhedron are comprised a number of places that must needs be visited. They are, to name the chief amongst them, Windsor, Frogmore and Virginia Water, Ascot, Sandhurst, Wellington, Wokingham and the little corner about Swallowfield rightly described as Miss Mitford's country. Yet it is also Charles Kingsley's country, for, although Eversley has the bad taste to be beyond the county boundary, in much of Kingsley's prose is to be traced the spirit of the Berkshire Forest, and he has many a tale to tell of the ways of the Berkshire broom-squires.*

Of these places the interest is in the main human, and none the worse or the less attractive for that; but the country also has a character of its own, a character gradually vanishing as

---

* 'Broom-squires?' 'So we call in Berkshire squatters on the moor who live by tying heath into brooms.' Charles Kingsley, *Two Years Ago*, Vol. II (1857).

London spreads out its tentacles, but still wonderful when we remember how very near London is. Hardly anywhere in southern England shall you find such vast expanses of barren and sandy heath, such ragged growth of firs and bracken and gorse, so much wild nature or so many solitudes. They are being invaded fast in these days. Trim villas and rows of houses rise as if by magic among the firs; at least three railway companies contend for the privilege, and the profit, of carrying breadwinners up to London every morning and back into the pure air when the day's work is done. Unaccustomed hands take to digging and planting; amateur gardeners struggle amain to make good the deficiencies of the soil. The forest, in fact, is disappearing gradually, but the process is very slow; for Nature is intractable and the earth is not responsive, and there will be plenty of forest open for matchless rambles and rides for many a long year to come. At any rate it would be churlish to complain, for it is too obvious to need argument that this exodus from the cities, this migration of children to districts simply overflowing with health, this bringing of a part of the rising generation face to face with Nature, is all for the good. Amongst other things it must serve to check, in part at least, that physical degeneration of our people of which we hear on all sides. [. . .]

Windsor, then is our centre, and first let us wander in the Home Park. The Long Walk passes from the castle along the eastern edge of Home Park, and then to Snow Hill and the very heart of the magnificent Great Park of 1,800 acres, stretching southward to Sunningdale, across Virginia Water and into Surrey, and at the south-west almost to Ascot, the most thickly wooded parts being on the west, near Cranbourne Tower, and on the south-east, near Virginia Water. It is, to put in a phrase, an altogether noble domain, possessing trees that are hard to match; and within its limits are contained Frogmore House, frequently occupied by the Prince and Princess of Wales; Cumberland Lodge, long associated with the names of Prince and Princess Christian of Schleswig-Holstein; Lower Lodge, said to have been built by Nell Gwynn; and the Royal Farms, including the Flemish Farm, for the King, like his father before him, is an enthusiastic and a judicious breeder of cattle, and Queen Victoria kept up all the agricultural enterprises started by the Prince Consort. [. . .]

A most pleasant way of travelling to Virginia Water is to take a coach from London, which involves a drive through some charming country having but one fault, to wit, that it is not part of the Royal County of Berks. It is just as well to approach Virginia Water from the north. The journey is more than worth making. True it is that the water and its surroundings are all artificial. Nature did not cause the wood-girt water to meander as it does. History has nothing to say to those ruins. The whole is simply a magnificent piece of landscape gardening, as landscape gardening does; it is now attaining quite respectable antiquity, and many of our kings, to say nothing of William, Duke of Cumberland, have been much attached to it. The truth of the matter is that Paul Sandby, the creator of the whole design, was not merely a gardener and favourite of the Duke of Cumberland, but a water-colourist of no mean repute and power, and a foundation member of the Royal Academy, whose views in 'aqua tinta' still command high prices. So the general plan of Virginia Water is distinctly good. Amongst its curious structures it has an interesting relic. In the belvedere is mounted a battery of artillery, and it is the very same battery that was used by the Duke of Cumberland against Charles Edward at Culloden. William IV caused a model frigate, now vanished, to be made and floated on the waters. In days when Queen Alexandra, as Princess of Wales, used to skate, Virginia Water was a favourite resort for her; and in these days, when shooting is to the fore at Windsor, it is a frequent venue for luncheon.

Let us have a kindly memory of this last-named Duke of Cumberland, the 'martial boy', the victor at Dettingen and Culloden, who outlived his popularity, who even got a worse name than he deserved, and as we proceed to Royal Ascot let us remember that he earned the gratitude of generations to come as the founder of Ascot Races, and as keen a sportsman as ever lived in England. Hardly less eager was Henry, Duke of Cumberland, whom we find among the subscribers to the Gold Cup in 1771. It would be wrong to describe the greatness of Ascot as a meeting, and it is unnecessary to follow its growth from strength to strength under royal patronage. Suffice to say, without fear of contradiction, that in Ascot Berkshire boasts a racecourse of worldwide celebrity and quite *sui generis*. Ascot is not so popular as Epsom, not quite as aristocratic as Goodwood, its course is one on which the 'going' frequently leaves much to be desired. Still, it is emphatically a great meeting, fitly described as the State event in the annual history of the sport of kings. Need it be added that, with the exception of Goodwood, Ascot is, from a scenic point of view, far and away the most choiceworthy of English racecourses? It is just the wildness of country and the sterility of the hungry soil, the main causes of Ascot scenic beauty, that make it difficult to keep the Ascot course in proper order. It is not an ideal place for a racecourse as such; on the other hand, it is an ideal place for men and women to reach from London in order to see horses run and to meet one another. Finally, it is within easy access of Windsor Castle. So the advantages more than counterbalance the drawbacks, and Ascot will surely live so long as horses are matched against one another for speed.

From Ascot you may go through the pine country to Bracknell, a quiet village in the heart of it, and turn left to Easthampstead, of almost forgotten fame. Few there are now who remember that there was a royal residence at Easthampstead whence the hapless Richard II was wont to start a-hunting in days before treachery and rebellion drove him from the throne – there is much forest left hereabouts still – or that James I resided at Easthampstead in 1622–3; for James, too, was a mighty, or at any rate an ardent, hunter. In these days the two things to do at Easthampstead are to enjoy the fresh air, and to forgive the modernity of the church for the sake of the beautiful Burne-Jones windows it contains.

Hence we pass, still in the pine country, undulating and at its best, by way of Caesar's Camp (just like a hundred places of the same name) to Wellington College. Here you will find none of the architectural charm marking Eton or Winchester; indeed, the buildings may almost be called unattractive. You will find something nearly as good, a school for English boys in a situation that, if it had but a river, would be absolutely ideal; you will find manly lads, many of them, as befits the eponymous hero of the school, intended for a military career, growing up with as much of wholesome *esprits de corps* as may be discovered at the oldest and greatest schools. If there is no long delay here over Wellington College, that is in no sense to the disparagement of Wellington. It is, from one point of view, in the happy position of having no history. It was not founded by an eccentric enthusiast and it has never trembled on the verge of bankruptcy. There, amid the rhododendrons and the Wellingtonias and the pines, are reared generations of boys before all of whom is set the grand example of the great duke. All of us have met them in the wider world, and have observed how conspicuous most of them are for manliness, straightfor- wardness, and absence of affectation.

Two miles away, or a little more, in the same kind of coun- try, although preserving less of its original character, is the Royal Military College, whither many of the pupils of Welling- ton migrate. We are here on the confines of the settlements arisen since the establishment of Aldershot. They have their uses, but they are very far from being lovely. It is, however, worthwhile to go from Sandhurst to Finchampstead, on the borders of the county and almost on the bank of Blackwater, for the sake of crossing the Finchampstead ridges. The church too, standing clear of the village to the north-west, and on a hill a hundred feet higher above the sea than the road leading through the village, is distinctly attractive. In all the adequate maps will be seen, a mile or so north of Finchampstead, lines of uncompromising straightness indicating a Roman road. This is the old Roman road from Silchester, only partially within our purview, to London. From Silchester it starts as if it had been drawn with a ruler; then it becomes more difficult to follow, but north of Finchampstead, through the woodland known as California (one knows not why) and along the 'nine-mile ride' it goes absolutely straight to King's Beeches and Sunningdale. Of this last place, since it has come in accidentally, it may be said that it is a typical and well-to-do settlement in the pine country; and that is enough.

These places might just as well be visited from Wokingham – which is picturesque and old-fashioned – as from Windsor. Hence you may go to see Binfield, keeping Pope in mind the while, remembering that he wrote here, amongst other things, *The Rape of the Lock* and, more appropriately, the Pastorals. A little to the west of Wokingham lies Bear Wood, the house standing on an eminence, and house and estate a monument of the position won by the Walter family as faithful servants of the public and honourable conductors of a great newspaper.[†] The Walter family is one of which Berkshire may be justly proud. The house contains some notable treasures of art, and hard by is a large piece of artificial water, where, as an epitaph in the

----

† The first John Walter (1739–1812) was the founder of *The Times*. The Walter family still owned the newspaper when this volume of the *Highways and Byways* series was published, although the paper was sold to Alfred Harmsworth, later Lord Northcliffe, in 1908.

church records, he who should have been John Walter IV, of Printing House Square and Bear Wood, 'died rescuing his brother and cousin from the frozen lake at Bear Wood, Christmas Eve, 1870'.

Why is Bear Wood so called? Here, in the heart of Berkshire, we have Bear Wood and, near Wargrave, Bear Place, Bear Park, and so forth. The Saxon chroniclers called the county 'Bearrucshire'; Asser says that Berkshire took its name from 'the wood of Berroc, where the box-tree grows abundantly'. We know that the Romans were in the habit of importing bears for their games from Britain, and that bears were certainly not extinct in Britain in the tenth century. So, while Bear Place may possibly have been one of the sites of a pit for baiting bears, there seems to be no sufficient reason why the title of Bear Wood, beyond question of great antiquity, should not be due to a tradition that this once pathless wood was haunted by bears. It may be that here we have lighted on the explanation of the origin of the name of the county also. There is really nothing against the theory, except the fact that nobody seems to have thought of it before. Let us reflect that the tenth or eleventh century are but as yesterday when it comes to a question of the origin of place names, and, thus reflecting, let us ask what could be more likely than that Berkshire, with its huge tract of forest, was in very truth one of the last haunts of the savage bear in southern England, and that Bear Wood was called after its own bears. Sometimes, too, one comes across traces of forgotten fauna in the sayings of the people of the county, and in the games of children, which never change. The fact of the matter is that the traditions of these peasant folk are handed down from father to son, that time is as nothing to them. Our Berkshire peasants speak of the wars, always meaning the Civil Wars, as if they had been waged a century back at most. Their minds will not take in the idea of the lapse of centuries.

2
THE BORDER

———✦———

Andrew and John Lang, 1913

Jedburgh; Teviotdale; Selkirk

In all the Border there stands no place more picturesquely situated than Jedburgh, nor in historical interest can any surpass it. And though its ancient castle, and the six strong towers that once defended the town, have long since vanished, there remains still the noble ruins of its magnificent abbey, and other relics of the past, less noticeable, but hardly less interesting; whilst the surrounding countryside brims over with the beauty of the river, wood and hill.

Like its not distant neighbour, the more famed castle at Roxburgh, Jedburgh Castle as time went on became a stronghold continually changing hands: today garrisoned by Scots, tomorrow held by English, taken and retaken again and again, too strong and of importance too great to be anything but a continuous bone of contention between the two nations, yet more often, and for longer periods, in English than in Scottish keeping. Ultimately, its fate was as that of a land wilfully devastated by its own people to hamper the march of an invading army. If the Scots could not permanently hold it, neither, they resolved, should it any more harbour those vermin of England. Accordingly, when in 1409 the men of Teviotdale, wiping out the English garrison, retook the castle, they at once set about its final destruction.

Perched above the town on a commanding eminence that on one side sloped steeply to the river, and on the other to a deep glen or ravine, defended also, doubtless, on the side farthest from the burgh by a deep fosse, the castle must once have been of great strength – how strong as regards position may best be judged from the bird's eye view of it to be gained if one climbs at the back of Jedburgh the exceedingly steep direct road that runs to Lanton village. From this point, too, one sees to advantage the venerable abbey nestling among the surrounding houses, and can best appreciate the wisdom of the old monks, who chose for their abode a site so pleasant. A valley smiling in the mellow sunshine; a place to which one may drop down from the heights above where bellows and raves a north-westerly gale, to find peace and quiet, undisturbed by any blustering wind; a valley rich in the fruits of the earth, and wandering through it a trout stream more beautiful than almost any of the many beautiful Border 'Waters', a stream that once was, and now should be, full of lusty yellow trout rising under the leafy elms in the long, warm summer evenings. An ideal water for trout is Jed, and many a pretty dish must those old monks have taken from it, by fair means or foul; pity that woollen mills below, and netting, and the indiscriminate slaughter of fingerlings above the town, should have so greatly damaged it as a sporting stream.

Possibly upper Jed is not now quite so bad as it was a few years ago, but what of the lower part of that beautiful river? The same may be said of it that may be said of Teviot immediately below Hawick, or of Gala, and, alas! of Tweed below Galashiels. The waters are poisoned by dyes and by sewage, rendered foul by sewage fungus, reeking with all manner of uncleanness, an offence to nostril and to eye. Five and thirty years ago Ruskin wrote: 'After seeing the stream of the Teviot as black as ink, a putrid carcass of a sheep lying in the dry channel of the Jed, under Jedburgh Abbey, the entire strength of the summer stream being taken away to supply a single mill, I know finally what value the British mind sets on the beauties of nature.' What, indeed, are the 'beauties of nature' that they should interfere with the glories of commerce! Truly we are a Commercial Nation. What might Ruskin say of these rivers now that five and thirty years have passed? Compared to Teviot, ink is a fluid that may claim to be *splendidior vitro**, and Jed below the town is in little better case.

A few hundred yards from the abbey, down a back street, there stands a picturesque old house, robbed now of some of its pic- turesqueness by the substitution of tiles for the old thatched roof that once was there. It is the house where, in a room in the second storey whose window overlooks a pleasant garden and the once crystal Jed, Mary Queen of Scots lay many days, sick unto death† – a house surely that should now be owned and cared for by the burgh. It stands in what must have been in her day a beautiful garden, sloping to the river. Hoary, moss-grown apple trees still blossom there and bear fruit. On a pleasant, sunny evening of late spring when thick-clustered apple and pear blos- som drape the boughs and thrushes sing, and Jed ripples musically beneath the worn arches of that fine old bridge near at hand, it is more of peace than of melancholy that the place speaks.

Yet there is sadness too, when one thinks of the – at least on *this* occasion – sorely maligned woman who lay there in griev- ous suffering in the darkening days of October 1566. 'Would that I had died at Jedburgh,' she sighed in later years. She had been spared much, the Fates had been less unkind, if death had then been her part.

As one proceeds up Jed from the ancient royal burgh, prob- ably the first thing that forces itself on the mind is that the old coach road was not constructed for present-day traffic. In less than a couple of miles the river is crossed no fewer than four times by bridges which are curiously old-fashioned, and in the steepness of their ascent and descent conveying to the occu-

---

* Brighter than glass.
† She had developed an acute fever having ridden fifty miles in bad weather.

pant of a motor car a sensation similar to that given to a bad sailor by a vessel at sea when she is surmounting 'the league-long rollers'. Nevertheless the beauty of road and country are great, especially if one should chance that a visit is paid to the district when the tender flush of early spring lies sweet on Jed's thick-wooded banks, and the trout have begun to think at last of rising again freely to the natural fly. It was a heavily wooded district this in former days, and one or two of the giants of old still survive – the widespreading 'Capon tree', for instance (but why 'Capon' it passes the knowledge of men to decide), and the 'King of the Woods' near Fernihirst, a beautiful and still vigorous oak, with a girth of seventeen feet.

Of castles and peel towers over the Jedburgh district the most are utterly ruined, but Fernihirst still stands, and, over the hill towards Teviot, Lanton Tower, the latter now incorporated with a comfortable modern dwelling. Strange are the vicissitudes of places and of people. Over this Forest of Jedworth and here at Lanton, where of old too often were heard the blast of trumpet, shouts and oaths of fiercely striving men, the roar and crackle of burning houses, you will hear now no sound more startling than the 'toot-toot' of the Master's horn and the babble of foxhounds; for at Lanton Tower are the kennels of the Jedforest Hunt, and many a glorious run is had with this pack, sometimes in enclosed country, sometimes among the great round-backed Border hills towards Carterfell, over country that will tail off all but the best of men and horses.

As we ascend Teviot, after Jed its next important tributary is the Ale, not so named from the resemblance of its waters, when flooded, to a refreshing beverage. Sir Herbert Maxwell[‡] says that the name was originally written 'Alne' (as in Aln,

---

[‡] 1845–1937, seventh baronet, politician and author. He was the most prominent scholarly country gentleman in Scotland.

Alnwick). About Ancrum the Ale, like the Jed, beautifies itself by cutting a deep channel through the fine red sandstone of which Melrose Abbey is built. These channels are always beautiful, but Ale, otherwise, as we ascend its valley, is a quiet trout stream 'that flows the green hills under'. In my boyhood, long, long ago, Ale abounded in excellent trout, and was my favourite among all our many streams. It does not require the angler to wade, like Tweed and Ettrick; it is narrow and easily commanded. The trout were almost as guileless as they were beautiful and abundant; but I presume that they are now almost exterminated by fair and unfair methods. The Scot, when he does not use nets, poisons, and dynamite, is too often a fisher with the worm, and, as I remember him, had no idea of returning even tiny fish to the water, as James Thomson, author of *The Seasons* and himself a Border angler, advises us to do.

Guileless indeed, since old time has been the character of the trout of Ale. But they are better educated, if fewer in number, than they appear to have been eighty or ninety years ago. But they did curious things in the name of Sport in the earlier half of last century. Many of the methods of catching salmon that are written of approvingly by Scrope, that great angler of Sir Walter's day, are now the rankest of poaching, and are prohibited by law.

Further up, Ale rests in the dull deep loch of Alemuir, which looks as if it held more pike than trout. And so we follow her into the hills and the watershed that, on one side, contributes feeders to the Ettrick. It is a lofty land of pasture and broken hills, whence you can see the airy peaks of Skelfhill, Penchrise, the Dunion, and the ranges of 'mountains', as Scott calls the hills through which the Border Waters run. A 'Water' is larger than a 'Burn', but attains not to the name of the river.

Rule, the next tributary as we ascend Teviot, is but a Water, a pretty trout stream it would be if it had fair play. The question of fishing in this country is knotted. Almost all the trout streams were open to everybody, in my boyhood, when I could fish all day in Tweed or Ale, and never see a rod but my own. The few anglers were sportsmen. Since these days the world has gone wild on angling, the waters are crowded like the Regent's Canal with rods. Now I am all for letting every man have his cast; but the only present hope for the survival of trout is in the associations of anglers who do their best to put down netting and dynamiting. A close time when trout are out of season, we owe to Sir Herbert Maxwell.

As we ascend, the water of Teviot becomes more and more foul; varying, when last I shuddered at it, from black to a most unwholesome light blue. It is distressing to see such a fluid flowing through beautiful scenes; and possibly since I mingled my tears with the polluted stream, the manufacturers off Hawick have taken some order in the way of more or less filtering their refuse and their dyes.

Immediately after passing Ettrickbank, the road, coming suddenly out from a clump of trees, breaks into view of a wide and pleasant valley. Above, rising abruptly, tier upon tier in cheerful succession, trees and houses that blend into the smiling face of Selkirk. During the autumn flood salmon run the gauntlet of Ettrick's lower reaches, and in countless numbers congregate below Selkirk Cauld (or weir), where the difficulty of ascent acts as a partial check on their continued migration. On a day in the month of November, if there should happen to be a considerable flood in the river, this cauld is a sight worth going a long way to look at. A wide rushing sea of tawny, foaming water – a hundred yards from bank to bank – races over the sloping face of the cauld, and, where it plunges into the deep pool at foot, rears itself in a mighty wave, with crest that tosses in the wintry breeze 'like the mane of a chestnut steed'. From daylight till dark you may watch the fish – big and little, from the thirty-pound leviathan to the little one- or two-pound sea trout – in their eagerness to reach the spawning beds of the upper waters, hurl themselves high in the air over this great barrier-wave, then, gallantly struggling, continue for a while their course up the rushing torrent, till gradually they lose way and come tumbling back, head over tail, into the pool from which half a minute before they had emerged. It is like standing by one of the jumps in an endless kind of finny Grand National steeplechase; so many fish are in the air at once at any given moment that one becomes giddy with watching them. Probably a good many do in time accomplish the ascent, or perhaps get up by the salmon-ladders in midstream, but the great majority are swept back, over and over again. Those that make the attempt near the side, in the shallow water out of the main force of the current, are frequently taken in landing nets (by water-bailiffs stationed there for the purpose), and are carried up and set at liberty in the smooth water above the cauld. It must be confessed that a considerable number are also taken in this way, or with the help of a 'cleek',§ by poachers. The bailiffs cannot be everywhere; and a salmon is a temptation before which (in the Border) almost the most virtuous of his sex might conceivably succumb. The average Borderer, indeed, I believe would cheerfully risk his life sometimes, rather than forego the chance of a fish. 'The only crime prevalent [in Selkirk] is that of poaching,' says the Revd Mr Campbell, minister of the parish for fifty years, writing in 1833. There was one, greatly sinning in this respect, of whom nevertheless, because of his gallant end, I cannot think without a feeling almost of affection. He – with a fish where no fish should have been – was hopelessly outmanoeuvred by the bailiffs, escape cut off on every side, and only the river, red, swollen, and cold as ice, open to him. 'Here's daith or glory for Jockie!' he cried, and plunged into a torrent from which he came no more alive.

---

§ A large hook or crook.

A little higher up than the cauld is the Piper's Pool, where, until he was hit by a chance bullet that brought him rolling like a shot rabbit down the brae into the water, a piper stood piping that September morning of 1645, when Montrose and Leslie were striving for the victory. On the bank above, those inhab-itants of Selkirk who cared to run some risk – which was probably the whole community – took up their position and watched the fight as from a grandstand. There is no better vantage point imaginable.

3

BUCKINGHAMSHIRE

Clement Shorter, 1910

Aylesbury; Ivinghoe; Chesham; High Wycombe; West Wycombe; Stoke Poges

As the county of Buckinghamshire is only fifty-three miles at its greatest length, and twenty-seven miles at its greatest breadth, the visitor who approaches it in a motor car can see it quite easily from any given point in day excursions. He who uses a horse or bicycle or his own legs can become familiar with it from any one of five towns: Aylesbury, High Wycombe, Great Marlow, Buckingham and Olney. The county contains no very substantial commercial centres, and it is one of its charms that no industries have grown up to spoil the rusticity of well nigh all of it. It is essentially an agricultural county, and it was exclusively this until the eighteenth century, when the so-called cottage industries of lace-making, straw-plaiting and chair-manufacturing grew up. The two former have declined, while the last has grown far beyond the resources of tree wood obtainable in the district. The social aspect of agriculture may be summed up in the fact that the wages of the labourers were never more than one shilling a day in the eighteenth century, while they are three or four times that amount today. Wages then ran considerably higher in the Chilterns than in the Vale.

Let our first introduction to the county be from Aylesbury, now reached pleasantly from Marylebone by the Great Central

Railway in less than an hour. We find ourselves in a town with some small survival of its ancient picturesqueness, although all too little of its many historical associations is preserved for us today. Standing in the centre of the large market square we face the George Inn, while our back is to the Corn Exchange. A hundred years ago we should have faced the King's Head Inn, now buried in a side street, but worth a visit to see its old Tudor window, one of the few relics of an older Aylesbury. The George was built in the beginning of the nineteenth century. It is interesting on account of its ballroom with a music gallery and many pictures, although these last are not of great merit. It is supposed they were removed from Eythorpe House upon the demolition of that splendid residence by the Earl of Chesterfield in 1812. Having confidently expected to be made Lord Lieutenant of the county, as the then occupant was dying, Lord Chesterfield returned to lunch one morning to be greeted with the news that Baron Cobham had received from Pitt the promise of the Lord Lieutenancy. Chesterfield left Eythorpe the next day and never set foot in the county again. A year or two afterwards he gave orders for the destruction of the mansion. His rare treasures he removed elsewhere. There are a set of four hand-fire screens in the possession of the land-lord which show the positions of the pictures in the room. Most of the pictures are copies, and we may be sure that none of them are of value, or they would not have remained so long in this quiet corner of the country. These pictures go with the house, and pass with the freehold from tenant to tenant.

The King's Head is situated at the back of the George. Here we are in quite an old-world atmosphere – the sign, indeed, only commemorates Henry VIII, but the hall of this quaint inn, and its long window, visible from the street, have a much greater antiquity. The heraldic devices that are still to be seen on the window make it clear that it dates from the fifteenth century; and also make it clear that the house had something to do with religion. As a matter of fact, all the original inns of England were kept by religious communities, and were under control of the monasteries. The fine window in the King's Head extends across its principal room, now used as a bar, with heraldry that recalls Margaret, the wife of Henry VI, from which it has been inferred that the building was erected shortly after the marriage of that monarch. In the seventeenth century the King's Head issued its own coinage, or tokens, for small payments. This it did in common with mercers and other tradesmen of the town. Instead of doing the work itself, the government allowed them here, as elsewhere, to make their own 'necessarie chainge'.

In leaving Aylesbury by the Tring road, the old Akeman Street, turn off to the right for Weston Turville, a pleasant village, notable as the place where most of the so-called Aylesbury ducks are reared. The church is some way from the main road, prettily situated among trees. We found the rector with his family playing tennis in the rectory garden on the occasion of our visit, and he courteously sent his son for the key of the church.

At Weston Turville we can get into the Lower Icknield Way to Halton, the park of which is bounded on one side by the high road from Wendover to Tring. The park belongs to Mr Alfred de Rothschild. Halton Park and Aston Clinton Park adjoin, being separated by a canal. Here is another of the many houses of the Rothschild family in this county, and it has the pleasant characteristics that their domination denotes – an outlook of picturesque modern cottages, of comfortable homesteads, and of delightful stretches of parkland visible from the road.

Back on the Tring road we can leave to the left and follow the Upper Icknield Way to Ivinghoe. Sir Walter Scott borrowed the name of Ivinghoe for his incomparable story *Ivanhoe*. Scott went to Buckinghamshire for several of the names in his novels and he certainly visited Aylesbury. It is pleasant to be in Ivinghoe quite apart from the association with Scott's great novel, and many a cyclist has long since discovered the comforts of its inn and the picturesqueness of its neighbourhood. It is a tradition that Ivinghoe was once an assize town, but there is no evidence of this. At the moment it is a village with a population at the last census of 1,077 souls, as against 1,215 a century ago – before Scott gave it its worldwide fame. That that fame has brought no additional population but exactly the contrary is worth recording. The view of the Chilterns from here is exceptionally fine. [. . .]

There are many ways of reaching Chesham. If we desire to visit it from London we shall travel by train which will probably necessitate our changing at Chalfont Road Station, from which there runs a short branch line. If we are already at Amersham there is a direct road through Chesham Bois, and the whole distance is less than two miles. If we are at Great Missenden we can climb up to the church and follow a road on the left through the woods direct into the town.

Chesham is well within the Chilterns, which bound it picturesquely on one side. The church is strikingly situated, the churchyard is impressive, the river Chess, which rises here, is at odd moments quite pretty. We particularly note the fir trees near by the factory, where thousands of children's hoops and spades are turned out. But the growth of Chesham – unlike most places in the county it has tripled its population in a century – has not been made upon artistic lines. The struggling town which follows the high road over the hills to Berkhamsted is much of it called New Town and it is fatally new from our limited point of view. The manufacture of boots and shoes is the principal industry.

But there is a Chesham 'worthy' of importance. Many have assumed that the Mad Hatter was a creation of children's storybooks, immortalised in *Alice in Wonderland*. But there really was a Mad Hatter, and he lived at Chesham for many years. His story is written in the *Harleian Miscellanies*. His name was Roger Crab. He had his 'skull cloven' in the Civil War, and for some breach of discipline was sentenced to death by Cromwell. He was released, and then opened a shop at Chesham as a 'haberdasher of hats'. He took to vegetarianism and water-drinking, then considered sure signs of madness, and clothed himself in sackcloth. He was cudgelled, put in the stocks and otherwise maltreated. He wrote several pamphlets that demonstrate his insanity, *The English Hermit's Spade* being one. He died in 1680. [. . .]

The principal industry of High Wycombe is the manufacture of chairs, the material not only being derived from the neighbouring beech woods, but much of the actual manufacture being carried on in the heart of the woods. Not the least attractive feature in weekend walks through these woods is the glimpse obtained of the gypsy-like encampments in which the various parts of a chair are cut out by hundreds and thousands. The chair-making industry of today, we may add, extends far beyond the utilisation of the wood actually grown in Buckinghamshire.

High Wycombe is quite the largest town in the county, and may be recommended as a good centre for seeing Bradenham, the home of Isaac d'Israeli (thus it was always spelt before Benjamin reached distinction), and Hughenden, the home and burial place of his greater son. From the balcony of the Red Lion, Benjamin Disraeli, afterwards Earl of Beaconsfield, made many political speeches. Hughenden is but just outside High Wycombe on the road to Great Missenden. When we have passed through the street of straggling houses we are compensated by a delightful woodland road, with Hughenden Park on our left. We see a gate with a lodge and the path brings us very quickly to the church while we may observe the house very conspicuously from many points, although we may not enter, unless we have obtained permission from the present owner,

Mr Coningsby Disraeli, a nephew of the great statesman. We are struck by the absence of population at Hughenden. The usual village does not exist, but the goodly congregation on a Sunday is accounted for in that it is drawn from the neighbouring hamlets of Kingshill and Naphill, to say nothing of the fact that the stalwart pedestrian from High Wycombe often walks across to the service here. In the churchyard we are at once attracted by the railed-in memorial to Lord Beaconsfield and his wife, a granite tombstone in three portions.

We may enjoy a pleasant walk from Hughenden to Disraeli's earlier home at Bradenham. There is a footpath at the lower end of the park that leads through Common Wood to Downley Common, and thence across Naphill Common. Bradenham is a most pleasing village, of which the Manor House is the most interesting object. It stands near the church, a fine mansion which will come as a surprise to those who think of Disraeli the younger as a self-made man. In this house Isaac d'Israeli lived from 1829 until his death in 1848 at the age of eighty-two. We shall find his tomb in the church and we shall have seen a monument to him in Hughenden Park as we have passed from Bradenham. It was his friendship with Pye, the Poet Laureate, that led Isaac d'Israeli into Buckinghamshire. Pye had been a rich man but had fallen on evil days financially when the then owner of Stoke Park, William Penn, a descendant of the founder of Pennsylvania, presented him with a cottage on his estate. [. . .]

Perhaps the most oft-visited spot in England next to Stratford-on-Avon, so far as literary associations are concerned, is Stoke Poges churchyard. It is a favourite resort with the visitors to Burnham Breeches. And since the advent of the motor-cab, that has proved a not-infrequent method of seeing the picturesque locality that will ever be associated with the poet Gray. It is a delightful excursion in the summertime, when the churchyard abounds in well-kept rose bushes. A 'cloister' of modern creation leads from the church to the original manor house, a gamekeeper's lodge in the sixties of last century and now a concert hall. It was for a time the studio of Sir Edwin Landseer. You cannot walk through this 'cloister' from the churchyard, but you may approach the fragment of the old manor house through the stable by the side of the Farnham road.

As we approach the churchyard we are reminded of the poet by a stately, if tasteless, monument – a large sarcophagus, supported on a square pedestal with inscription on each side. It was John Penn, who lived at Stoke Poges in 1799, to whom we owe this monument. At the end of the churchyard, close by the wall at the east end of the church, we find the simple tomb under which Gray and his mother lie buried. He inscribed it to 'Dorothy Gray, the careful tender mother of many children, one of whom alone had the misfortune to survive her.' The famous *Elegy Written in a Country Churchyard* was begun at Stoke in 1749, and apparently inspired by three deaths. Gray's uncle, Jonathan Rogers, died at Stoke Poges in 1742, as did his friend West, and his aunt died here in 1749. In 1753 Gray's mother died. Gray himself died at Cambridge in 1771, and his remains were carried to Stoke Poges and placed in the same tomb with his mother and aunt. It was a quiet funeral for the author of one of the most popular poems in our language. The mourners were four in number. We can but contrast with this the thousands of annual visitors to this simple grave – all inspired by love of one short but immortal poem.

4

CAMBRIDGE
AND ELY

Revd Edward Conybeare, 1910

The University;
King's College Chapel;
Trinity College Library;
Ely Cathedral

In 1209, when the schools of Oxford were for a while closed by the government, as the outcome of a more than usually outrageous 'rag', large numbers of the students migrated to Cambridge. From henceforward, at all events, it attained European reputation in this respect, for in 1229, we find another batch of expelled students, this time from Paris, settling themselves here, and yet another swarm of Oxonians twenty years later. The earliest undergraduates were, at first, an utterly lawless lot, and made themselves most unpleasant neighbours to the 'burgesses' of the town. The student population speedily became far more numerous than the townsfolk. University lodgers thronged the private houses and the annexes, or 'hostels' as they are named, run up for their sole use by speculative landlords. These hostels gradually attained a more or less official recognition by the university, and paved the way for the setting up of colleges.

The test applied to students by the university before conferring upon them a degree was by public disputations in the schools, each candidate having to support or oppose some literary or scientific thesis. The memory of these wordy 'opponencies' is still preserved in the denomination of 'Wrangler' bestowed on the candidates who obtain a First Class in the Mathematical Examination for an Honour degree, and by every examination through which such a degree can be obtained being called a 'Tripos', from the three-legged stool which played a notable part in those old ordeals. The test demanded steadiness of nerve and readiness of wit, as well as mere knowledge; and, in all these, the scholar of a college, well catered and cared for, was far better equipped than his lawless, and often foodless, non-collegiate competitor.

At the present day, the colleges *are* Cambridge; and to the visitor their buildings completely out-bulk those which belong to the university. Each college consists of an enclosed precinct (to which the students are confined at night) containing blocks of apartments for Fellows, Scholars and Pensioners; a special lodge for the Master; a chapel; a library, and a hall, with kitchen and buttery attached. Here the Masters sit at the High Table on a dais across the upper end of the hall, and the students at less pretentious boards arranged longitudinally. All are bound to dine in hall, unless by special leave; but other meals may be in your own rooms, of which each student has a suite of three, in which he is said to 'keep'. All three are within one general outer door or 'oak', to be opened only by a latch-key, and 'sported' whenever the owner desires his citadel to be inaccessible.

Proctors perambulate the town after dark to punish wrong-doers, usually by a fine of 6s. 8d., or some multiple of that sum, the unit being a survival from medieval numismatics, as equivalent to half a Mark. For smaller offences the place of fines is taken by 'gating' for a certain period, during which the nocturnal enclosure of the culprit begins at some earlier hour than usual.

As a regular rule the college gates are shut at ten p.m. Once inside the gates the student is under no obligation to keep to his own rooms, but has the run of the college all night. He is bound, however, to spend his nights within the walls, and not even for a single night may he be absent without a duly signed *exeat* from the college authorities giving him leave.

All this is very unlike Continental or American university life, but is almost the ditto of Oxford. For Cambridge is the sister-daughter of Oxford. The earliest Cambridge college, Peterhouse, was not only suggested by the earliest Oxford Foundation, Merton, but borrowed its very statutes; and the development of the two seats of learning has twinned itself throughout the centuries to an extent unparalleled elsewhere in history. Of each distinctive feature, considered separately, the choicest specimen is to be found in Cambridge – the best college chapel at King's, the finest college hall and college courts at Trinity; the most characteristic and beautiful library at St John's. But apart from the university buildings, the town of Cambridge, with its narrow streets and mean public edifices, is hopelessly outclassed by the beautiful city of Oxford. Invidious comparisons, however, are, in the case of sisters, more than ordinarily odious.

Should the reader enter the town from the railway station he will have to face a mile or so of 'long unlovely street' to begin with. For when railroads were first made they were regarded with extreme suspicion and dislike by the authorities of the university. The noise of the trains, it was declared, would be fatal to their studies; the facility of running up to London would hopelessly demoralise the undergraduates; bad characters from the metropolis would come down in shoals to prey upon them. Thus the university strenuously opposed any near approach of this new-fangled abomination to its hallowed precincts. [. . .]

If we emerge from Queens' gate and turn leftwards, we have on one side the dark-red bricks of that college, on the other the like buildings of St Catharine's, while, at the further end of the street in front, our view is bounded by the white stone of the new gateway of King's. The whole effect is delightful. Through this gateway we make our way into the Premier college of Cambridge (this rank is one of the privileges due to the Royal Founder), and soon find ourselves face to face with one of the most beautiful views of the world. Before us spreads a spacious lawn, the most extensive in existence. (A current story tells how a millionaire, who boasted that his money should make him a lawn as perfect, was discomfited by being told that to attain such perfection 'you must mow and roll it regularly for 400 years. That is what has been done here.') The north side of the Great Court is formed, as Henry VI decreed, by his glorious Chapel, the most magnificent in the world, which now rises before us in all its grandeur as we behold it across the Court.

And if the outside view is impressive, that which greets us when we enter is absolutely overpowering in its majesty. The sense of space and repose; the up-running lines of the shafting catching the eye whithersoever it turns, and leading it up to the myriad-celled spans of the vault; the subdued light through the pictured windows staining the venerable masonry; the great organ, upborne by the rich oaken screen, dominating the whole vista, uplifting indeed to heart and sense alike. And when to this feast of visual harmony is added the feast of aural harmony, when the clear and mellow voices of the choir blend with the majestic tones of the organ, we can understand how the inspiration of the scene has thrilled poet after poet, not Tennyson only, but Wordsworth, and even Milton, Puritan as he was, yet more. [. . .]

We proceed northward till we reach the fine iron gate which bears the escutcheon of Cambridge's mightiest college, Trinity, a college more than twice as large as any other. Like London, which an Indian visitor once described as 'not a city, but a herd of cities', Trinity may best be described as a conjoined herd of colleges, for it was created by the amalgamation of no fewer than nine earlier institutions. All these colleges and hostels alike were seized upon by Henry VIII, when that rapacious and unprincipled monarch desired to pose (in 1546, a year before his death) as a Pious Founder, and go down to posterity as a benefactor. His professed object was 'to educate Youth in piety, virtue, self-restraint, charity towards the poor, and relief of the distressed'. His alumni, in short, were to be made as opposite to himself in character as possible.

On entering Trinity Library, built by Sir Christopher Wren in 1675, what first catches our eye will be the window at the southern end of the room, with its painted glass so unlike anything to be seen elsewhere. It is, in fact, unique, having been made in the middle of the eighteenth century by the discoverer of this particular method of staining glass, who kept the process secret – a secret which died with him, and has never been recovered. The subject is weird. The University of Cambridge, represented as a lady in a somewhat scanty robe of yellow, is presenting Sir Isaac Newton to George III (who did not come to the throne till 1760, many years after the great philosopher died), while the transaction is being recorded by Francis Bacon, Lord Verulam of Elizabethan fame!

Beneath this window is Thorwaldsen's fine marble statue of Lord Byron, one of Trinity's greatest poets. This was originally intended for Poets' Corner in Westminster Abbey, but the Dean and Chapter of the period so strongly disapproved of Byron's morality that they refused it a place there. Apart from his poetical genius, he as little deserved to be honoured in Trinity Library; for, as an undergraduate, he not only accomplished the apparently impossible feat of climbing by night to the roof (which others have more than once done since) but abominably disfigured the statues upon it, in which he has had, happily, no

* In his first year, Byron seems to have been rather unimpressed by Trinity: 'This place is wretched enough – a villainous chaos of din and drunkenness, nothing but hazard and burgundy, hunting, mathematics and Newmarket, riot and racing.' In his second year, however, from which his roof-climbing adventures date, he embraced this sort of life unreservedly.

imitators.* Nocturnal exploration of the college roofs has been so favourite an amusement amongst undergraduates that not so long ago a book was actually published entitled *The Roof-Climber's Guide to Trinity College*. Every eminence in the college has been scaled, save only the Great Gate Tower. The Hon. C. S. Rolls†, who was afterwards the first man to fly from England to France and back, and who fell a martyr to his zeal for aviation, was, in his day, the most daring and systematic of all Trinity roof-climbers.

*

It may be unenterprising to come to Ely by rail; but yet there is no approach that can give us a finer impression of the Minster than we gain by our first view of it from the train, whether we arrive from the north or from the south. In either case we have been travelling over flat dull country, when suddenly there stands up before our eyes the 'stately fane' of which we have heard so much, and our first impulse is to show her some token of reverence. We take a good look at the pile of building before us, and we resolve not to forget our first sight of this our new friend.

Leaving Ely station, our best course will be to walk toward the Cathedral taking the second turn to the right. This brings us into a commonplace street where, however, we should notice on our right a row of thatched cottages, with their overhanging upper storeys, that have survived from olden days. Just opposite these cottages is an iron gateway which invites us into the Cathedral 'Park', an undulating piece of ground some sixteen acres in extent grazed by cattle and sheep, its highest point

---

† Charles Rolls (1877–1910), co-founder of Rolls-Royce, and the first Englishman to be killed flying an aeroplane.

being an artificial mound, now densely clothed with trees, called Cherry Hill. Grassy hillocks rise between us and the Cathedral; and we gain an impression as of some great ship riding majestically over ocean billows. The church, indeed, is actually about the size of a large liner, and the green swells of the park are not unlike in magnitude to those of the Atlantic. Turner's painting of Ely Minster gives this same ship-like impression of the place, thus embodying the history of this wondrous pile. It has in truth weathered many a tempest, has been wrecked and built afresh, has sunk and been restored, and is preserved for us still as a holy and classic House of God. There is a delicious harmony in it all; in the intricacy of the masonry, in the very colour of the stone; and we admire those builders of yore who, while respecting the work of their fore-fathers, did not hesitate to deal with their material according to their own fuller light and skill. Perhaps we shall doubt as to calling the topmost octagonal tower wholly in keeping with the base of the steeple; yet if we had the power we should not have the wish to alter it.

The tourist must walk round the Cathedral outside. He will then be perplexed by the anachronisms before him; he will see Perpendicular windows inserted in the Norman aisles, Deco-rated tracery in Early English masonry; he will observe this from without more plainly than from within, and he will realise how the monks who designed and built it all had a firm belief in themselves, and in their own age, so that they did not shrink from what we should now count as acts of Vandalism. They no more hesitated to displace the works of their fore-fathers by their own, than we hesitate to light our houses and churches with electricity, instead of being content with the gas that was good enough for our grandparents.

Those who desire it can climb to the top of the western tower, and if the day is clear they will be well rewarded by a superb view over the 'boundless plain' below; towns and hamlets, steeples and spires, spread beneath us, nor must we forget the railways, with their kindly evidence of modern life at its fullest. To the east the horizon is bounded by those East Anglian uplands which nurtured Etheldreda for her great work here. But, beyond almost any other, this is essentially a man-made landscape; its salient features are not hills, but buildings, not rivers but lodes. Peterborough, the sister Abbey-Cathedral, is in view twenty miles away to the north-west, and many a church of note and beauty is prominent within nearer range, including the towers and spires of Cambridge fifteen miles to the south.

It is well that we should realise how much the preservation of this stately steeple has cost. Ever since the central tower fell in 1322, sacrists, priors, monks, bishops, deans, have lived in constant terror lest what had befallen the central might also befall the western tower. We can read how they have braced it with iron and wood, how they have weighted it with bells, how they have lightened it by removing its wooden spire, how they have buttressed it, how they have plastered it. Century after century they have continued the repairs, sometimes making mistakes, but never asking the question, fatal to all good work, 'Is it worthwhile?' There it stands, surveying its vast plain for thirty miles around, with its air of unbroken security.

5
DERBYSHIRE

J. B. Firth, 1905

Chatsworth; Baslow;
Longstone Edge; Matlock

Chatsworth – both House and Park – is usually described in superlatives, and for once the language of seeming exaggeration is not ill employed. For, all things considered, Chatsworth is perhaps the most beautiful as well as the most imposing of the great houses and great parks of England. The situation is perfection. The wide rolling moors spread away high above it and behind it to the east. They break into woods at their edge – beautiful woods where every tree seems to find just the soil and sustenance it needs – and then they dip in sharp, yet not steep, declivity to the rich parkland in which Chatsworth stands, with the Derwent flowing pleasantly through the mid-valley. Along the left bank of the river, from the Baslow entrance to the Park to the bridge near Beeley, this exquisite range of woods continues, while on the right bank the ground is less regular in outline, and rises more gradually up to the plateau dividing Chatsworth from Haddon. Yet here, too, as one looks down from such a vantage spot as the Wellington Monument above Baslow, the main impression is of woods, and the whole valley looks a green vista of delight.

It was the remarkable contrast between the rich luxuriant Derwent Valley and the barren moors between it and Chesterfield – the usual road of approach – that impressed most visitors to Chatsworth in the old days. The sudden descent into the smiling valley was as astonishing to them as the towers of Venice rising from the waste of waters.

The Chatsworth Hobbes knew, and where he spent so many years as the honoured recipient of Cavendish hospitality, was the Chatsworth which Bess of Hardwick built and where Mary Queen of Scots dwelt as a prisoner. Of that mansion practically nothing remains, for the new one was built on the old site. However, Queen Mary's Bower has happily been spared. It stands below the House, close to the bridge over the Derwent, a grey stone building, to which access is obtained by a flight of thirty steps rising over a moat of varying width. Two old yew trees growing within the bower throw their shade over the entrance gate, a third flourishes in a corner, and in the centre stands a fine sycamore with spreading branches. No spot could be more romantic, built up from the placid moat three or four feet at its deepest, surmounted with its crown of foliage and haunted with memories of the Queen of Scots.

The sixth duke was the patron of Sir Joseph Paxton. As a boy Paxton ran away from an uncongenial apprenticeship, and was found on the road by a Quaker named Hooker, who kept the nursery gardens at Chiswick. One of Hooker's patrons was the Duke of Devonshire, who took a fancy to the young gardener and told him casually that, if he wished it, he might have a place at Chatsworth. A few hours later Paxton set off from London in the Yorkshire coach, and arrived at Chesterfield at three in the morning. He walked the nine miles to Chatsworth, climbed over the wall, reconnoitred the grounds before anyone was stirring, and then presented himself at the housekeeper's room for breakfast. And before the meal was over – so legend saith – he had made up his mind to accept the duke's offer, to remodel the gardens, and to marry the housekeeper's niece. And so he did.

The Great Conservatory at Chatsworth is usually spoken of as the building which suggested Paxton's Crystal Palace. That is an error. The real prototype is the small Lily House, which stands before the head gardener's villa, by the kitchen garden in the Park. Paxton was one day talking with John Marples, one of the duke's agents and an uncultivated genius who knew nothing of science and rules, but could conquer any engineering difficulty by sheer native ability, and, pointing to Lily House, said 'Could you build it from here to Chatsworth?' 'Certainly,' answered Marples. 'Then it's done,' said Paxton, and slapped his leg. And so the idea of the Crystal Palace was born. Paxton had the inspiration, but Marples translated it into glass and iron.

Paxton laid out the Italian gardens fronting the river, and his name is indelibly associated with the whole hundred and twenty-six acres of pleasure grounds, with the Victoria Regis House, and the Great Conservatory. There is, to my mind, a touch of megalomania in this colossal glasshouse, and it only bores me to be told of its miles of piping and acreage – or is it mileage? – of glass. The sixth duke used to drive a little carriage with four ponies and outriders through this conservatory, and he had milestones – think of it! – in his garden walks to tell him how far he was from home. This from the Whig noble, whose bust graces a real antique pillar from Sunium! Well, we all have our foibles.

As for the House itself, which is most generously shown to the curious and thronging public, I have no room to describe its contents. Moreover, I always find that going over these lordly houses – as one of a 'party' – is a most chastening experience. You wish to linger, but must not; the guide shepherds you from room to room, and the tired finger indicates, and the uninterested voice describes, the things in which you take not the least concern. A canoe given by the Sultan! A malachite clock presented by the Emperor Nicholas! A magnificent set of ivory chessmen! These things move me not. I always think of the hours I might spend there with the right *cicerone** — at leisure and in quiet.

In days gone by the ladies of the great House used to watch the chase from the upper windows of the Hunting Tower; now the top of the hill is given up to woods and game preserves. Here, too, lie the lakes, the largest of which works the great Emperor Fountain below, a perfect Paradise for wild fowl. Green drives branch off at either side. Among them you may wander at will, so you but keep to the paths and drives, and there is no shadow of excuse to quit them, for they conduct you to the very arcana of the woodlands. Here by a gate-side some keeper had made his gibbet, displaying the mouldering, mummified carcases of five weasels. By their side dangled a hawk and other birds of prey which I was not naturalist enough to distinguish. One wonders if these gibbets are efficacious. Are the weasels frightened to repentance as they look on their dead fellows? Who shall say? But they who think on these things cannot do better than linger in the retired woods above Chatsworth House, where one can roam for miles by taking the various walks which present themselves at every turn and side. Specially worthwhile is to keep high up and follow along the edge of the woods above the valley, till, beyond a small forest of ancient and decaying oaks, you quit the Park through a gate by the Parkgate Farm, and then find yourself on the moorland, with Harland Edge on your left hand. There you reap reward in superb views down into the valley of the Derwent, and across the desolate expanse of Beeley Moor, which itself drops down over Fallinge Edge into a broad terrace of green pastures, and then descends in handsome woods to the level of the stream.

On the border of Chatsworth Park stands Baslow, a pretty

---

* Guide.

village of some importance. Despite its distance from the railway, it is one of the best touring centres for this side of the county, for it lies within easy walking distance of Rowsley, Bakewell, Ashford, Eyam, Grindleford Bridge, Hathersage, and the noble moors, whose fine edges overhang the Derwent Valley from Baslow to the Vale of Hope. The village is curiously divided in twain. At the Bridge End the Derwent is spanned by a humped bridge, still steep and placed at an awkward angle to the road, yet much steeper in the old days, as one can see from the curious stone toll shelter on the left bank, the floor of which is evidently higher than it used to be. The church stands by the side of the stony bed of the river. It was restored some half-century ago by ruthless hands, which swept away nearly everything that was old, save a few ancient sepulchral stones and a heavy whip, which the dog-whipper plied on stray curs if they ventured within the precincts. The other half of the village lies on the Bar Brook, near the entrance gates to Chatsworth, with one or two picturesque old inns and a variety of other hostelries, which are the goal of the Sheffield and Chesterfield brakes that daily cross the moors to Baslow in the summertime.

From Baslow it is a pleasant afternoon's ramble to visit the familiar landmark of Longstone Edge, which stretches across from the Wye, near Cressbrook Dale, to the Derwent at Calver, some five miles in length and rising to nearly thirteen hundred feet at its highest point. The old road from Bakewell to Sheffield lies at its foot, lined on either side by trees which form an exquisite avenue. I could find no one who knew when or by whom these trees were planted. Yet the man who had the thought and the will to set such gracious trees to transform a bare road into a thing of beauty deserves the kindliest remembrance. Nowadays trees are rarely planted – they are not utilitarian. But the difference!

✳

The approach to Matlock along the main road through Darley
Dale is most disappointing. As road, river, and railway draw
together, we reach the commonplace outskirts of the town,
spoilt by aggressive limekilns, quarries, and all the paraphernalia of industry in its ugliest form. When we emerge we are
close to Matlock Bridge, an ancient structure which, as I saw
it, was in the throes of being widened. Matlock Bank stretches
away up the steep hillside to the left hand – a prosperous-look-
ing place of little interest, unless your tastes lie in the direction
of hydropathy and the buildings where it is cultivated. Fifty or
sixty years ago Matlock Bank was a bare expanse with few
houses. Crossing the bridge, we follow the main road – now a
street of commonplace shops – till we soon pass under the railway and enter upon one of the most beautiful reaches of
Derbyshire. We do so with high expectation. The fame of Matlock's beauty has gone forth to the uttermost parts of the
earth. For a whole century writer after writer has assured us
that the charms of romantic Matlock are irresistible; that its
combination of river, rocks, and woods is matchless. Let us
quote Ruskin's glowing eulogy:

> English *pater familias* – think of what this little piece of mid-
> England has brought into so narrow compass of all that
> should be most precious to you. In its very minuteness it is
> the most educational of all the districts of beautiful land-
> scape known to me. The vast masses, the luxurious
> colouring, the mingled associations of great mountain
> scenery, amaze, excite, overwhelm . . . the mind cannot
> choose where to begin.

Many years have passed since Ruskin penned that. If he could
revisit the well-loved scene, would he suffer the written word

to stand? I think that those who best know Ruskin's work and feel qualified to speak, however diffidently, in his name, will agree that if he could walk from Matlock Bath to Cromford, the old man's indignation would rise at every step till, by the time he reached the turn of the road at Cromford, he would be bubbling over with fury and rage and would scarify those who so complacently wrest his generous praise to the ignoble uses of advertisement. Ruskin would not mince his words; and making no allowance for delicate susceptibilities, he would tell the Matlock people in scorching words that they have suffered their beautiful country to become vulgarised. Let the truth be told for once! Nature has done for favoured Matlock all she can; she has lavished upon her her very choicest treasures. And in return for these bounties, what have the guardians of the dale done for Nature? They have deliberately degraded Matlock Bath into a tripper's Paradise, and encouraged the railway companies to let loose daily in the summertime among its sylvan beauties a horde of callous rowdies, who envy Attila his destructive secret, whereby the grass never grew again where once his foot had been planted. The debasing influence of the day-tripper is everywhere visible in Matlock. His trail is unmistakable. His litter is omnipresent. And even when no long trains are standing empty in the sidings waiting for the hour of return, the mark of the tripper is daubed all over Matlock. He has tastes which must be catered for – the ugly phrase is here appropriate. The shops deck themselves out with vulgarities and banalities to please their patron. His eye is supposed to be dim; therefore, nothing but what is gaudy will attract him. His ear is so accustomed to the roar of machinery and the din of streets that there must be a bawling salesman on the pavement to shout crude invitations to buy. It is these shops, these refreshment bars, these permanent preparations for the coming of the tripper, which ruin a place, and, once begun, the descent to Avernus becomes a veritable glissade.

Every shop, all down this short reach of the river, seems either a cheap eating-house or a cheap spar-house, where the stranger may purchase a memento of his happy day, and obtain a bewildering choice of perfectly useless and futile ornaments. Again the situation is charming, but what with the bawling of the drivers of brakes and waggonettes, the attentions of the pushing salesmen, and the tawdriness and vulgarity of their wares, one is glad to get away around the next bend.

We are now in the old part of Matlock Bath – the South Parade. It is a glorious site for an inland watering place, but the main road is frankly detestable. Such desecration – for desecration it is – is pitiful. At every step you are adjured to go and see some miraculous cavern, or dropping well, or giant stalactite, each the greatest wonder and marvel of the Peak. When trade is brisk, you may hear every few minutes shrill, hysterical laughter and cries of uncontrolled joy, blended with the rush and rattle of strident wheels. It is a wanton outrage to one of the fairest scenes in England.

Happily, there are signs that the people of Matlock Bath are seeing the folly of so short-sighted a policy, and schemes of considerable magnitude are on foot for improvement of the district. It is proposed to acquire gradually the entire river bank, which unfortunately belongs to a large number of small owners, each of whom has hitherto done that which he liked with his own. It is proposed to build a Pump Room and Baths on the Buxton and Harrogate model. The thermal water from the Grotto Spring in the grounds of the Royal Hotel would thus be properly utilised, half the flow of water – which is four hundred thousand gallons a day – being guaranteed in perpetuity to the town. If that were done and stringent control were exercised over the enterprise of individual ratepayers, and the railway companies were discouraged from flooding the place every summer day with trippers, Matlock Bath might hope to win back some of her vanished prestige.

6

DEVON AND CORNWALL

Arthur H. Norway, 1897

Beer; Teignmouth; Torbay; Paignton; 'White ale'; the Lizard; Helston

The pleasantest way to Beer is over the western cliff by a steep and broken path from Seaton. From the summit of this crumbling white chalk bluff there is a singularly fine view up the valley of the Axe, winding in dim luxuriance till it is lost among the hills of Shute; and one has scarcely turned away from this rich prospect of inland beauty before the path drops rapidly to a deep and narrow cove, hardly seen until one is immediately above it, and suggesting irresistibly by the seclusion of its situation certain pursuits which brought to the fishermen of Beer for many generations more profit than favour in the eye of the law. There is no harm in speaking of these matters now; for Beer has been this many a day like the sinner that repenteth, and is rather pleased to detail its former transgressions, feeling perhaps that a certain spice of devilry handed down from former days is an agreeable relief to the more prosaic occupations of the present time. But it is certainly not more than fifty years since the whole community of Beer – men, women and children all alike – was desperately addicted to smuggling, and found its glory and its chief delight in eluding the vigilance of the revenue officers; and it is a curious instance of the changed conditions of life in England that law, which never was otherwise than reluctantly obeyed on the western coasts of England until the present century was far advanced, has at last succeeded in tying down the restless energies of the men and women of Beer to the peaceful pursuits of trawling and the manufacture of lace. [. . .]

When the perspiring rider comes warily down the last crooked hill from Dawlish, he will doubtless find Teignmouth looking extremely beautiful. It should be visited in the spring, while the sky is still a little watery, while the clouds floating over Haldon have density and weight, and their shadows lie darkly here and there upon the sea. Then the colour of that wide and sunny bay is at its loveliest. Far away in the east the white cliffs of Beer and Seaton gleam and shine, and a soft blue line behind them can be followed out to sea till it is lost in haze just where we know that the Chesil beach and the Isle of Portland lie.

To some of us who love the west it seems as if it were at Teignmouth that it properly begins. For here is the first of the true west country ports – a little town huddled in the warmest corner of the hills, where neither west nor east wind can bite it or molest it, a tidal estuary left almost bare twice every day, a harbour of floating seaweed and green limpid water, where half a dozen ships lie canting over in the shallows, a race of honest, kindly, slow-speaking people, to whom the soil and climate seem to have communicated their own warmth and geniality.

It is time to pass onwards, crossing the harbour by its long wooden bridge, and climbing the hill road which crosses the shoulder of the Ness, so lofty that the view extends not only far out to sea on one hand, but on the other stretches out over a fine broken country of hill and valley rising at length, on the blue horizon, into that great barrier of jagged Tors which hides the wonderland of the moor, that great boss of granite, that wild central table-land out of which Devon draws its rivers, its keen fresh breezes, and the greater part of its vast store of tradition and romance.

Now this road is dangerously seductive. Here is Labrador, when we have hardly got up the first hill, calling us off the road to clamber down its steep cliff path and sit in the pretty tea house, where so many lads and lasses go from Teignmouth on summer evenings to eat cream and whatever fruit may be in season, and talk of heaven knows what, while looking out over a sea view as fine as any it is possible to find; here is Watcombe, which owns the best red potter's clay in England, as the Romans knew; and Babbacombe, where man has tried to paint the lily, and has spoilt it in the process, as he always does. We must go past them all, towards Hope's Nose, looking down upon the great expanse of all Torbay lying at one's feet.

It is a very noble and moving view which lies below. High precipices of limestone wall the bay upon the nearer side, broken into masses of green verdure, and cut by terraces and lovely gardens over which the eye runs from point to point still catching some new beauty, still dwelling on some fine contrast of rich plantation and dark crag and gloomy pinewood skirting the rich purple of the ocean, till wearied by the gleam of the white rock, it drops upon the sea. Far across the wide bay a few smoking chimneys catch the eye.

Need I say that Torbay is like the Bay of Naples? Why stick at such a statement when you hear it all about you? All English bays are like the Bay of Naples. Bideford Bay is like it too, while St Ives' bay is as like Naples as twin sisters, having even a little Capri at the entrance. What could be more exact? Why go abroad when all the beauties of the Mediterranean are five hours from town? I do not wish to carp, but I am weary of hearing of the Bay of Naples. Torbay is far too beautiful to need the help of any such comparison, and need wish nothing better than to be like itself.

Now the weight of historical associations in Torbay is all upon the western side, at Paignton and at Brixham. It is not William of Orange who forms the chief glory of Paignton; nor is it Miles Coverdale, who is fondly thought to have translated the Bible in an ancient tower by the church. Still less is it the church or the exquisite chantry it contains. Of all these distinctions the man of Paignton is modestly conscious; but what makes him swell with pride is the recollection of the Paignton Pudding.

It is in a note on the 1680 autobiography of Dr James Yonge that we find our first reference to this mighty dish. 'Paynton held her charter by a Whitepot – whence Devonshire men are soe called – which was to be seven yeares making, seven baking and seven eating.' Now the doctor may or may not have been right in saying that the term 'Whitepot' adhered to the men of Devon. Certainly the Cornish call them 'Dumplings' when much irritated, and the Devon men retaliate with the injurious epithet of 'Pasties', and then peace is no longer worth hoping for, but both sides proceed to argue with their fists. But to return to the pudding. It may or may not be a 'Whitepot', but it certainly does not occupy seven years in either making, baking or eating. In fact it is only once every fifty years that the construction of the pudding is undertaken. It was made in 1809, and it may be interesting to append the recipe: 400 pounds of flour, 170 pounds of beef suet, 140 pounds of raisins and 240 eggs. Picture what a mountain it must have made! Fifty years later, in 1859, the pudding had grown even larger. [. . .]

At Torcross the road turns inland, and runs onward towards Kingsbridge. This is the heart of the South Hams, a district not very clearly defined, but including the greater part of the country which lies south of the moor between Exeter and Plymouth. It is a cider country very famous once for the quality of its liquor, and still noted for its excellence; though it somehow happens that cider does not fetch the price it did, and farmers are making less and less. However, if good cider is becoming scarce in the South Hams, there is another liquor on which the thirsty traveller can fall back, somewhat uninviting in appearance, it is true, but of very high and ancient repute at Kingsbridge, where it is chiefly made. If it indeed be true that 'white ale' was once the staple drink of western England, we may fairly congratulate ourselves on having given one proof of progress in shaking off our national attachment to this thick heady liquor, which perhaps is the same as appalled Andrew Borde who tried to penetrate into wild Cornwall 350 years ago; but found the ale so bad that he had to give it up. It looked, he said, 'as if pygges had wrasteled in it'.

And what is this delectable drink? Why, that is declared to be a secret, known only to one family, and jealously guarded through successive generations. All the outer world knows is that eggs are in it, as well as some mystical ingredient called 'grout'; that it looks like some extremely nauseous doctor's draught; that it flies quickly to the head; and that the sooner the South Hams grow as wise as Cornwall and the rest of England, and consign all this nasty liquor to the limbo of the past, the better will be the judgement formed of their good sense. For it would be a rare and monumental folly to lose cider, and retain white ale.

*

The Lizard Peninsula is almost, if not quite, the wildest and most solitary district in Cornwall. The deep estuary of the Helford River on the one hand, and the Loe Pool on the other, give it some degree of character of an island promontory. It is the most southerly land in England. It contains no town save Helston, which lies at its entrance; and nearly all its centre is occupied by the great waste of Goonhilly Downs, a tract of country which, however interesting to the botanist, or to him who gloats on legends, is sufficiently savage to have been a terror to travellers of ages not very remote from our own, and is still a perplexity even to natives, when the sea mists envelope it with light wreaths of vapour, and the familiar land-marks seem to melt away, and drift by as impalpable as the fog. It has a coastline of great magnificence and beauty in the eyes of summer visitors, but pitifully dreaded by the mariner, and there is hardly one among its rocky coves or iron precipices to which some story does not cling of a night of death and terror; so that when one walks around the cliffs they seem a trifle ghostly, as those regions must where, since the beginning of time, scarce even a winter storm has blown itself out without sending some tall ship crashing to her doom. And it was not only the fury of the sea and wind that sailors driven on this coast had cause to dread, for the cruelty and greed of man wrought in the same direction; and this is one of the districts in which the old tales of wrecking cling most persistently. In this isolated region a wild and lawless population was left to follow its own impulses, unrestrained by contact with men of other ideas; and the result was a life vivid enough to set any man's imagination working, as he follows the cliff paths.

On the eastern range of cliffs the caverns which pierce them are mostly accessible only by sea. As for the cliffs in the contrary direction, the wise man will walk along them all the way to Helston. There is scarce a yard which is not fine and striking; while almost at the beginning of the walk lies Kynance Cove, which some assert to be the finest in all Cornwall. It is beyond all doubt a place of singular beauty. It is approached through a rocky gorge, whose deep sides are golden with sweet-scented furze, and in whose bottom a rapid stream gushes over boulders, foaming into little cascades and reedy pools, and so courses onwards to a high rocky wall down which it leaps into the sea. In the bed of this stream the stones of serpentine, polished by the rushing water, gleam with points of fiery red; and the steps cut in the rock beside it, by which one goes to the beach, are like those of a king's palace, so green and ruddy are their streaks and veins.

It is the eve of Helston Flora day, and unless I reach the Angel ere night, I may well find myself crowded out from that old hostelry. When I reach the wide hilly street of Helston the lamps are lighted in the porches of the hotels. All night I am lulled by the song of running water, for the one beauty of Helston is a double stream which gushes fresh and copious down either side of its precipitous main street; and early in the morning the sound of a band awakes me to the consciousness that the festivities of Flora day have begun. I dress hastily, and get out to find the volunteer band perambulating the town, playing in slow time, and with a strongly marked accent, that quaint old hornpipe tune which will be familiar enough before the day is over. A crowd of men and boys marches with the band; but Helston has not got its blood up yet, and they step out gravely, keeping time as if it were a solemn duty, while none but a few impulsive youngsters seize each other by the waist and twirl round to a clumsy dancing step. The general opinion is that the time for these levities has not come yet; and thus the band goes quietly about, and the women stand in their doors tapping out the time with restless feet, and laughing merrily as the crowd goes by.

A little later in the morning brakes and carriages begin to arrive in crowds. Enormous numbers of people throng the streets, booths are erected by the footways, and such mountains of sticky things are being piled on them as may serve to give happy moments to all the boys and girls of western Cornwall. Down in the meadows by the river at the foot of the town a circus tent is being put up as fast as the crowd of children will permit; and by and by the procession goes through the streets. It is historical and educative. First comes William the Conqueror, all clad in a silver armour a little battered, as the corselet of such a mighty warrior would naturally be, his half-fed destrier neatly ticketed on the flank with the designation and date of his illustrious rider. William II follows him, wearing a splendid ermine cloak, beneath which a pair of very ordinary blue serge trousers peep forth rather quaintly; and after him come riding solemnly a long row of English monarchs as far as Richard II, where a hiatus occurs, and we skip suddenly to Queen Mary, her of Scots, and lastly her reigning Majesty and Empress throned high on a triumphal car, which has been rigged up with unsparing grandeur. Truly a very moving pageant, though a little incomplete!

But how this sight has drawn the people out! Burly farmers in corduroys and gaiters, smart servant girls and farm wenches in new straw hats and bright pink bodices, labourers in their ill-fitting Sunday clothes, a sprinkling of ladies in gay summer dresses, a countless multitude of boys, a party of sailors from the *Ganges* – all these seething to and fro, pushing, struggling, shouting, laughing, swearing, cracking jokes upon each other, swaying every way at once and trampling each other down the centre of the street. Outside the corn market the throng is at its densest, for from that point the first party is to start at one o'clock on its time-honoured errand of dancing round the town, thus celebrating the old spring festival which has been kept in Helston with hardly a break since the days, so very long ago, when the faith and reverence which it excited were real and living.

This is why the streets are dressed up with green boughs and garlands and strings of flags; and this it is which has drawn all this mad weltering impatient crowd out of the scattered hamlets and lonely farms of a thinly populated countryside. There is a long delay; but at last the policemen rush out of the corn market and charge everybody in violent excitement. The booming of a drum is heard. The volunteers in uniform emerge and form up as well as the crowd allows them. Now the band has begun solemnly, yet gaily, to play the ancient well-marked melody. The crowd surges back, and the party comes tripping down the steps, looking by no means joyous, but oppressed with the consciousness that the most venerable institution of their mother town is in their hands to maintain or disgrace. And now they dutifully twirl each other round, and smile and try to look as if they were at ease; and so the whole procession sweeps round into a street where they disappear bodily into the back door of a shop, while a few minutes later those who are able to see anything at all in the press behold them issuing triumphantly from the shop door, ducking their heads to avoid the swinging hams and sausages, headed by their music trumpeting loudly for very joy at having got over their first fence and left none of their number in the ditch. High spirited and joyful they all are as they emerge, and they change partners outside the shop door on the pavement, and go on again, disappearing and emerging, among the shouts and laughter of the crowd. And indeed there is something highly quaint in the sight of those uniformed musicians with their train of top-hatted men and bright-dressed ladies marching solemnly into the kitchen entrance of some quiet house, while the crowd fights and quarrels as to where they will come out.

But the crowd cannot forget itself as they do. No one copies them. It is a good-tempered throng enough, but now it has no joyousness, no verve, it is afraid of looking foolish, and, indeed, is more than half convinced that the dancers are a pack of fools, and they themselves who stand squeezing each other in the street the only wise ones.

How different this might be were the spirit of the ancient ceremony not yet dead! Can no one even now revive it? Then this solemn capering, all weighted and burdened by the fear of ridicule, might become what it was once – an act of joyousness and true rejoicing with one's neighbours over the glory and the beauty of the spring. There is room enough in modern life for such a spectacle; for a day set apart on which for once the heavy weight of labour and responsibility might be shaken off their shoulders by all ranks and classes, making open profession together of a joyousness which clears the heart and sweeps away the mists of winter and ushers in the season of warmth and sunshine in which all things equally begin to bud and blossom.

7

DONEGAL
AND ANTRIM

Stephen Gwynn, 1899

Carrick; Slieve League;
Glen Columbkille

The road from Killybegs to Carrick is one you cannot well miss, for telegraph wires will guide you the whole way. Very little of it is really level, but it is fairly divided between uphill and down. I rode it on a Sunday, and for my sins had to carry my baggage, as Carrick, like London, has no Sunday delivery of letters*; extremes meet. Also I had driving rain and a head of wind and soft roads; and under these conditions I was almost an hour and three-quarters on the way. At first you are by the sea, then you turn inland, and wind your way over very wild mountain; but the shapes of everything were lost in what we in Ireland call a Scotch mist, though we all know Scotland has no monopoly of the article. At Kilcar you may leave the telegraph posts and turn to the right for about a mile, when you will meet the posts again, and they will take you over the wildest of all these wild hills into Carrick. I never saw anywhere so many wild flowers as among these marshy meadows. Somewhere on the other side of the hill leading down to Kilcar I had noticed the finest patch I ever saw of the beautiful white bog bean growing in a swamp to the right of the road. Bog-cotton was everywhere through the heather, of course. But this

---

*Throughout his tour by bicycle (often referred to simply as the 'machine'), the author sent his luggage on by mail car, when possible.

hillside about Kilcar was simply flooded with bluebells: growing, not in the shelter of trees or hedges – for trees and hedges
there are none on these wild moors: but the ocean winds which
sweep the heads off whatever resists them deal gently with the
soft bluebells and let them carpet the open meadows to the
colour of an Italian sky.

When you crest the hill, the village with its Roman Catholic
chapel lies directly below you: you cross the Glen River by a
bridge, come up the little street, and at the head you will see
a low, comfortable-looking house with trim white verandah;
that is the Glen Columbkille Hotel.

There is a great deal to be said for staying at one place
instead of attempting perpetual motion; and if you adopt the
usual British formula of a compromise, there is no better place
to stay in for a week than Carrick. Besides, it is an excellent
spot for anglers. Brown trout fishing is free to all guests on two
rivers and three lakes. Salmon and trout fishing is free also,
provided you take out your licence in the hotel. The licence
taken there will be available at any other river in the county.
You are allowed to keep your fish, and with luck you should
get plenty.

But the essential thing for you to do is to see Slieve League
and Glen Columbkille. Leaving the hotel, one walks down a
road which follows the swift and rocky course of the Glen
River seawards for about two miles; then a track turns off to
the right up which ponies can carry a lady almost to the very
top. A few hundred yards further on a road branches away also
to the right, towards what simply appears to be a very high
mountain with a sharply serrated ridge defined against the sky.
The other side of the mountain is a precipitous cliff varying
from 1,000 to 2,000 feet, and part of the serrated ridge is One
Man's Path. All the water you can see from here is the estuary
winding down to Teelin Harbour, and beyond that the mouth
of Donegal Bay with the Sligo mountains showing blue on the

far side. The road goes on for a considerable way and turns into
a path up which a donkey can travel; I made the journey in
company with a man who was going up to cut turf. Here in
Glen Columbkille they get their firing free, but they have to go
a far way for it in some cases. A few of the more fortunate can
cut on their own farms: my companion had to ascend at least
1,000 feet before he reached his own particular bog; yet there
are plenty less lucky than he, for they have not all donkeys to
carry the sods. He was a fisherman by trade and belonged to
the crew of a yarl, one of the row-boats which go out to fish
for cod, ling, and mackerel off this rocky coast. They never go
far from Teelin, as it is the only safe place to run to. Most of
the fish caught in this way is sold to cadgers or travelling hawk-
ers; the Congested Districts Board make no objection to this
trade provided the price given is at least sixpence a dozen
above what they give at the curing station. My friend seemed
to envy the more fortunate crews of smacks who take to the
nets and go round to Galway Bay or Downings Bay in Sheep-
haven; but he had 'an old father and mother that had no other
son but him', and they objected to these protracted and risky
cruises. On every smack is a crew of eight; six Irish and with
them two Scotchmen, who are regularly retained by the Board
at a fixed wage to teach the others how and where to shoot
their nets and how to mend and keep them. It is a school of
technical education, and one sorely needed, for the Irish have
never at any time used the sea for peace or war: and the men
seem to take to it.

These details, I confess, seemed to me more interesting than
scenery, and when my acquaintance broke off to show me a slab
called the Giant's Grave with some old wives' story attached
to it, I headed him off antiquities. But when one reached the
cliff edge and saw the sea 1,000 feet below and the Connaught
coast stretching away in its interminable line, one felt there
was something to be said for scenery. The extraordinary beauty

of the scene was given by a sight which must be common at that point. It was blowing half a gale, the bay was full of spindrift, and the sun striking on this made a rainbow right below us, arched against sea and cliff. I never realised what intensity of colour was before.

From this point you begin a really stiff climb, following the edge of the cliff in its upward winding. The stiffest of the actual climb is over when you get to One Man's Path. Here the cliff top is literally a narrow edge of stone about two feet across, mounting very steep for about fifteen yards. It must be done on hands and knees. On your right inland is a very steep slope running down towards a tarn; on the seaward side is practically a straight drop, but only over a heathery slope. It is my opinion that if you fell off One Man's Path on the landside you would roll down with little damage, and that if you fell off on the seaward side you would be able to stop yourself by clinging to the heather. My guide – for I took the gentleman with the ass as a guide – was of a very different opinion; and there is no doubt that although the cliffs here are not absolutely plumb – as they are at Head and Horn Head – you could toboggan down them with every certainty of a speedy run to the bottom. But One Man's Path is nothing to be afraid of. Your guide, if you have one, will industriously try to frighten you, and then flatter you when you have got across. All I can say for mine is that he was genuinely afraid, for he declined to carry my macintosh over the place, on the grounds that his boots were bad; and I had to wear it, which gave me an insight into the difficulties of cliff work for ladies.

Tourists should be careful to believe what they are told about the dangers of Slieve League when it is capped with mist. Under these conditions a guide is indispensable. Anyone who wishes to walk back across the mountain will find it rough work, and possibly dangerous, even on a clear day, to people who do not understand bogs. The mountain is full of hares, which add charm of wild life to it, and everywhere one is haunted by the pretty little wheatears, a bird strange to English eyes.

Having seen Slieve League, it is your next duty to see Glen Columbkille and Glen Head, perhaps the only piece of coast scenery that can hold its own for grandeur with the famous cliff. There are three ways of doing this. Either you may continue to stay at Carrick; secondly, you may go to Glen and put up at the inn there, which is a very clean little public house, the sort of thing which is common in England but rare and deserving of every encouragement in Ireland; or, thirdly, you may take the Glen on your way to Glenties or Ardara. I started from Carrick with rain threatening and the usual headwind; pushed the machine nearly all the way for a matter of two miles up a road – which on a calm dry day could be easily ridden – following the course of the Owen Wee River. Then I came to a bridge, and kept straight on past many cottages with dogs that necessitated an occasional stone. I came to Lough Auva which was being lashed by the westerly wind. Here I stopped and fished the lough for an hour or so; if you care to know the bag, it consisted of two trout of which the larger might have weighed so much as one ounce: they are both growing bigger and wiser as I write. An old watcher who hailed me to see my pass for the fishing comforted me with the assurance that it was only two miles to Malinmore, and that I would go down 'like thunder'. I did not make so much noise as thunder, and I was much below the pace of lightning, but still I had a downward slope. Past a coastguard station at Malinmore I had the wind nearly behind me and sailed along cheerfully.

Suddenly the road turned and there Glen Head rose before me – a huge cliff shrouded in mist at the top, and two great rocks standing up at an angle as if slices had been cut off the cliff and fallen apart. It was impressive to the point of startling one. A truly terrible coast it is, and there are not many of us who would like to have a son engaged in fishing there. Down the road you spin and here for the first time since I entered the county from the south, I saw what is familiar all the way to Horn Head – seaweed used for manure. I ran through the town and up to the little inn; there I left my bicycle and asked the landlord to find me someone who would show me the antiquities of the Glen. For this Glen, wild as it is, in perhaps the most inaccessible part of Ireland, whether by land or sea, was the peculiar sanctuary of Ireland's greatest missionary, St Columbkille, who founded numberless monasteries in Ireland before he went to Iona and set to evangelising the barbarous Scots and Britons. English people when they hear this suppose that it is some sort of joke; but the historic fact remains that, from the beginning of the sixth century to the end of the eighth, Ireland was the University of Europe just as Greece was in the late days of the Roman Republic.

John Gillespie, who showed me over the place, will no doubt do the same for you if you ask him; he is lame, but to judge from my experience can tire out most walkers on our mountains. One of the most interesting things in the Glen is a cave in the cemetery of the Protestant church which was discovered by chance by men digging a grave not long ago. It is an artificial underground passage leading between two underground rooms. The roof is constructed of immense transverse slabs of stone. Still more interesting are the old remains of huts, roofed in likewise with huge stones. One of these, alas! is, by a utilitarian generation, converted into a pigsty. What they were for is a matter for conjecture. My guide set them down as pagan.

The day was misty, but Gillespie remarked that I might never be there again, so up the Head he took me to the Sturrell or Spire point. On the way up my companion discoursed of many things, the praise of the Congested Districts Board chiefly. What they have done for the fisheries was not news to me. He was of opinion, also, that the homespun industry was a real source of profit to the peasants, and if this last year was not as bad as the early eighties, that was thanks to a potato spraying system that the Board had introduced. We plunged along the cliff front in the driving mist, and ultimately struck a road leading out to the Sturrell itself, which is a high conical piece of rock, with a limitless drop below it. At this point the youths of that side of the Glen are in the habit of climbing down the cliff face in search of strayed sheep.

Coming down we passed Columbkille's holy well. As we were there and tasting the water, I thoughtlessly asked Gillespie if he had ever been to Doon well. 'Once,' he said with a curious intonation; and I knew instantly what I might have guessed, that he must have been taken there in the hopes of a cure. He hurt his knee at 'hurling', from a blow of the hard wooden ball, and is very lame indeed. To that circumstance, no doubt, he owes an exceptional taste for education. There were few things that did not seem to interest him, for he had the temper that makes of so many Irishmen either scholars or wanderers, though living in this out-of-the-world place.

I had tea – very good – at the little public house, took my machine, wheeled it laboriously up a mile or so of hill; found a level of a mile at top, then a generous descent of about four miles, the whole of which to the hotel may be coasted, and it is barely needful to pedal again even once. This is all very well when the road is dry and clean, but whizzing down among the stones and on a muddy surface I was thankful to escape a sideslip. I ran also into a flock of sheep – but gently; and there is always the losing hazard of a pig or a cow. That is why coasting is hardly safe in Donegal: the reader may take the warning.

8

DORSET

Sir Frederick Treves, 1906

Shaftesbury; Iwerne Minster ('the Village of the Future'); Lyme Regis

The Shaftesbury of today is a bright, pleasant and healthy town, perched on the bluff end of a ridge. The best sight of Shaftesbury is from Melbury Hill on the south. From this height it appears as a steep green ridge capped on the skyline by red-roofed houses and church towers and by comfortable clumps of trees.

The town has some 2,000 inhabitants, and its disposition is of the simplest. A hot and tired-looking road hurries in from Salisbury, climbs over the hill, and, dropping down upon the other side, pushes on towards Sherborne. In its unsteady passage across the top of the ridge it makes the wavering High Street of the settlement. A few side lanes on either side complete the plan of the place.

Most of the houses, of stone and red brick, cling to that austere simplicity of design which marks the habitation a child draws on a slate – a thing of four symmetrical windows, a central door and two chimneys giving forth a curling smoke. There are, however, modern villas which would not disgrace the suburbs of Stratford-by-Bow.

At many a point in the streets of this windswept town will be a bright gap among the houses whence is a sudden view of the limitless valley. In any street you may come unexpectedly upon a steep, green-walled lane which drops down over the cliff to the plain as a rope ladder would drop from a tower. Not the least headlong of these lanes is Gold Hill. It is a cobbled way, slow to climb, at the summit of which are the not unpicturesque Town Hall, the crumbling church of St Peter's and the Sun and Moon inn.

The ancient church of St Peter's is the most conspicuous object in the High Street. Faded and pitiably senile, its stone is corroded by centuries of keen wind and biting rain, while its tottering doorway and porch stand by the church as emblems of venerable poverty. The deserted sanctuary seems to be shrinking into the earth; so close are its windows to the very pavement that the curious child can peep in at the empty nave.

On the southern edge of the ridge is a delightful wooded walk, called Park Walk, from which extends a view surpassed by few in England. This meditative avenue is on the very edge of the height, and it is said to have been a walk in the Abbey Park. The view from the Abbey terrace is across a vast, verdant, undulating valley of the richest pasture land – a plain without a level stretch in it. It ever rolls away into shallow valley and low hill, with now and then a wooded height or the glittering track of a stream. The land is broken up into a thousand fields, fringed by luxuriant hedges. In every hedge are many trees; trees follow every buff-coloured road, and gather around every hamlet or cluster of farm buildings. It is a country of dairies. Everywhere are there cows, for the smell of cows is the incense of North Dorset.

At Shaftesbury, as at many another Dorset town, the dweller in cities can see something of the charm of the life of little towns. There is a curious absence of traffic in the streets, and a sense that the place is deserted. Everyone walks in the road, and from the tramp of their feet on the crisp way it would seem that shoes here are of heavier make than in cities. In London the passing crowd is dumb, for all are strangers. Here each knows the other, so that scarcely a soul goes by without a word of greeting. The boys in the streets are whistling a tune which was popular two years ago; many people stand at street corners, as if waiting for someone who never comes; most of the men carry sticks, and most of the women baskets.

There is a personality about the place which is lacking in those great cities which never slumber nor sleep. In the morning the town wakes up. The householder opens his front door and stands out in the road in his shirtsleeves to appraise the weather. The idle apprentice takes down the shop shutters and – between intervals of gossip – places buckets, spades, tubs, horse-collars and other goods, according to their kinds, upon the edge of the pavement. The sexton strolls by to toll the morning bell. A leisurely man drags a drowsy horse to the blacksmith's to be shod, and in a while there is the sound of a hammer on the anvil. A passing gig, that started from some farmhouse at sunrise, interests the waking town. It may carry a dairymaid on her way to a new situation, a couple of milk cans, or a confused heifer under a net.

A man proceeds to sweep the road with a besom made of a bundle of twigs according to the pattern of centuries ago. He shows a willingness to converse with everyone who will stop to pass the time of day with him. As something of an event, a miller's cart, with a team of four fine horses, climbs up the High Street. They may have come so far that they appear to be foreign. There is always a vain, boastful dog with the waggon, who clamours that the town should stir to see his horses, his wain, his waggoner and his sacks, all of which he regards as of unequalled magnificence.

In the evening the town goes lazily to sleep. The yawning shops close reluctantly, the long shadows of the setting sun fall across the drowsy street. The children have vanished. The lovers have come back from the lanes arm in arm. A tired dog is asleep in the centre of the road. Lights go out in the windows one by one, until the place is silent and dark. The visitor from the city falls asleep, lulled by the unwonted odour of a blown-out candle and of a pillow that has been embalmed in lavender. Possibly about midnight a single horseman trots into the sleeping town, and in a while two horsemen clatter out again along the same road. From which it may be known that an anxious man has come in from the country to fetch the doctor, and is taking him back as if by the bidding of some habeas corpus.

*

On the Blandford road is Iwerne Minster, a village of some size, beautifully situated, and possessed of many charming old cottages. It must at one time have been very picturesque, but it is in the process of being metamorphosed into red brick. The low thatched cottages are gradually vanishing, to be replaced by bold houses of gaudy brick and tiles.

Iwerne serves to show one phase of the future – the well-to-do, unblushing village of red brick, which for the bread of quiet beauty offers the stone of harsh unseemliness. It is impossible to complain of this with any show of reason. The low thatched cottage embedded in creepers is to a varying extent unhealthy; it is probably damp, is certainly ill ventilated, and usually lacking in light and the first needs of sanitation. The red brick house can claim to be 'hygienic', but by some ill fortune most things that are hygienic – whether they be clothing, food, or buildings – are unpleasant and unsightly. Even the hygienic person, with his fusty undergarments, his dismal diet, and his axioms about drains and traps, is not attractive. It is unreasonable to require that the inhabitants of villages should occupy unwholesome dwellings merely to please the aesthetic tastes of the passer-by. The exquisite old thatched cottage, with its tiny windows of diamond panes, must go, for the man of drains has spoken, and with it will vanish the most characteristic feature of rural England.

That the unhealthiness of the gracious old cottage is no matter of surmise is enforced by the evidence of poor health among villagers. The men, who live in the open air, may be hearty enough, although they are not always so robust as they look. The stay-at-home women, on the other hand, are very commonly the subjects of anaemia and not infrequently of tuberculosis. The life of a really poor woman in a remote village must be woefully and injuriously dull, and those who spend thousands of pounds in providing holidays for city folk might remember that cottagers are not exempted from the need of change simply because they live in the country. In support of this I may quote the following paragraph from a London journal:

> Those who view the increase of insanity in these islands with alarm are apt to attribute the deplorable growth of lunacy to the pressures of modern life, and especially the struggle for existence in great cities. They picture the simple countryman living the 'simple life' in reasonable content, and keeping a sound mind in a healthy body, while the dweller in crowded areas succumbs to nervous strain. Upon this picture the fifty-ninth report of the Commissioners in Lunacy, just issued, turns the hard light of facts. According to this summary, it is the countryman who goes mad sooner on the average, while the much-pitied townsman, in spite of strain and competition, remains sane enough to be called upon to look after him.[*]

One remark I overheard at a small wayside station will,

---

[*] *Daily Telegraph*, 12 September 1905.

perhaps, impress the town-dweller with the isolation of some village lives. A woman, who had evidently walked far to take the train, having deposited her great bunch of flowers and queer parcels on the bench, exclaimed with great fervour, 'Oh! How nice to see a railway station once more!'

*

From the windy summit of Timber Hill, beyond Charmouth, the white high road drops down headlong into Lyme. From the height it is possible to look down upon the town as from the battlements of a tower. The place looks exceedingly small as it stands on the narrow ledge between the downs and the sea. So wide is the expanse of the Channel that the tiny settlement is dwarfed to a mere patch of colour on a beach. Lyme, from the heights, is nothing more than a jumble of red roofs, from which rises a grey church tower, and from which trail into the sea the curving tendrils of the cobb or pier round a clump of schooners and brigs.

The houses, like the Gaderene swine, appear to be running down a steep place into the sea. At the end of the street they are only prevented from tumbling into the ocean by a sudden sea wall, over which they hang unsteadily. Just a few escape and wander along the beach. Lyme-of-the-King is a very undecided town, a place of wandering and unrealised ideas. The main street on its way to the shore wavers to and fro like a drunken man. The lanes are in disorder, as if they could never determine which way to go. There is an esplanade or marine walk, but it has neither orthodox beginning nor end. It starts, in a way, with an assortment of houses, a new red-brick building, an ancient thatched cottage with a bow window, and a pompous villa. It then lapses into a green bank of bushes, fir trees, and a wild undergrowth, a garden or two, and the blankest of blank walls. Finally it takes to houses again, but in the form now of a solid clump.

There is a piece of sea wall by the stream which seems to have been built at ten different periods from ten different points of view. Many of the houses of Lyme are ancient and very picturesque. They are all irregular, however, for the unmethodical seaport seems to have changed its mind many times as to its intentions. At present it is carrying out a rustic attempt to found a seaside resort.

The old fossil shop nearby, 'patronised by Prince Alfred', is as curious a house as any in the town. Here can be purchased, at the same counter, fresh prawns or fossil ammonites, filleted soles or pieces of a saurian's backbone. Some few million years ago the vicinity of Lyme Regis was a favourite resort for saurians, fearful monsters, who have never been seen when living by the eye of man.

The cobb or stone pier is the chief glory and delight of Lyme. It is a sturdy work, laid down on mysterious lines and bearing a resemblance to no marine structure of like intent. It combines in one series of stone banks the functions of a breakwater, a quay and a pier. It has somewhat the curve of a shepherd's crook, with an adventitious tentacle of masonry projecting from the summit of its bend. It wanders into the water in a hesitating manner which is quite in keeping with the uncertainty of the town. The cobb, or a cobb, dates from the time of Edward I, since when it has been many times destroyed by storms and as many times rebuilt. The present work belongs to 1825, when it rose afresh from the ruin wrought by the memorable gale of the previous year.

The most curious quarter of Lyme Regis is that which crowds about the banks of the Buddle River. So very narrow is the stream that the houses upon the two sides of it nearly touch one another, especially as they are brought nearer by overhanging storeys propped up by ruffianly-looking timbers. Certain of the dwellings are built actually over the stream, so that the halting watercourse runs partly through a tunnel and partly by a dark gully between precipitous house backs. The dwellings, faded and sinister-looking, would appear to keep to such simple old customs as the emptying of slops and rubbish out of windows. This obsolete riverside place is particularly evil-looking at night. There is a suggestion of trapdoors, of dark entries, and of dungeon-like, mouldy cellars. It has been — if the stories are true — a smugglers' alley of the fine old cutlass and pistol type. To the imaginative it is a water lane of muffled footsteps, of dark lanterns carried with suspicious slowness, of hoarse whispers and an occasional low whistle, of sudden lights at dirty windows and of ropes mysteriously lowered into the gloom.

9
EAST ANGLIA

William A. Dutt, 1901

The Fens; Dedham Vale

No greater contrast can be imagined than that between Fenland in summer and Fenland in winter. Today it is a sunlit but somnolent district. The cattle on the fens, glad to avail themselves of any streak or patch of shade, stand close under the hedges and willows and scarcely stir amid the seeding grasses. The larks' songs are only faintly heard – they are almost lost in the vast expanse of sky. The meadow pipits are even less audible; the *chizzit* of the wagtails is heard at such long intervals as to suggest that even those active, dignified little dyke-rangers are enjoying a noontide siesta. Since the bargee vanished into the alehouse near Brandon Creek Bridge, I have not seen a human being, though there are snug little homesteads dotted about the lowlands. But presently I hear a sound which indicates that there is human life not far from the riverside – a sound characteristic of these lush pastures. It is the musical clinking of milk pails. At first I cannot discover whence it comes; but suddenly, from behind a weather-beaten cattle-bield, emerges a figure which might have stepped out of the pages of *Tess of the d'Urbervilles*. It is that of a fair young milkmaid, who is carrying to a neighbouring farmstead a couple of pails nearly brimming with frothing milk. She carries them in the old country fashion, on chains attached to a wooden yoke which rests upon her shoulders. A lilac sunbonnet, despite its capaciousness, fails to conceal the warm flush exertion has brought to her cheeks, nor does it wholly hide the delightful disorder of her dusky hair. The weight of the brimming cans must be such as would make many men glad to set them down every hundred yards or so; but so long as she is in sight she keeps on walking at an even pace. Such a stalwart maid would, I fancy, in the old days have been one of the first to shoulder spade and start for the bank that weakened under stress of storm. She disappears behind a hedge of sallows and elders, and I am left alone again in the midst of the fens.

Such is the aspect of a part of the Great Level today. Let me try and picture it on a winter day, when the floods are 'out' and many acres of shallow water are frozen and able to bear the weight of a thousand skaters. (Fenmen will assure you that, so far as England is concerned, it is only on the Great Level of Fenland that you have a chance of indulging in real skating; and everyone who knows what the district is like after a succession of sharp frosts will agree with them. Where else can skaters go for an out-and-home run of over seventy miles in a day, as has been done between Earith and Wisbech?) The whole Level, except where the sweepers have prepared the ice for a winter carnival, lies under a white coverlet of snow; willows, gateposts, and every other inanimate stationary object which rises above the snow, glistens with rime frost; the snow itself sparkles as though dusted with diamonds. Since about nine in the morning a continuous stream of skaters has flowed towards the ice, Lynn, Ely, Littleport, Wisbech, Downham, and many of the Fenland hamlets each contributing its quota to the crowd of pleasure-seekers. For the latter it is a great day. Not only are they able to take part in one of the healthiest and most enjoyable pastimes, but they are to witness an important skating match between some of the best-known experts in Fenland. As the time for the races approaches, the crowd distributes itself along the borders of a course roped off for the event of the day. The competitors wear close-fitting jerseys and breeches; some are bare-headed, others wear a kind of maltster's cap. Each man has supporters ready to back him against all comers; during the interval between the appearance of the racers and the starting of the race his merits and demerits are fully and freely discussed. While the race is going on the excitement is intense, and the ice around the course suffers in consequence. The winner of every heat receives an ovation; hats and sticks are waved, skaters able and awkward cut the queerest of capers, and the frosty air resounds with shouts of acclamation. The final heat is contested amid so deafening a din that one wonders how it is the competitors are not unnerved by it; but they go about their racing with set, stolid faces, as though the result were a matter of absolute indifference to them. Yet it is amazing what activity and endurance they display, what long strokes they take, and how sharply their skates cut into the ice. (Old 'Turkey' Smart used to take strokes averaging fourteen yards, and was known to have made them eighteen yards 'with the wind'.) That wide swinging of the arms, which distinguishes the Fenland skaters from all others, adds much to the racer's speed; but it is to sheer strength – splendid muscular development of back, thighs, and legs – that the fenmen chiefly owe their prowess. When you see them win races you may know that their success is due to hard training – to trench-digging and ploughing on the peaty fens.

So the fenman's life today, while it has its hardships, such as long hours of exposure to drenching rains, scorching sun, and biting blasts, is not without its pleasures. On one thing, at least, he has good cause to congratulate himself: he is no longer subject to the attacks of ague, that 'Bailiff of Marshland' whose shivering fits were so frequently inflicted upon the old-time slodgers and bankers. Dugdale* was much impressed by the difficulty the fenmen of his day had in living a healthy life.

---

* Sir William Dugdale (1605–1686).

'What expectation of health can there be,' he asks, 'to the bodies of men where there is no element of good? The air being for the most part cloudy, gross, and full of rotten harrs, the water putrid and muddy, yea, and full of loathsome vermin; the earth spongy and boggy, and the fire noisome by the stink of smoaky hassocks.' Many of the victims of the joint-racking 'Bailiff of Marshland' became habitual opium-eaters: until a comparatively recent date the sale of opium in the Fenland towns was greater than anywhere else in England. Now that the fens are practically all drained the dwellers in Fenland are no longer slaves to the drug; except, maybe, for a few old marsh folk who use it to 'soothe a blank senility'.

*

Words cannot convey the charm of lovely Dedham Vale. Its beauty is too subtle to be grasped in detail, too various to be described in general terms. Just now, as I lean against a field gate beside the Flatford road, it is full of lights and shades and overhung by slowly drifting clouds. Where the shadows lurk the outlines of the trees and homesteads are hardly definable; even the borders of the fields and pastures are scarcely perceptible; but where the sunlight falls every waterside willow and poplar, every cottage, hedgerow and farmstead stands out clear and beautiful, each a picture in itself. Subject to the clouds' drift, the swathes of light and shade steal in quick succession through the vale, and presently the tall square tower of Dedham church – so conspicuous a feature of Constable's picture of the vale – reveals itself amid a grove of trees. Around the church lies the village which gives its name to the vale, and beyond it and the slow-flowing river are the Essex cornfields. Go into the National Gallery and look at Constable's *Cornfield* and you will see one of these Essex fields. In the foreground of the picture is a winding lane, beyond which the yellow corn is

bathed in sunlight. Through an open gateway you see the corn-
stalks bowing before the wind. Beyond the field is Dedham
church. Beside the lane is a brook into which the brambles dip
their bending briars, arching from banks where wave the white
umbels of wild parsleys. Along the rough waggon track a dog
drives a flock of sheep while their young shepherd lies down
to drink of the waters of the brook. In the neighbourhood of
East Bergholt are many such lanes, bordered by oaks and elms,
and hedgerows draped with bryony. They tempt you to leave
the highroads and by-roads; but if you yield to the temptation
you find it hard to retrace your steps, for every turning reveals
some fresh alluring charm. One such lane branches off from
the Flatford road and seems to lose itself in the Dedham Vale;
but the road leads down to the river. And it is towards the river
I ramble after leaning for an hour or more over that field gate
on the uplands above the vale. But like most strangers in this
enchanting country I find it impossible to hasten. For the road
suddenly becomes an arboreal cloister into which the sunlight
filters as through the leafage of a dense wood, and again I am
a laggard wayfarer, loitering as though I had a lifetime in which
to find my way to Flatford Mill. A noontide twilight lurks in
this tunnel of sylvan greenery; moths which shun the daylight
are abroad here at midday; even in winter, when the trees are
leafless, this bit of road can never know full daylight, so closely
interlaced are its overarching boughs. I begin to think that
Nature never meant men to discover Flatford, so made the
approach to it one of captivating charm.

But I have determined that no witchery of Nature shall keep
me from seeing Flatford Mill, and when I emerge from the
mystic noon-gloom of this sylvan shadowland I have freed
myself of the last of her magic spells. Before me lie the open
levels of the Stour valley – a wide plain of pleasant pasture-
lands where cattle are grazing amid whispering sedges and
gleaming willows. As I cross the rustic wooden bridge which

spans the river a little way below the mill I hear the rushing of water over a weir, and following the footpath by the riverside I soon come to the lock gates. A few steps further and the mill itself comes in sight on the opposite bank of the stream. It has altered little since Constable painted it nearly a hundred years ago; but the trees which then gave it a sylvan setting almost hide it now, and to see it clearly I have to cross the river again. But the old wooden lock is quite unchanged, and so, too, is the towing path which was one of the artist's favourite haunts. Giant burdocks, pink hemp agrimony, dingy figwort, and large-leaved comfrey grow close beside it, and it is fragrant of water mint and almond-scented meadow-sweet. A more peaceful scene one cannot imagine. Not a jarring sound breaks the spell of its quiet beauty. The stream flows silently until it falls over the weir, and even then its voice is as soothing as that of a summer breeze among summer leaves. Now and again a rat rustles in the sedges or a fish makes a faint splash as it rises to the surface of the mill pool. Brilliant-hued dragonflies flash like living gems above the bright green water-weeds, beautiful as the flickering sun-gleams which steal through the willows to the stream. A lad who came down to the river to fish has fallen asleep on the bank, where he lies half concealed by mauve-flowered water mints. His rod has fallen from his hand and its line is entangled with a patch of stout-stemmed hemlock in the stream. His stillness reminds me that Constable, while paint-ing here one day, sat so still that a field mouse crept into his coat pocket.

Dusk descends with almost tropical suddenness upon the Stour valley, for when the setting sun reaches the uplands' high horizon the shadows steal quickly over the lowlands. As soon as the light fails little wisps of mist appear, marking the wind-ings of the river. Slowly the mist spreads over the meadows, lurking close to the ground, so that the trunks of trees are hidden while their branches are unconcealed. The grass and flowers are soon saturated with moisture, and the briars fringed with mist-drops which shower down at the slightest touch. Then it is time to leave the lowlands and seek a clearer and drier air; so I retrace my steps to East Bergholt. Under the dense leafage of the sylvan part of the Flatford road the gloom is now at its deepest, and a man who bids me a gruff 'Good-night' passes unseen; but when I reach the gate over which I got my first glimpse of the Vale of Dedham a surprise awaits me. For there I see the moon rising and slowly filling the vale with silvery light. The effect is weirdly beautiful; it is aerial, nebulous, phantasmal; for the whole valley is now white with mist. From my point of vantage I can almost believe I am on a mountain top and looking down on cloudland, and that the dark blotches which are really trees are glimpses of the earth beneath the clouds. Nature has drawn a white coverlet over the sleeping earth – a coverlet which, in the moonlight, seems made of the very drapery of dreams.

10

ESSEX

———◆———

Clifford Bax, 1939

Southend

Yesterday several hundred whitebaits were buried with fitting pomp. The Southend Chamber of Trade was revelling in its annual whitebait feast and, according to *The Times*, the little victims were played into the dining room by a fanfare from 'trumpeters of the Royal Artillery in full dress'. Other specimens of a harmless tribe enjoyed an even more august fate, being presented, we are told, to the Minister of Agriculture and Fisheries, the Lord Mayor of London, and the Prime Minister himself.

Seeing that the pier, the remoteness of the sea at low tide, and the presence of many winkles have made Southend so famous, especially among music-hall comedians, it is interesting to find that in 1804 an Essex historian dismissed it in a hundred words. 'Southend,' he said,

> 'is a small village, pleasantly situated on the acclivity of a well-wooded hill, at the mouth of the Thames, nearly opposite Sheerness. Within the last twelve or fifteen years, it has obtained some repute as a bathing place; and though previously little known, has been since advancing in importance. An Assembly Room has been erected for the use of visitors, as well as a row of respectable houses for lodgings; and a new theatre is in contemplation. At a little distance from the village is a *Stone*, placed as a boundary mark, at the extent

of the jurisdiction of the Corporation of London, over the river Thames.'

Again, it is startling, and a little grievous, to find that Miss Austen permits one of her characters to say, 'It was an awkward business, my dear, your spending the autumn at South End instead of coming here. I never had such opinion of the Sea Air.' I do not know how many people were living in the 'small village' when Miss Austen was writing *Emma*, but as against a mere 8,000 in 1881, Southend has now, if the *Alphabetical Railway Guide* does not mislead us, some 120,000 inhabitants. It has also one faithful visitor whose name is likely to be associated for a very long time with the 'small village' — the well-known hippophile, Mr James Agate.*

Agate, however, does not see Southend from the pit or gallery. To rent a bungalow, or to hire a room in some massive hotel, is to flavour Southend as little, as though, seeking to appreciate the comedy of the Surrey crowd, we were to sit upon a bench in the pavilion at Kennington Oval. To understand Southend completely it is necessary to go there in August and to stay in Mrs Bloater's† lace-curtained apartments. Here a man may find himself occupying a plain but hygienic bedroom, with 'view of sea' if he is lucky enough to resemble the giraffe. He will need, it is true, to rise early if he means to recline for more than two minutes in Mrs Bloater's bath, nor should he be squeamish if he finds that a certain portion of that bath might with advantage have been re-enamelled. After all, if the tide is in, he can always join the hearty throng which makes a rite of its 'morning dip'. In any case, he would be a

---

* 1877–1947; as well as being one of the most popular theatre critics of his day, Agate was an expert on horses.

† The author adds his own footnote here: 'That is not her true name, but it is a near-truth.'

very churl if he were to criticise the exiguousness of his breakfast, for even Mrs Bloater must live, or so she maintains; and
although the rasher may be a burnt offering, the visitor will not
be starved of 'human interest'. Mr Spriggs, Mrs Spriggs and
the two small sprigs are delightful examples of English honesty
and goodwill. They look with awe upon little Teddy Trile, the
jockey, for Trile has been photographed so often for the papers.
They feel, in the simplicity of their hearts, that Mr Trile's opinion of the European situation must be worth more than their
own because he is famous. And then, there was poor Miss Macintosh, foredoomed from birth to be a spinster, but a spinster,
as we discovered, with very harsh views of those who will not
spend Sunday morning in church.

Mrs Bloater presided, of course, at our table, nor did any of
us hear her complain even once that blancmange had appeared
as our 'sweet' for five days out of the seven. Mrs Spriggs
wanted to protest, but Hiram K. Lovejoy prevented a civil war
at 'Cosinook' by assuring her that blancmange was, as the word
suggests, very good for the complexion. Joe Trott, a publican
from the Midlands, raised the spirit in everyone by telling us
that 'it don't matter *what* you eat, believe me, so long as you
enjoy it'; and there may be some truth in his philosophy.

It was Joe Trott who took me on to the celebrated pier.
Southend does not encourage the slot-machines which enable
a ravenous male to learn 'What Happened When Mabel Put
Out the Light', or even to see 'What Happened When Agatha
Goes to Bed': and Joe, I may as well admit, was disappointed.
'I came south,' he said, 'hoping to get a bit of fun,' and we all
know that life in the Midlands is not sumptuously fulfilled.
Nevertheless, Joe Trott and I, before we trudged to the very
end of the pier, beguiled ourselves by having our fortunes automatically forecast (Joe was informed that he would soon meet
with a dazzling blonde, and remarked 'My wife's a blonde —
or so she says'); by engaging, at a penny a side, in an almost

paralytic football match, and also by watching a house burn. I did not tell Joe Trott that, according to Erewhon Butler‡, everybody hopes that the fire will win. He had, I think, not heard of Butler.

By this time the sun, though not sinking, was in a decline; and Joe suggested that we might be wasting the privilege of being alive if we did not taste a few Southend winkles. So we did that. And it was then that he told me – you never know what you might hear next – that Mr Spriggs, despite his upright demeanour, had for several years been living in sin. I expressed my horror, as was right. 'Yes,' said Trott, 'he's keeping two establishments, though how he does it I can't imagine. Lucky devil!' After the winkles we were in high spirits. We felt that Trile, although he was so popular with the picture-papers, could not withstand us and that there might be some intricacies in the European situation which he had overlooked; and it was in that brave mood that Joe and I convened for our high tea at six o'clock.

Trott was one of those innumerable men who suppose that their opinions are as important as the opinions of a Cabinet minister. He argued with the jockey as though their exchange of views could really modify the map of Europe; and there, just opposite me, sat Mr Spriggs, little guessing that I knew the black secret of his double life. It is astonishing to watch the fervour with which two Englishmen will engage in political combat – even to the point of detesting one another – and yet the rational onlooker is well aware that only five or six men in the kingdom can seriously affect its future.

After our high tea Mr Spriggs proudly drove his wife and me to the neighbouring village of Prittlewell. The little sprigs were making mud pies close to the pier and under the supervision

---

‡ Samuel Butler (1835–1902), author of the 1872 satirical novel *Erewhon*.

of Miss Macintosh. Spriggs ought never, I guessed, to have bought any car, but a car was as necessary to his self-respect as a Sam Browne belt is to that of an officer. Albert Spriggs, I discovered, was a hairdresser who cut hair in Epsom; and it was soon clear that his tiny car was a symbol of his masculinity. True, it was not built for long legs, but both the Spriggses have short legs, and the car did at least deliver its burden at Prittlewell. Unless the reader had consulted *The Place Names of Essex*, he would never, perhaps, have realised that a stream prittles; but no sooner will he hear the word than he must know in a flash that every stream has prittled since Eve met Adam. The name, we are told, signifies a babbling stream. Mrs Spriggs, not without cause, repeatedly told us that the village was sweetly pretty. Mr Spriggs, with that hunger for knowledge which most of us have detected in the conversation of hairdressers, wanted to see the church, and here we were able to appreciate something of Norman handiwork and a good measure of excellent building done in the fifteenth century. We also gazed with awe at the Roman tiles incorporated in one of the doorways, probably by Saxon masons, but Mrs Spriggs disconcerted us by saying, at the sound of the word 'Roman', that the government ought to prevent Signor Mussolini from tampering with English churches. Prittlewell is now merely a quiet adjunct to Southend, but for centuries it was the more important place. Sea-bathing, we must remember, is a fairly modern pleasure, and, a hundred years ago, an exotic indulgence. Had it not been so, the Brighton band would not have played the national anthem when George III stepped from his bathing machine.

As the evening was long and golden, we packed ourselves once more into the car, and visited Leigh and Hadleigh. The church at Leigh has been so altered that it did not long detain us, but we looked with admiration at several brasses, including an early one (1453) which mentions a certain

Richard Haddock. The most exciting incident in the history of this quiet and respectable place was the discovery, in 1892, of a skeleton under whose neckbone lay seven silver coins of King Alfred's minting. In the westering light the wide view from the church door was one to remember in hours of world-weariness. When we came to Hadleigh, Mr Spriggs appeared to be more excited by the scant ruins of the castle, built in 1230 by Hubert de Burgh, than by the church, and here again we were charmed by the landscape that lay before us and the reddening cloudscapes above us. There, far away across the estuary, lay the foreign fields of Kent.

From Southend an enterprising visitor, if able to wrench himself away from the delights of the pier and the thronged promenade, with all its effervescent human interest, may easily see at Shoeburyness our Navy in the making; and is it not always exhilarating to look upon soldiers, airmen and sailors – young fit men who, although they would never permit us to say so, are England's defence of her arts, her science, her commerce and her liberty? Moreover, only a little way from Shoeburyness lie those attractive islands Rushley, Potton, Havengore and New England; only a little eastward, the wild fragment of England which, misleadingly enough, is called Foulness Island. Worley refers to it as a 'dreary island'. When, however, we know that the name does not apply to the climate, but to the wild birds, or fowls, who find Foulness a better feeding place than any upon the grey savannahs of the sea, we shall suspect that the island would seem far from dreary to an ornithologist; and indeed it is one which needs not to be dreaded by a man who can endure the conversation of his own memories and thoughts.

By this time, however, the hairdresser's wife had become anxious about her offspring, and so, hunching ourselves into the car, we returned to our base. Southend was just lighting up. Many thousands of children had just gone to bed, dreaming happily, we may hope, of oranges, pierrots, mud pies and the sea; and those of the adult visitors who were not already in the picture houses, were snuffing up the fine air of Southend as they walked and joked along the immense parade. A faithful observer ought to admit that if we join that ever-moving throng we shall not be able to assert confidently that the English are a beautiful race, but he would also conclude, I believe, that the English, though unsubtle and satisfied with rudimentary forms of humour, are easy-going and kindly.

II

GALLOWAY
AND CARRICK

Revd C. H. Dick, 1938
(Second Edition)

The Nick of the Balloch;
Shalloch on Minnoch; the Merrick

The road to Barr branches off the Girvan Valley road and after passing Penkill Castle climbs to the height of 695 feet. Just beyond the summit there is a place called Peden's Pulpit on the left side of the road, where a stone marks the scene of some of the Prophet's preaching labours. The road then winds downwards – this section is known locally as the Corkscrew – into the hollow where Barr lies among its trees and waters, 300 feet below the pass.

A very few days in Barr are enough to make one aware of its rather unusual attractions, and I stayed there for almost a month. The place is in touch with civilisation on the one hand and, on the other, is an outpost towards the wilds. A bus runs between it and Girvan, but there is no regular bus traffic passing through it. In half an hour one can board a train or bus at Girvan for the ends of the earth, while in less than this time one can be plunged deep in the lonely quiet of hills where the chief sounds are those of purling burns and bleating sheep and calls of grouse, peewits and an occasional black-headed gull. The Stinchar flows past the end of the village between well-wooded banks, receiving up and down its course here and there a tributary rippling gently under the shade of trees or thrown violently down a rocky gully. Barr is indeed a beautiful nook among closely enfolding hills with tall larches, birches, ash trees and other woodland giants shading the little streets, the grounds of the churches and the banks of the Gregg Burn.

I had to wait only three days for a dry forenoon. Meanwhile I was very comfortably lodged in the King's Arms Hotel, and if there had been need for soporific aid at night, this would have been supplied by the murmur of the Gregg Burn coursing rapidly in those rainy days past the front of the house.

I set off on my bicycle under a dull sky, leaving the village by the road that runs up Stinchar Glen to Pinvalley farm. Four miles from the starting point one turns sharply to the right where a fingerpost announces that here is a road to Newton Stewart. Besides Pinvalley farmhouse I had to open a gate where the road began to climb and made a note of that gate as a danger to be remembered if one should be descending from the Nick of the Balloch in the dark.

The track is the narrowest possible shelf consistent with being a road at all, and winds up steep pastoral slopes that descend on the right to ever greater depths as one mounts higher and higher.

A strong wind blowing down the valley made riding the bicycle impossible. This was no loss. Walking gave one more leisure to observe the mountains on the other side and the little glittering cataracts converging to make the Balloch Burn. The steepness and depth of the hillsides reminded me of the great passes between the Clyde and the Nith. There was also a suggestion of spaciousness here from the vista provided by the upper valley out of which the Balloch Burn was descending between the Balloch Hill on my right and the Glengap Hill on my left with, highest of all, the Haggis Hill filling the distance.

Soon the upper part of the Balloch valley was shut out as I came abreast of the Glengap Hill rising on the other side of the Corn Roy Burn, and my attention was now drawn to a cut in the skyline before me that looked as if it might be the Nick at the head of this tributary glen. In a few minutes I mounted the bicycle and so reached and passed the summit; but as the descent towards the junction with the road from Straiton began, there was to be no free-wheeling, for the still contrary wind came swirling along the mountain with great force. The ground now ran down abruptly on the left as it had formerly done on the right, and then, after a wide hollow where amid the brown moor I traced the earliest trickling feeders of the Minnoch Water, rose to a ridge on the other side of which was the glen of the road from Straiton; beyond that was the greater Rig of the Shalloch; while behind that, again, were the more northerly of the mountains that make the western front of the central mass of the Carrick and Galloway Highlands – Shalloch on Minnoch, Tarriefessock, Kirriereoch and the Merrick.

I soon saw below me the windings of the road from Straiton towards which the track that I was following was gently descending. A few yards short of their meeting point, the Rowantree Burn passes under bridges on both of the roads, and on its left bank is a rowan tree, probably not the first to give its name to the place, and I hope that it will not be the last to support the name.

At the angle of the roads are the slight remains of the inn and toll house. These were not coaching roads, and the only traveller's reference that I have found is in Sir Herbert Maxwell's *Evening Memories*, where he tells how when he was a boy of ten years[*], he was taken with his father and mother on some country house visits:

> At that time there was no railway nearer than Ayr sixty miles on the north and Dumfries seventy miles on the east. We travelled post in our big yellow carriage, with luggage atop and boot and rumble filled, over the wild mountainous

---

[*] In 1855.

region between Newton Stewart and Straiton, through the lonely toll bars of Suie and Rowantree, and so to Ayr. My mother whiled away the time by telling me the gruesome story of the Murder Hole.

At the schoolhouse, a mile farther on, I got directions for finding the Murder Hole. In an article contributed to *Good Words* by Sir Herbert Maxwell is given the only eye-witness's description that I have seen:

> There was a natural pit of unknown depth, with a narrow mouth, peering into which one might see – nay, may see to this day – inky water lipping to the green moss growing around the orifice. This murder hole has never revealed the full tale of its secrets, for it cannot be cleared out; but it was to its depths that the remains of the victims were one by one committed.

Since this was written the hole has been filled up to prevent its being a danger to children and sheep; but the site can be seen in a hollow of the moor just below the sheep-rees of Craigenreoch.

The powerful wind that had opposed my upward journey to the Nick of the Balloch still held and, as I returned towards the Nick, swept me before it. At the summit the depth of the glen was abruptly revealed, and although I had come up that way a few hours earlier, it gave me a shock of surprise, something like the startling effect that John Keats knew on seeing Ailsa Craig suddenly; but the road is narrow enough and, after passing the summit, steep enough to demand close attention on either bicycle or car, and I found myself taking little note of the scenery. On another visit a few days later I saw also, beyond the hills, the Isle of Arran, the intervening Firth of Clyde, and the Peninsula of Kintyre.

The brakes were in use during almost the whole of the descent. One of my most memorable bicycle rides was from the capital of Venezuela to the port of La Guaira. Then it seemed as if my fingers must be permanently stretched through the strain of holding the brakes. The descent from the Nick of the Balloch is not nearly so long, nor is it so steep, but it brought vividly to mind that earlier adventure.

After once scrambling up by the Nick and coming out upon the high, windy spaces, I was allured to repeat the journey and cross the Minnoch Valley to the mountains. Especially attractive was the rarely climbed Shalloch on Minnoch; its outline from easterly points of view, as I had hitherto seen it most often, is so striking.

Three days after the journey to Rowantree the sun was shining in the morning, and although the weather forecast was not encouraging, I took the Nick of the Balloch road again. At the house of Shalloch on Minnoch the herd's wife detailed one of her ten children to guide me to the Session Stone, a large slab on the edge of the right bank of the Shalloch Burn, where Covenanting preachers are said to have led the worship of congregations during the Persecution. It is easy to believe the tradition. On the other side of the burn is a level space with a curved bank behind it that would make a good auditorium on a still day or in a westerly breeze.

We made our way up the glen under a darkening sky, the weather seeming to fit the pathetic associations of the place. As we tramped over heath and moss amid scattered boulders, I told my young companion that it had been a custom of the herds in these parts to trample on the peewit's eggs whenever they found them, and that it had arisen in the days when our Covenanting forefathers had been hunted on the hills by dragoons and had had to meet with the utmost secrecy when they wished to worship God as faithful sons of the reformed Church of Scotland. Their reason for the destruction was that the peewit, alarmed by their presence, was very apt by its outcry to betray them to their enemies. Even in the nineteenth century instances of the practice occurred on the part of herds who did not know its origin. My guide had not heard of it.

From the Session Stone I took a fairly direct course towards the summit of Shalloch on Minnoch. As I climbed the long, easy slope, the weather became gloomier, the threatening clouds that were not being borne inland from the Atlantic making a grand, though not a welcome, spectacle. The threat was soon fulfilled in falling rain. As I turned and looked southward, the far-spread lowlands with an occasional clump of little hills and here and there a sullen-looking loch or a dark plantation were turned to a purple-grey that seemed to be verging on black, and there darted into my mind the Hebrew tradition about a darkness that once fell upon the land of Egypt.

I was too far up the hill to think of turning back. Just before I entered the cloud zone, I got a glimpse past the north-east front of Kirriereoch of a large part of Loch Enoch on its high shelf, a sight that after an interval of many years was worth the endurance of much mist and rain. My flimsy waterproof did not save me from being pretty thoroughly soaked from the waist downwards; but I knew that there was an abundant supply of hot water in the bathroom of the hotel at Barr and was sure that the herd's wife at the bottom of the hill would give me as many cups of tea as I wished, even if I had not complimented her on the handsome contribution that she had made to the population of the country!

Honour had been satisfied with two ascents to the Nick of the Balloch under my own power. When at last, in the middle of July, there came a fine day that I could devote to the Merrick, I used a motor-car to save time on the preliminary journey to the herd's house of Tarriefessock. The undulating floor of the Minnoch Valley was saturated with the recent rains and, wishing to keep my boots and stockings dry for at least the first half of the day, I took them off and walked barefoot. The only discomfort was caused by the hard stems of the frequent bog-myrtle, and these could usually be avoided. This, however, was a very slow way of crossing the country, and on reaching some rising ground near the farther side of the valley, I made better speed with my boots in their proper place.

I held on up the right bank of the Kirshinnoch Burn with the grim northern front of the Merrick before me. From this approach the mountain looks like a megatherium risen from the primeval slime, but now well washed by the rains of the millenniums. On reaching a double bend that made a place of shelter from the wind blowing up the glen, I had a bathe in the burn, a sunbathe on a rock in the midst of the singing water, and a light luncheon, a programme that made a good preparation for the real ascent. The sky was now somewhat overcast, but there was abundance of diffused sunlight, and much more extensive views were opened up than from Shalloch on Minnoch on that day of gloom. Among the greater birds that may be seen in this wilderness the golden eagle can still be named; but he comes only as a visitor taking an occasional glance at an old home of the family.

I left the summit by the Fang of Merrick, a very narrow spur falling northwards at the east end of the mountain. So narrow and so steep is the descent that it is almost like coming down a ladder.

Descending into the glen of the Kirshinnoch Burn, I took the right bank because I should thus get a better view of the mountain that I was leaving. On passing an accumulation of boulders it occurred to me that here was a likely home for foxes, and so it must have been for ages, for 'Kirshinnoch' means 'the foxes' crag'. But more noteworthy than these details was the northern front of the Merrick overhanging one in this narrow glen, almost vertical precipices alternating with driblets of scree as if the monster were baring his teeth and slavering at the thought of a victim.

12

GLOUCESTERSHIRE

Edward Hutton, 1932

Bourton-on-the-Water;
the Slaughters; Stow-on-the-Wold;
the Swells; Chipping Campden;
Broad Campden

From Little Rissington I went down near two miles to Bourton-on-the-Water. Someone has absurdly called this charming and mainly Georgian village 'the English Venice'. Bourton is as charming as its lovely name, with its bridges over the water, its grass beside the way, its placid air and broad street, and its beautiful trees. You may eat well there in an English way, you may play cricket, and there is a cottage hospital if you should be ill, and all looks prosperity and content. As my predecessor, the author of that charming book *By Thames and Cotswold* says, 'The church might have been quite comfortable, and Georgian too, like its tower, if someone had not set himself to make a new Gothic erection of it.'*That is well said. And how delightful it would have been to find a Georgian church here in Bourton Vale! Such things are none too common anywhere, and, indeed, cruelly rare in country places. The barbarism of destroying lovely eighteenth-century work, to substitute the jerry-built humbug of yesterday and today, could only have

---

*William Holden Hutton (1860–1930), also the author of *Highways and Byways in Shakespeare's Country* in this series.

been attempted by people who had lost not only all sense of beauty and fitness, but also all sense of morals. What is a momentary breaking of Friday's abstinence to a contempt for all beauty and a destruction of the excellent work of our fathers, to substitute the execrable fake of yesterday and today? Is not Pride the capital of all the capital sins? I should like to hear a bishop on these points, if bishops were not often the worst offenders. [. . .]

Well, let us get on to the Slaughters.

Bourton-on-the-Water
That's next door to Slaughter.

Lower Slaughter, I regret to say, has suffered in the same way as Bourton: the church was practically rebuilt in 1867. However, the old Transitional arcade between nave and aisle remains. It was a chapelry annexed to Bourton, and the register dates only from 1814. Here from the seventeenth century lived and died the Whitmores. Passing up through the churchyard, we come to a fine old manor house, among the lovely things of England, a thing almost to venerate, now a farmhouse in Upper Slaughter, that dates from Elizabeth and earlier, and its beauty more than compensates for the new church. Here after the Dissolution dwelt the Slaughters, an ancient family which took its name from the village, which itself may commemorate in its cruel name some battle with the Saxon pirates, or with the Danes‡. Such things are not to be thought of today in Lower Slaughter, which is a very trim village, with jolly little bridges over the stream and a great air of well-being and con-

---

† Another theory, much less dramatic, is that 'Slaughter' derives from the Old English 'slohtre', meaning 'muddy place'.

tent. Upper Slaughter is like unto it, even to the extent of having rebuilt its church.

Stow-on-the-Wold is very much what its name suggests. It stands on a hill near 800 feet high – is, indeed, the highest town in the Cotswolds – and is open to all the winds of heaven.

> *Stow-on-the-Wold,*
> *Where the wind blows cold.*

It seems to look down on everything. Stow-St-Edward, it used to be called, in kindlier phrase, for its church is dedicated in honour of the Confessor, and its once-famous fair was held upon the feast of that saint, 13 October, which has now become (for the fair) 24 October with the New Style.‡ This was a fair for horses, cows, sheep and cheese – Defoe, in his *Travels Through Great Britain*, says 20,000 sheep were sold here – but is now chiefly devoted to ironmongery and hops and whatnot, the horse fair taking place on 12 May (Old Style 1 May)§, the feast of saints Philip and James.

The Fosse Way runs right through Stow marketplace, which was in its great days larger than it is now, and, indeed, roads from all over Gloucestershire seem to meet in Stow-on-the-Wold. Its great days were, of course, the great days of Cirencester, Fairford, Northleach and other towns of the Cotswolds, when the Cotswold sheep, bred for their wool – you never see them now – were the source of the wealth in these hills, and found the money to build all the great Perpendicular churches which the rich wool-staplers set up in their pride in all these towns. Splendid lanterns they are, but somehow they lack the attraction of the older churches, and never

---

‡ The Gregorian calendar.
§ The Julian calendar.

seem to have expressed the religious awe and devotion inherent in the humbler Norman, Early English and Decorated sanctuaries, which were built not as a boast of so transitory riches where moth and rust corrupt, but for the glory and love of God. All the same, let us be glad of them, for very glorious they are, and for very long now we have not been able, and for very long we shall not be able, to match them. So it is at Stow-on-the-Wold. [. . .]

My immediate pleasure and business was to visit the Swells, which both lie in the valley westward under Stow. I reached Upper Swell by the meadow path about Abbotswood, a modern house. Upper Swell is a very beautiful village, and can boast of a manor house to vie for beauty with the Old Manor of Upper Slaughter. This lovely house, with its beautiful porch and gables, is later than the Old Manor at Slaughter – it seems to date from late Tudor or even Stuart times – but it is perfection, a beautiful work of the English Renaissance which somehow has a more human and perhaps more homely quality than houses of its date in France or Italy. Who would not ruin himself for such a house? Who would not willingly live and die in the shadow of such beauty?

I took it gently up the long hill into Stow, having enjoyed my morning's stroll. After luncheon at an inn, where it was now neither too early nor too late to obtain refreshment – these are very important matters in the kindergarten they are making of England – I set off downhill again for Oddington, eastward in the widening vale of Evenlode, till I came to the church in the secret vale near the inn, half a mile under the village. It stands quite alone, and might be called the beautiful church near the wood; so alone, so silent and so beautiful it is that one wonders whether it has not been happily forgotten by men since the sixteenth century, and whether if one came early enough, or at Easter, or All Souls, or Christmas, one might not find the Mass still being said, and the sacred Latin tongue and the tapers, and be perhaps the only living man among that cloud of witnesses crowding chancel and nave and aisle – since every Mass is said not for the living only. But it was summer when I came by, and already afternoon, and no priest was there nor any company to sing Vespers over Evenlode: only a bird sang, a woodland bird, and over all that peace brooded the voice of a dove. This little church of St Nicholas, which was long neglected and in ruin, is, I read, now in the care of the Society for the Preservation of Ancient Buildings. Remains of mural paintings, including a spoiled Doom, have been brought to light in the restoration.

The whole of the great northern promontory of the Cotswold, with Chipping Campden, its lovely capital, and the rich vale at its feet, is a *presqu'île* – indeed, an island – separated from the rest of our county. It is true that there is a narrow strip of land, a mere gully, a few hundred yards wide between Campden Ashes and Springhill which is for ever Gloucestershire, but Campden and all that great headland and beyond to the Avon, a country some ten miles by eight, can only be approached from alien soil. I don't like to say it, I can hardly bear to think of it, but the fact has to be faced: in case of war with Worcestershire, Warwick or Oxford, Campden might have to be abandoned. It would then become *irredenta*, and in the long political struggle for its redemption which would follow, filling generations and perhaps ages with intrigues, plots, assassinations, propaganda, patriotism, spying, rhetoric, blackmail, sentimentalism, blasphemy and treason in this best of all noble causes, only disaster could overtake the Empire, whether by then it remains British or, as some think, has again become Roman. This question of our northern frontier is a very serious matter. Why have the sodden Midlands, with all the filthy and immoral industrialism of their Birmingham, their Cowley, their Stourbridge, thrust down into us – our Eden, our demi-Paradise? Is it envy and egoism only, or mere vulgar, bulging, awkward parvenuism and new riches: just the old barbarian, the old Adam, the old jackass, wicked-ness – in one word, the Foreigner. [. . .]

Chipping Campden is unquestionably the finest of those Cotswold towns which got their riches and their beauty from the wool trade; Cirencester, Fairford, Lechlade, Northleach, Stow-on-the-Wold – none of them can really vie with her. Lying as she does in a fold of the Cotswold, where the hills grow narrow between the great vales of Gloucester and Eve-sham and the valleys of the Stour and the Avon, Campden is as it were caught in a knot, where Cotswold, hung with woods, doubles back about the valleys of Knee Brook, with the vale of Red Horse to the east. It is today still a stately town of one fine street, full of houses mainly of the late sixteenth and seven-teenth centuries, all preserved by good fortune and perhaps a little self-conscious contrivance, to the great pleasure of those who are, after all, only passers-by. That street is one of the glo-ries of Gloucestershire, and the great fifteenth-century church is as fine as anything of its kind in the county.

That noble and very English street, nearly a mile long, and wide too, gets its beauty and dignity from the fine old stone houses which are ranged along it: Grevel's House, built, it is said, by William Grevel, 'the flower of merchants all', about 1380, with its two-storied panelled oriel, its fourteenth-century doorway, its gargoyles; the (modernised) Court House, and the Market Hall, which lends the High Street so much picturesque-ness, built in 1624 by Sir Baptist Hicks. Then there is the Grammar School, rebuilt in 1628, but founded, it is said, by John Ferby and his wife in 1487, and the Almshouses, founded by Sir Baptist, in the southern end of the town. Yes, when Campden was a busy place in its great centuries, it must have been a sight to see. Even today we may recapture there something of the splendour of the unmechanised, non-industrial England (as we understand 'industry') when agriculture in its various forms was still its chief business.

Many are the pleasant walks about Campden. You have only to gain the ridge above to see all the world laid out at your feet, with its shining towns and villages, from the Malvern Hills to the Severn Sea, with Evesham, Tewkesbury and far Gloucester glittering in the rich and famous Vale between Severn and Cotswold.

Then there is the little Norman church at Broad Campden that must on no account be missed. It brings us back to an older England than that which Campden shows. One of the local *illustres* was Captain Robert Dover, founder of the Olympic games on Cotswold. He built a house at Stanway, and early in the reign of King James I founded the 'Cotswold games', which he kept going till the Civil War put an end to them and Merry England together; but they were revived under Charles II, and continued till 1859, when 30,000 people, 'the scum of the Black Country', attended. With the King's licence to choose a good place, Dover chose the hill half a mile outside Campden which still bears his name. There, arrayed in a discarded habit of the King, he superintended the games for many years and distributed the prizes annually on Whit Thursday. Ben Jonson, Drayton and other poets wrote verses on this festivity, which were collected into a volume and published under the title *Annalia Dubrensia*, now a very rare item for the Gloucestershire collector. The prizes were valuable, and five hundred gentlemen wore 'Dover's yellow favours'. The games consisted of wrestling, cudgel-play, the quintain, leaping, pitching the bar, playing at balloon, walking on the hands, a dance of virgins, hunting a hare which must not be killed, and horse racing.

Also at Broad Campden you may ruminate on the passion that some men have for Letters and Antiquity, and how, in the face of the most appalling obstacles, they will pursue it and let it possess them. Such a man was George Ballard, born here of mean parentage in 1706. His mother was a midwife, and he was, on account of weak health, apprenticed to a stay-maker. His fate was, as it ever is in such cases, early upon him. As a boy he showed a taste for learning, and especially, we read, for the study of Anglo-Saxon, so that he would read far into the night. Hearing of this, Lord Chedworth, 'and some gentleman of the hunt', offered him an annuity of £100 a year for life. Alas, gone are those generous souls! Would I had known you and excited your generous spirits! You have left, I fear, no successors, and fox-hunting, they say, with England, is on its last legs.

13

HAMPSHIRE

D. H. Moutray Read, 1908

Southampton; Winchester;
the Test Valley

Much of the history of Southampton is the history of her shire, and that, again, in great part is the history of England. Even to refer to most of it is beyond our compass. It is a great tale, endless as the lip, lip, lip of waters when the tides ebb and flow over the grass-wrack that trails above the ooze of the foreshore and gives such wonderful colours to Southampton Water. Many a time have I seen it, from the deck of a liner, from yacht or launch, from either bank, and from the Island that acts as a breakwater with its grim white cliffs to the south between the outer seas and these sheltered waters, and the only thing that is ever the same is my surprise. Nor is this only because of the endless variety the vagaries of our island climate bestow in colouring and atmospheric effect: the surprise is there on a grey day, when all colour is washed out in a sad drizzle; it is there when one steals by under the mystery of night, with a glimmer of lights on either hand, and their multifold reflections gleaming on the heaving darkness beneath; or when the bluest heaven is mirrored on an unrippled surface, and the church spires rise white above rows of villas and trees that spread away over the hills to fade into the blue-grey distance. This is Southampton, one of our great ports, where commerce holds successful and busy sway, and, withal, its setting is rest the most absolute. To have stood on a trooper's deck when the long lines of khaki-clad figures filed up from train after train on a mission of war, and looked from the orderly disorder to the unchanged imperturbable quiet with which it was all encircled, is to have touched the quintessence of contrast.

And contrast is everywhere. Electric trams jangle past centuries-old masonry. Rows of villas, their bricks hardly set for newness, spread ever-increasing lines by and through avenues of venerable elms. From the gardens where the town children play, and where rhododendrons make a gorgeous display of blossom in their season, you may pass to the busy streets that lead to warehouses and docks, or by the old wall with its arcade and mouldering turrets; or from the cellars of thirteenth-century wine merchants, to the fo'c'sle of a German liner and its bizarre crowd of alien emigrants, of strange speech and foreign costume, chaffering by pantomime gestures with itinerant sellers. In fact, turn which way you will, if you seek contrast there is plenty yet for your finding, though modern 'improvements' have done their best to sweep away the remnants of the old town. Even the Bargate was in danger when the trams were brought along the High Street – it interfered with traffic: that sufficed, it must go. *Punch* amongst others came to the rescue, the roadway was lowered, and now the trams pass under the Norman archway in the core of the thirteenth-century gateway. It is a compromise, but the Bargate has been saved, and some day the local authorities may practically apply a great Irishman's theory when it was suggested a tree that interfered with his house should be felled – he could build another house, but not grow another tree – so it is possible to make another road, but never to replace the venerable Bargate, with its heraldic treasures, its stories and romances.

Above Bar the street becomes more and more modern, but Bargate Street leads westwards to Arundel Tower and the glory of Southampton, the grand old walls. The beautiful embattled Arcade is noted by every writer as unique. The fourteenth-

century arches set against the old Norman masonry are
mementoes of Southampton's blackest day of trial and shame,
the French raid of 1338. The good folk of the town were at
Mass one Sunday morning in October; the bad were presumably either non-existent or asleep, for up Southampton Water
to the Gravels swept a fleet of foreign galleys from Normandy
and Picardy, Genoa and Spain. There was harrying and hanging, fire and, sad to say, flight.

One might go on indefinitely wandering around Southampton's streets and corners, there is so much to remember, and
many a good tale or romance to recall: the docks and their
manifold interests, the busy wharves, trains and shipping,
freight and passengers, stacks of timber, warehouses piled with
bales, an ever-shifting scene: the gradual return of prosperity
– there were but thirteen ships, not counting coasters, connected with the port at the end of the eighteenth century, now
there are more than as many shipping companies! The coming
of the P&O liners opened a new phase in life to Southampton.
Officials came perforce to live where their duties required
them, and old Indians, retired officers and civilians, in part
attracted by the mildness of the climate, in part by convenience, settled in the vicinity, till the streets grew more gay than
they had been once the fashionable world deserted the town
for newer watering places and foreign spas.

*

In sooth the best approach to Winchester is a debatable matter.
My first, from the Forest, is now only a memory of bad roads
and disappointments; my next, other than by rail, was from
Farnham, and along the Pilgrim's Way; but, as a dramatic introduction, this is again unsatisfactory. You are in Winton before
you see it, and there is nothing to suggest the mother-city of a
nation till you have crossed the irregular High Street and come

down the narrow passage by the City Cross to the Cathedral. Then the sudden transition from the bustling little street with its quaint houses, its shops and traffic, to the elms and the lime-shaded quiet of the Cathedral precincts, the long, stately, grey pile, the venerable walls and red-brick houses, creeper-smothered, of the Close, is dramatic enough.

Trams – thank goodness! – do not jangle down Winchester's streets, but the old city has lost more than one could willingly spare of her ancient buildings. But, indeed, in view of her stormy past, it is wonderful, not that Winchester has few, but that she has any traces of antiquity to show. Cradled in her river valley, reft through the chalk backbone that stretches across the county, Winchester has watched the rolling up of page after page of our island story. Venta Belgarum developed to Win-chester, the centre of Anglo-Saxon civilisation, government and culture. Royal city, busy mart, educational centre, all of these she has been, and something of each remains with the old city of memories today. To me, it never seems that the old ages of Hampshire are as sentient in her cities as on her wild free Downs, and in forgotten corners of her valleys, where you may get very far away from sight or sound of aught modern. So one may most feel the age of Winchester when standing above her, say on St Catherine's Hill, especially when the sun sets behind the further ridge of downland and mist gathers in folds of grey along the valley. As night deepens it might be a vision of old Winton, and the bugles at the barracks are the trumpets of knightly retinues, till a motor coughing along the highway, or the rumble of the boat-express from Southampton, recalls one to the actualities of twentieth-century scurry.

Only a century ago the beacon fires on St Catherine's stood ready with a nightly guard, to light the pile, should a signal flame from the south-east give warning the menaced French invasion was become a dire reality. Among the orders given to the watch was one 'to be civil to the college boys when at their exercise on the hill, but not to allow them into the hut, or to pull the straw off the beacon'.

Though St Mary's College was not the first school in England it was the first modelled on college lines, where the boys and their education constituted the *raison d'être* of foundation, and thus furnished the pattern for our public schools today. Before Henry VI arranged the statutes of his Eton College, he spent studious days in Wykeham's school, examining the statutes and observing his methods. *Manners makyth man.** There is no lack of success to prove it. Men who left their mark on more than one generation are not far to seek if the roll of names be studied. For Wykeham was concerned with manners in the broadest sense – there were to be no half measures, for what a man is will his manners be, and it was the making of men the old master-builder had at heart when, in the city where he had himself been educated, he founded his school in connection with his Oxford college.† The buildings are solid and well fitted for their purpose; there is little ornate about them, yet they are not lacking in structural beauty. Alterations and additions have of necessity been made since the foundation stone was laid on 26 March, 1387; nearly nine years after Wykeham obtained a Bull from Pope Urban VI for 'a college of seventy poor scholars, clerks, to live college-wise and study grammar, near the city of Winchester'. He built for all time, for, even when these solid grey walls and sturdy timbers have crumbled to dust, the work of Wykeham and his sons remains, till time ceases, knit into the fabric of the Empire's life.

*

---

*The motto of Winchester College.
† Wykeham founded New College in 1379.

Wide stretches of lonely country, rolling expanse of grassy down broken by dark woods, or long strips of coppice beside a roadway, and the greenest of green valleys where the Test and her tributaries wind through marsh and meadow: such is the country that lies between central Hants and the Wiltshire border, a country intersected by road and rail, yet that retains much of the peaceful charm of old-world days when rush and bustle seem to have been words without meaning. But it was never remote from beaten tracks, and even before the coming of the Iron Horse valley and down were cut through and across by important highways; roads from Salisbury to Winchester and Andover, and the old Roman causeway from Cirencester to Winchester meeting at right angles in the green heart of the downlands the coach road from Basingstoke to Stockbridge.

From Woolbury Ring one may get a wonderful panorama over all this green country and the valley of the beautiful Test, which of all our colourful corners possibly stands first, as certainly it does for variety of scenery. Even at midsummer the wealth of colour is indescribable. Spring displays hues of a fresh beauty and clearness that excel even the rich colouring when autumn turns the greens and yellows of down and cornfield to opulent bronze and gold, when the beeches exchange their deep greens for shimmering copper tints, and the elms flaunt every yellow against the red and brown of maple and oak. Wild flowers are everywhere, the deep hedges are buried in blossom each May, and burdened with berries by September. As for the water-meadows in the valleys, and the wild stretches of swamp or common through which the clear chalk streams twist in and out among the flowery borders, filter through beds of willow-herb and reed-mace, are lost under a tangle of sedge and sallow, divide into a dozen rills and channels, unite and broaden into wide and shallow lakes with a hundred reedy islands, as the wayward currents will, they have charms unending to those who find their pleasure in the wild life of Nature's gardens.

There is choice, therefore, for diverse tastes and fancies hereabouts – history and archaeology, sport and scenery. The flower lover may revel in the wealth of blossom and seek on the Downs that stretch towards Winchester for many a treasure. There is the rare round-headed rampion; the writer found some growing by the road over Worthy Down, and in the same neighbourhood were the burnt orchis, the broad-leaved and white helleborines, the beautiful butterfly orchis, and over a dozen others of that quaint and delightful tribe. There are orchis in the valleys also, the spider, a variety of the marsh, and the sweet-scented, besides less uncommon beauties in the wet meadows and by the riverside, where water-fowl nest in the sedges, and the gay yellow iris and the great masses of glorious mimulus succeed the golden marsh marigolds and exquisite pink and white blossoms of the buckbean by the forget-me-nots in every hollow and along every ditch. Here in springtime the weird drone of the drumming snipe rings over the swamp where his mate sits on her grass-lined nest in some dry reed tuft, while swifts and swallows rival his 'flightsmanship' as they wheel and dart with dizzying ceaselessness, and the sedge warblers vie with the lark and both are beaten in persistency by the cuckoo!

The peaceful water meadows are connected with brothers of the angle and their gentle art. In Tufton the lane crosses the river by a bridge that has often tempted me to linger when the whirr of a Nottingham reel comes from the riverside. Swiftly the clear water glides over the bed of waving water weeds; a flight of duck breaks from the reeds in the upper reach; here, there, everywhere, as the interlacing circles show, trout are rising for their evening meal. Whurr! Whurrrr! Someone is having good sport down there behind those grey-green willows by the clump of tall poplars where the river bends.

Plump. Splash! Fancy suggests a whopper, a very grandfather of trouts is rising yonder by that pollarded willow – or was it a water rat? Trout do not run to any great size in the upper waters of the Test, judging from those of my acquaintance. Our introduction usually takes place at the breakfast table! For records of monster trout one must wait till Romsey is reached; though between Longparish and Stockbridge they run up to three pounds and over. But the strictly preserved Test fishing is too well known to need comment, suffice it that, in the words of a local writer, '"Veish is the curiosest things as is" – and, like all unfathomable things, endowed with an irresistible and unfailing charm.'

14

HERTFORDSHIRE

Herbert W. Tompkins, 1902

West Hertfordshire

After a most enjoyable stroll across the little breezy Langley Common, through narrow winding lanes, and besides fields of corn I came back again just now into the road from Bucks Hill to Chipperfield. Here, close to an orchard where many beehives stand beneath the trees, I have been sitting down to make a few notes; to listen to the bees whose 'murmuring small trumpets sounden wide', and to the yellow-hammer who is calling persistently for a *very very little bit of bread and no-oo cheese*. It is another grand stretch of common that I cross soon after resuming my way, where for an eternity forest trees and furze have fought for supremacy of the soil, and the great battle of evolution is still waging. A fine old manor house is at Chipperfield, so spacious and so inviting that you can hardly observe it and keep the tenth commandment. Forest and furze have been cleared by the hand of man from before the village, which skirts the common on the east and the north; at the west angle of the common stands the church, approached from the east through an avenue of limes, and from the north through some fine lych-gates. Some of the oldest cottages in the village seem to be those at the northern end down by the Baptist chapel and the Royal Oak – houses of equal importance in the eyes of their respective supporters. A gentleman who shows his appreciation of the tropical warmth by walking in his shirt-sleeves, and whose appearance is strongly suggestive of Mr

Richard Swiveller*, tells me that the village of Chipperfield is well known to certain patrons of the 'fancy', and that 'the common is just the place for a walk before breakfast with a weighted stick when you're getting in condition.' I gather from his somewhat disjointed remarks that promising young boxers are sent here to train, but, although loquacious enough, he is careful to mention no names either of houses or men. Our ways soon part, but not before I have impressed him visibly by stating that the 'Coffee Cooler' was trained at Wheathampstead, and that I lived in the village at the time.†

If in these highways and byways in western Hertfordshire I fail to reap 'the harvest of a quiet eye', the fault is surely my own. Here, or nowhere, I may cultivate the art of sauntering. I am confident that to saunter in a pretty district, where the mind is kept occupied but not excited, is the finest of all tonics. De Quincey was sure that young ladies would take longer walks in the country if they knew how the practice enhanced the beauty of their eyes. The diminutive, opium-eating moralist was a great walker himself and would have rejoiced to see such tall, strong, handsome young women as I meet in the long street of Bovingdon. The village lies scattered upon the slopes of two hills, the centre being in the deep between the two, and the church of St Lawrence a few steps eastward from the main street. The most conspicuous object in the village is a well, now in disuse, with a pentagonal roof supported on pillars of timber. But I must take the road to Hemel Hempstead soon; so I bestow but a cursory glance upon the parish church, with its pinnacled tower and ivy-clad walls, and chat for a few

---

* The character from Dickens's *The Old Curiosity Shop*.

† The author is possibly referring to Frank Craig (1870–?), a New York middleweight boxer who in 1894 came to England to fight and stayed for over twenty years.

moments with a little maid who has brought a handful of marsh marigolds to place on 'Daddie's grave'.

It is a pleasant stroll through the suburban Marlowes to Hemel Hempstead. There is an abundance of wild flowers in trim gardens, unusual variety of cottage architecture, a high wooded ridge that shuts in the landscape upon the western side – and there is also a motor car. I wish people would refrain from naming rural highways and byways after London thoroughfares. I should like to enter this old town and climb its hilly High Street without passing Cornhill or Cheapside, especially as Hemel Hempstead, like Sion of old, is beautiful for situation. After sauntering through those streets of classic nomenclature, I turn to the left at the Posting House, go up Bury Hill, pass the Jolly Drayman and, looking back, have a good view of the little town called by the Saxons *Hamelamestead*. Above is a sky 'deeply, darkly, beautifully blue'; eastward from the town the hills are covered over with corn. People wishing to vegetate in the provinces might go very much farther and fare worse.

Here, as in other towns in Hertfordshire, paper is made, and there is a trade in corn and in straw plait – the latter, I am told, a fast dying industry. These last few days I have sometimes seen a woman or a child plaiting before their cottage, but twenty years ago I met them everywhere, holding the short straws between their teeth, and plaiting deftly and swiftly as they talked. In those days the plait was woven thus by thousands of hands, and brought from almost every village and hamlet in the county to the larger centres and there 'made up'. Indeed, the centre of this industry in England has, for two hundred years, been in the counties of Bedfordshire and Hertfordshire, for wheat grown hereabouts yielded excellent straws, bright in colour and of great strength. Twenty years ago the yearly output of the English straw-plaiting trade was about £4,000,000, but even then foreign materials fought against the straw of the Home Counties and hats of palmetto fronds were made at St Albans.

Market day here is Thursday, where there are sales of fat and store stock. Yesterday was the annual Wool Fair. The parish was formerly a 'Bailiwick'; the high bailiff was elected annually, on St Andrew's day, and there was, I believe, a praiseworthy custom of dispensing mulled port on that occasion at the expense of the new high bailiff. This evening the High Street is bright with colour as the promenade of a watering place, for it is Saturday and young ladies are finishing the week with critical inspections of their neighbours' dresses. But the best of pleasures pall; presently the idlers of the High Street disperse to their homes and I seek the quiet precincts of the fine old church of St Mary, where a mower is wetting his scythe in a far corner of the churchyard.

*

That Tring is an 'ancient town of England' is, I believe, indisputable; but this morning I have been wondering how it has contrived to conceal its antiquity. A bird's eye view of the disposition of the streets of Tring would readily convince you that the town grew up in the 'golden days, long, long ago', for it is dotted and dispersed irregularly around four main, twisted streets; but few of the houses are of great age. An hour's ramble from street to street has brought to my mind, with undesirable vividness, memories of Shoreditch and Whitechapel rather than of any other town. I have been peeping up courtyards and under arches, and trespassing in Willow Court and Tabernacle Yard and Denmark Place, where clusters of tiny cottages are hidden away under the very shadow of inns and in the rear of shops; where groups of children are playing at fivestones or squabbling about nothing, and women are at the wash-tub with their sleeves rolled up, or gossiping from door to door with their arms a-kimbo.

Had I visited Tring some years ago I might have sought out one who knew many a snatch and legend of the district. This was old Betty, a well-known person in this far west corner of Hertfordshire, who went 'a-fagging' every wheat harvest, and was over one hundred years old when last she gleaned in the fields near here. Farmer and labourer alike knew old Betty; she was fond of her snuff and, when asked how she did, invariably answered that she was well enough, but her box was empty. There was a touch of Meg Merrilies‡ in her too for she would rail on occasion against those who endeavoured to enclose common land, plough public footpaths, prosecute the poacher, or infringe the gleaner's immemorial rights. I am told that she died in her hundred and tenth year, and was hale and reasonable to the last.

Friday is market day in Tring, and if you had entered the town early in the morning, when the trade in hand-woven plait was at its height, you would have met on every side women coming in from the surrounding villages to sell their handiwork to the Luton dealers. But there is no market here today, and very little bustle or stir in the short High Street. Indeed, as I saunter from the corner of Akeman Street to the Robin Hood Inn, I see nothing out of the common order of things, saving only a sundial over a shop on my left-hand side, which has told the time o' day since the year 1773. So I retrace my steps and find myself in a long and narrow passage that leads me to Tring Park, in the midst of which stands the home of Lord Rothschild. Originally erected by that master-builder, Sir Christopher Wren, the house has been renovated and

---

‡ A half-crazy gypsy character who appeared in works by John Keats and Sir Walter Scott.

transformed. It is said that the Merry Monarch himself stayed here at times and that Mistress Nell Gwynn stayed here sometimes too.

If there is a more delightful spot in which to take one's ease than Tring Park I should like to know it. Rich, undulating pastures stretch on all sides from the house, crowned on the western side by a grandly wooded hill. The voices of the cuckoo and the dove seem to fill the whole park, stroll where I may. This, considering the quiet seclusion and the time of year, is perhaps no matter for surprise; but I am surprised indeed to come upon a dozen cassowaries and a kangaroo, near the footpath to the museum. The kangaroo is watching me, as he rests his chin upon a wire fence; but he can make nothing of me, and bounds away towards a large elm, where he regards me furtively for some time from the other side of the trunk. Crossing a little valley I am presently in the shadow of many spreading chestnut trees, then in a fine avenue of beech and yew, edged on either side with young berberis and fir. Another pathway leads me to higher ground, where many hundreds of tall beeches stand shoulder to shoulder; beneath them are thousands of tiny seedlings, rooted in the rich leaf-mould, the deposit of many autumns. How quiet, how fragrant, how impressive it all is!

Lovely byways these, indeed. From morning to evening I have roamed in the dense hazel woods around Lord Grimthorpe's estate at Batch Wood near St Albans, in the beautiful glades of Bricket Wood, in the Beech Hanger at Selbourne, in the Parkhurst and St Leonard's forests, in the glades of dwarf oak at Saundersfoot on the coast of Pembrokeshire, in the solitudes of the New Forest at Malwood and Lyndhurst and Fordingbridge; but I assert without hesitation that these walks on the wooded hillside at Tring are as beautiful as any of the spots that I have named. Early in the morning young school girls, their satchels on their shoulders, trip through these woods on their way from Wiggington to Tring. Emerson says that whilst we send our boys to school they educate themselves at the shop windows. Surely the daily walk through woods like these may become a more lovely education.

It is half an hour's walk from the town to the railway station at Tring. After passing the signpost on the Berkhamsted road, a long descent, shaded by many trees on the southern side, leads me once again to the towing path of the Grand Junction Canal. Here, however, the scene is not like that of the usual canal side, but far more picturesque. I have passed through a little gateway near the bridge, and scrambled down a most precipitous path to the waterside, where the steep banks on either side are covered with birch and larch and beech, and where wild roses, growing on the very edge of the water, strew it continually with their pink petals, now falling fast. The waters of this canal are in many places clear as a running stream; but the barge that passed just now, parting the masses of floating weed as it went, has left in its wake a muddy turmoil. A train hurrying northwards with its freight of human lives passes through the station as I clamber up the steep, a fact which I note because it is the last train I shall see for a day or two. These roads take me almost immediately into an open country, smiling brightly in the morning sun, and girt round with wooded hills in the far distance. I see the village of Aldbury straggling across the valley.

Aldbury is one of the few villages in Hertfordshire which has preserved its stocks to this day. The villagers are very proud of these stocks that stand beside the pond on the green, under the shadow of an enormous elm. They are not so perfect as they were recently, for one day some holidaymakers drove down to Aldbury and did their best to destroy as much as possible before leaving. They unfastened the stocks, pelted the upper board with stones and brickbats, and then flung it into the pond. After damaging the lower branches of the elm they turned their attention to the church, romped around the graves outside, and finding the door open, filled the sacred building with ribald shouts and broke portions from the limbs of the effigies. A vivid description of all this horseplay is given to me by a very civil Aldbury man, who adds that, had not the men of the village been in the fields at the time, those holiday-makers would have been roughly handled. Grandsires in Aldbury used also, many years back, to repeat strange stories of the ducking stool that stood close to the stocks for the correction of scolds and other naughty women; but stories and ducking stool alike are things of the past now.

15
CENTRAL HIGHLANDS

Seton Gordon, 1948

Loch Ness

During many centuries the River Ness has flowed unchanged yet ever-changing through Inverness. This river, so short in its course, is nevertheless in times of flood one of the most mighty in the Highlands. Its waters never freeze, even at the margins, and on a morning of hard frost it is interesting to see the majestic Ness flowing seaward, with waters steaming like those of a hot spring in Iceland. Here in winter many water ouzels fly backwards and forwards, or sing their low song, or plunge beneath that rapid tide and search the stones of the riverbed for aquatic larvae. In December, January and February, eager salmon, fat and silver-sided, from the deeps of the Atlantic enter the Ness and pass swiftly through to Loch Ness, thence to the clear foaming waters of the Garry, where they are sometimes caught with the fly on days of January so cold that the angler's line freezes to the rings of his rod. They are also taken in Loch Ness in this chilly season, but the Loch Ness salmon are believed to be a different race from those which enter the Garry.

Along the south bank of Loch Ness there is a good road from Inverness as far as Inverfarigaig and Foyers (where the splendid Fall of Foyers supplies power for aluminium works), but at Foyers the road leaves the loch-side and climbs to Whitebridge, continuing on high ground until Fort Augustus is almost reached.

The road from Inverness first skirts the River Ness, and

reaches the loch at Dores. Before Loch Ness was deepened for the passage of ships and its level considerably raised for the Caledonian Canal, the loch could be crossed at Dores at the Bona Ford.

Near Inverfarigaig rises Dun Dearduil, an ancient *dun* or fort that is connected with the Celtic heroine Deirdre, or Dearduil as she is sometimes called. I know of no *dun* in the Scottish Highlands in more inspiring surroundings. The hill on which it is built is cone-like and on three sides a sheer precipice. Beneath the hill flows the River Farigaig, a Highland river of swift rushes and deep, peat-stained pools, and along the river weeping birches sway graceful boughs.

I saw Dun Dearduil on a winter's day, when the leafless birches and cold ground, iron-hard from long-continued frost where the snow had gone from it, increased the heroic character of the scene.

The ascent of Dun Dearduil should be made from the southeast, for the ascent is comparatively easy from that quarter, and the rocky bluff on which the *dun* is built is seen at its best. Little is now left of the actual *dun*, but the great stones which formed its outer foundations are still in place. Because of the view alone, the ascent of the bluff will more than repay him who makes it. I know of no view which brings out so clearly the grandeur of Loch Ness, which is seen stretching away east and west into the haze of distance. Nor have I found a view which gives a greater dignity to the ruins of Castle Urquhart, although they are some miles distant and on the far side of the loch. On the winter day when I stood on Dun Dearduil I thought that Castle Urquhart rose like some magic castle, dark and mystical, upon a promontory that from my viewpoint seemed very lonely, and almost surrounded, so it appeared, by dark storm eddies which moved across Loch Ness on the icy breath of the winter wind.

Rather more than a mile to the west of Inverfarigaig and

Dun Dearduil is the Fall of Foyers, where Dr Johnson found 'all the gloom and grandeur of Siberian solitude'. Although Foyers itself has changed greatly during the past twenty-five years, the scene at the great fall has lost nothing of its dignity and grandeur. On this winter day the beauty of the scene was enhanced by the fairy-like wall of ice which had been built up on either side of the cascade, and the falling water, filling the deep gorge with tumult, disappeared almost at once beneath the ice which held the pool below. I was interested to see that the water lying above the ice at its edges was deeply stained with peat, and I thought this noteworthy, because there are few Highland rivers or burns which maintain their peaty character after a prolonged spell of frost.

From Foyers the road rises, and crossing the high ground and passing near Loch Tarff, descends again abruptly to the level of Loch Ness at Fort Augustus. Fort Augustus as a military station has disappeared. Where the fort stood is now a well-endowed Benedictine abbey. Lord Lovat bought from the government the fort and the farm attached to it, and the present monastery was completed and opened in 1878. The old fortress has now become part of the abbey. The old tree planted in memory of the battle of Culloden is still alive. The tradition that Jacobite prisoners were hanged on this tree is, I understand, incorrect; they were shot on a piece of level ground which is now the cricket field of the abbey.

The return journey to Inverness can be made along the north side of Loch Ness, by the new high-road from Fort William to Inverness. The scenery along this road, particularly in late spring or early summer, is especially fine. The graceful weeping birches leaf here earlier than in most parts of the Highlands, and are in all the beauty of their young foliage when the trees of Glen Moriston and Glen Urquhart are bare as at mid-winter. Broom beside this road comes into flower early. I have seen golden fields of broom here in April, although on the higher ground this plant does not flower until June. When, on damp rocks beside the Loch Ness road, broom and primroses are blossoming together, the blending of gold and yellow is most attractive. The road passes above the grand old ruin of Urquhart Castle, a ruin now in the care of the Government Department of Ancient Monuments.

From the neighbourhood of Urquhart Castle of recent years the strange but now well-attested creature, the Loch Ness monster, has on a number of occasions been seen. There is in my mind no doubt that such a creature – there may be more than one – does exist in Loch Ness. Among a number of reliable witnesses who told me that they saw the monster was the late Captain Grant, of the MacBrayne paddle steamer *Pioneer*, which regularly plies on Loch Ness during the summer months. From Captain Grant's observations – and from the observations of other reputable witnesses – it would seem that the strange creature is timid, and that the sound, or vibration, of a steamer's screw or paddles causes it to submerge while the ship is yet a considerable distance off. Mr Goodbody of Invergarry House and his daughter watched the creature for forty minutes through a stalking-glass. The Loch Ness monster is indeed no recent 'find', although at the present day it is known to a much larger number of people than ever before. The chief reason, I believe, why many more people now see it is that the new high-road along the north shore of Loch Ness gives a much better view of the loch. But there is another reason. Before the monster became, so to speak, public property, those who saw the 'unchancy' creature decided that the less said about it the better. They realised that they would be laughed at, or pitied, or would be set down as addicted to a 'dram'. So long as half a century ago, to my own knowledge, children were told by their nurses that if they persisted in naughtiness the loch monster would take them. I heard of a well-known resident on Loch Ness-side who one day, after rowing down the loch in his small boat, appeared at a friend's house white and shaken, and asked for brandy. His friend for some time vainly endeavoured to ascertain the cause of his distress, to receive an answer, 'It is no use my telling you, for even if I did you would not believe me.' But in the end, when prevailed upon to unburden himself of his secret, he said to his friend, 'As I was rowing down the loch some creature came to the surface beside me – and all I can say is that I hope I may never see the like again.'

Most of the large and deep Highland lochs harbour, in the legends of the country, creatures which, as described in old books and writings, in their appearance resemble the Loch Ness monster. A peculiarity common to them all would appear to be their humps. The monster of Loch Morar, deepest loch in Scotland with a depth of 1,080 feet, and a floor no less than 1,050 feet below sea level, had a special name; it was known to Gaelic-speaking Highlanders of the district as Mhorag, and appeared only before a death in the family of MacDonell of Morar. May it not be that in the monster of Loch Ness we have a survival of an ancient race which, living for the most part under water and being of a timid disposition, has existed in comparative obscurity during successive centuries?

Hills rise steeply from Loch Ness throughout the length of its northern shore. Looking west up the loch from the neighbourhood of Inverness, the most prominent of these hills is graceful Mealfourvonie (2,264 feet). Professor Watson gives the Gaelic name of the hill as Meall Fuarmhonaidh, Hill of Cold Moor. It doubtless received its name because of the cold, upland country which lies around it on every side, except towards Loch Ness.

Looking up Loch Ness, it can be realised how straight is the depression of the Great Glen, a depression which coincides with a line of fracture of great geological antiquity, and one which has been subjected again and again to disturbance and displacement. Even at the present day, earthquake tremors are more frequent here than elsewhere in the Highlands.

Let us now return to Dores, and instead of travelling along the shore of Loch Ness, ascend the hill road to Kildrummond, then make our way east along the moor road which ends at Inverness. In the neighbourhood are the high-lying lochs, Ashie and Duntelchaig. On the moor near Loch Duntelchaig are cairns which are believed to mark the ancient graves of warriors. The late Neil Fraser-Tytler of Aldourie, in an interesting booklet, *Tales of Old Days*, notes that on the moor east of this loch a ghostly battle has often been seen. Soon after dawn on a May morning is the most propitious time for watching that ghostly fight. In 1870–71 it was clearly seen, and the suggestion was made that it was a mirage of the fighting in France. But the battle has been seen since that time.

> Large bodies of men in close formation and smaller bodies of cavalry facing an attacking force advancing from the east, wounded men clapping sphagnum moss to their wounds and tearing off strips from their shirts to bind it on – all this has been seen. On one occasion a man cycling to Inverness saw three horsemen on the road in front of him. He followed them for some distance and then, when rounding a sharp bend in the road, he ran into and through them. He fell off his bicycle in astonishment, and on getting up he beheld the phantom armies.

A couple of miles to the south lies Loch Ruthven. The country around Loch Ruthven is wild and attractive, and in spring and early summer the air is filled with the trilling songs of curlews. The cuckoo calls from the birches, and lapwings wheel and somersault. It is a country very different from that of Loch

Ness, and in winter may be for weeks snowbound and in the grip of frost when on the shores of Loch Ness, 800 feet below, the ground is snowless and the air comparatively mild.

16

WEST HIGHLANDS

Seton Gordon, 1935

Ben Nevis

Ben Nevis, reaching a height of 4,400 feet above sea level, is the highest mountain in the British Isles, being rather more than 100 foot higher than Ben MacDhui, chief of the Cairngorm range. It stands at the head of Loch Linnhe, in Lochaber.

The derivation of the name Nevis is uncertain. The Gaelic name of the hill is Beinn Nimheis, and popular tradition describes it as the Hill of Heaven. The River Nevis probably named the hill, and some believe that the name is identical with the Old Irish 'neim', and may mean 'the venomous one'. Glen Nevis and its river had a bad reputation in the old days. It has been written of as 'a glen on which God has turned his back'.

The old people were awed by the darkness and gloom of Glen Nevis, from which the Ben towers mightily to the clouds. The pastime of mountaineering was then unknown, and it must have been rare indeed for any man to have climbed the hill. Then came the time when an observatory was built on the summit of Ben Nevis and for the best part of half a century hourly observations, both by day and night, were made here. The observers had thrilling experiences. The winter hurricanes, sometimes blowing at speeds of over two miles a minute, threatened to sweep them, with the furiously driven snow, over the great precipice that dropped sheer from beside the observatory. The record of one of the observers (*Forty Years on Ben Nevis*, by W. M. Kilgour) is a book which all who love the Scottish hills should read, and it sometimes recalls the

Everest expedition on a smaller scale. Northern Lights, St Elmo's Fire, Glories, Fire-balls, wonderful rainbows spanning the heavens, the blackness of an approaching storm, all these things were watched with appreciation by the small band who lived together in their mountain fastness on the Roof of Scotland.

The observatory, alas, has been abandoned, but it was built so firmly that it should stand for many a day. Its reports in these days of flying would be of considerable value, for it stands in path of the storms which approach us from the Atlantic.

One summer night that I spent on the summit of Ben Nevis remains as a clear memory. When I reached the plateau the sun had already set in the glens beneath me, but the hilltop was still bathed in its last rays, and the lingering snow-fields were faintly pink in its glow. The low sun passed just above the Cuillin summits in distant Skye, so that their jagged peaks stood out in sharp relief , and finally sank below the horizon beyond the hills of Knoydart. For fully three-quarters of an hour after the sun had set, its rays still shot high into the northern sky, and throughout the short night the horizon west and north held the afterglow, while in the east a waning moon struggled to pierce the mist with her silvery rays.

By dawn the face of the landscape had changed. During the brief hours of dusk a pall of white mist, creeping stealthily west from the distant North Sea, had covered all the Highlands. From this vast sea of mist the tops of the highest hills rose clearly. Never, either before or since, have I seen so unusual and wonderful a sight. Before the sun rose upon it the mist was grey and cold. Very gently the sun warmed that ocean of mist, so that a rose-coloured glow suffused it. On this glowing aerial sea the shadow of the Ben was thrown for many miles towards the south-west. On the hilltop scarcely a breath of wind stirred, but several thousand feet below me the cloud moved westward, and during its slow journey towards the Atlantic assumed in places the form of gigantic billows which rose above the average level of the mist sea as they flowed over some insignificant hill that barred their way. Even at ten o'clock the vast cloud canopy was still unbroken, and now reflected the rays of the sun with brilliance. High above the mist to the east the Cairngorm hills were visible; Cairn Toul (4,241 feet) being especially prominent across fifty miles of the Scottish Highlands. To the southward of it Loch na Gar, on the King's forest of Balmoral, climbed above the cloud. Of all the peaks rising from the mist sea, Schiehallion, 'fairy hill of the Caledonians', was the most striking, its tapering cone rising grandly to the blue of the sky. West, the two peaks of Cruachan just topped the cloud, but here the level of the mist was higher, and hid all but the summits of the highest hills. Sgurr a' Mhaim, across Glen Nevis, raised its crater-shaped corrie to the bright sunshine, and through my glass I saw two stags reach its ridge, and look down into the white ocean of cloud beneath them.

There are few flowering plants on the plateau of Ben Nevis, for the season of growth here is a very short one, but a small colony of plants of the starry saxifrage (*Saxifraga stellaris*) flower here at an elevation of 4,300 feet above sea level. This is, I believe, the highest point at which any flowering plants are found in Britain, for it is slightly higher than the summit of Ben MacDhui, where the cushion pink (*Silene acaulis*) is found.

I have stood on the summit of Ben Nevis on fine clear days, yet I have still to look forward to seeing the hills of the northern coast of Ireland. The distance is so great that it is only very occasionally that these distant hills are visible. The observatory staff have placed it on record that they *can* be seen on days of extreme visibility.

The climb I have described was in the middle of July – at the height of summer. Another day on which I climbed the Ben was in May. Summer that year came early to Lochaber. The birches, swaying their young green leaves in the soft breeze, were happy in the warmth of the sun. Fields of wild hyacinths scented the air. Only on the brow of Ben Nevis did winter linger. Down in Glen Nevis the river flowed low and clear. Glen Nevis is on the eastern border of Fort William. The climber takes the road up the east side of the glen, and at a farmhouse finds the beginning of the path to the hilltop. The ascent is easy and daring spirits have even driven motor cars and motor bicycles to the summit of the Ben, but this is not to be recommended. The ordinary mortal will be thankful if he reaches by his own unaided power the highest land in the British Isles.

As I climbed, this May day, Ben Nevis seemed to tower to the blue sky, and the strong sun gleamed on its great snow-fields. The bleating of lambs was heard. Beside the springs of clear water the green leafy rosettes of the starry saxifrage took the place of the pink flowers of the lousewort which had been seen at lower levels. On the path a ptarmigan's feather lay, but no voice of bird was heard that day upon the Ben which rose, grim and mighty, from a flower-strewn base.

From the halfway hut the view was already remarkable. Delicately pencilled on the north-west horizon rose Rhum. In the middle foreground was Loch Eil, its waters pale blue and calm. A herring drifter steamed out from the Caledonian Canal, and steered away for the open sea and the summer herring fishing in the Isles. I continued to climb, and at the 3,500-feet level entered the country of the snows. At first the snow lay in small fields, but before I had arrived at the height of 4,000 feet I was walking across an unbroken expanse of glistening white. Ben Nevis, like most hills, is deceptive. The summit appears close at hand and the climber is cheered. But now, as he thinks to stand on the summit, yet another snowy slope rises ahead of him, and this too must be surmounted, painfully and slowly, if the snow be soft. Many insects rested on the snow cap. The warm wind had carried them up from the lower slopes and they had alighted on an inhospitable waste. Across the snow they crept. After sunset they would have neither the power to rise nor the knowledge where to fly to escape the frost, and few would survive the night. Across the abyss of Glen Nevis Sgurr a' Mhaim rose. Its eastern crater-shaped corrie where I had seen the two stags on a midsummer day years before was now filled with unbroken snow. Bidean nam Beann, highest of Argyllshire hills, rose from dark Glen Coe, and near it was Beinn Bheir.

Great clouds, inky-black and menacing, approached the plateau of Ben Nevis. They hid the sun; they curled and eddied, with primrose edges and awe-inspiring centres. A twilight fell on the Ben. From white, the snows changed to pale grey and themselves appeared intangible and cloud-like. Across this Arctic waste rose a line of stone cairns that used to guide the observers to the summit in mist and snow, in the days when the observatory was occupied. At last I was close to the hill-top. Along the precipice a great cornice of snow extended into space. It was impossible to know whether I was standing above firm ground or was suspended by the frozen snow over an abyss of 2,000 feet. No Arctic tundra could have been more lonely. There must have been an average depth of twelve feet of snow on the hilltop. Yet in the glen beneath me the birches were in leaf, and violets and wild hyacinths were growing among the uncurling bracken fronds.

From the unbroken snowy surface the flat roof of the abandoned observatory and its chimney projected a few inches. The roof might have been a large flat rock. It was sun-warmed and pleasant to sit upon. Here I rested, looking over a wide country of hill, glen and sea, smiling and sunlit.

West and north rose hill upon hill. Beyond Lismore, low and green, was the Isle of Mull. Its highest hill, Beinn Mhor, was the only peak, north, south, east and west, on which a cloud rested. Beyond the cliffs of Gribun in Mull I fancied I could make out Iona. Far beyond Ben Resipol of Ardnamurchan rose the isles of Coll and Tiree on the hazy Atlantic. A hundred miles distant from where I sat were the hills of South Uist in the Outer Hebrides. Hecla, Corodale, the long ridge of Beinn Mhor — all were distinct. Bearing north, the Cuillin hills formed the horizon. So clear was the air in this direction that each sharp top could be distinguished. Upon Sgurr nan Gillean a snow-field shone. The glass showed the Inaccessible Pinnacle of Sgurr Dearg rising black against the sky. Even the great cairn on the summit of Beinn na Cailliche was visible. A sea of prim-rose mist, drifting before a northerly wind, swirled about the slopes of Glamaig. To the south the view was not so clear. Schiehallion was seen, but was less imposing than she had been on that early morning when I had watched the sun shine upon the aerial sea. To the east the Cairngorms were in strong sun-shine. Cairn Toul I recognised, and Brae Riach with its snow-filled corrie, and, across the depths of Lairig Ghru, the shoulder and summit of Ben MacDhui. It is a far cry from Iona, Coll and the Outer Hebrides to Schiehallion and the Cairn-gorms — from Jura (seen on the horizon southward) to the Cuillin of Skye and the hills of Ross-shire.

The ascent of Ben Nevis had been arduous. The descent was swift and easy. Down 2,000 feet of the hill I was able to follow a snow-filled gulley. The gradient was so steep that it would have been scarcely possible to have descended here under ordi-nary conditions, and at times I seemed in danger of disappearing over a snowy precipice. The snow, however, was soft and gave excellent footing. I heard beneath my feet the rush of a hill torrent, flowing unseen through a snow tunnel. The snow was blinding in the intensity of its light. I glissaded quickly down this almost vertical snow slope, and as I moved had the curious illusion of being suspended in space. Near the halfway hut I came upon the path and here, looking back, I saw great thunder-clouds gathering above the Ben, but the lower slopes of the hill were in brilliant sunshine.

That night, from the birches of Loch Eil, I looked back on to Ben Nevis. Above the lesser hills it towered, massive and imposing. In the evening light the great cornice fringing its summit was lemon-tinted. The lower slopes, snowless and in shadow, were of a deep blue. A thunder-cloud lay beyond the summit of glowing snow. Thus Ben Nevis appeared at the coming of summer. In June the snows on its crown gradually lessen, and disappear in July, but there is one snow-field in the north-east corrie which has never been known to melt, and they say in Lochaber that if snow should disappear from the Ben, the hill would revert to the Crown.

17

KENT

Walter Jerrold, 1907

Sandwich; Deal; Kentish Hops

Sandwich, quaint old Cinque Port of tortuous streets and ancient houses, suggestive by its very name of a dim, historic past, and of modern golf links, lies on the right bank of the Stour at its extreme southerly bend. As we approach it, the town, dominated by the curiously topped tower of St Peter's Church, has the look of a foreign city. Over the river is a toll bridge and a quaint (restored) barbican spans the road, upon the wall of it being set out an elaborate scale of tolls, providing for payment from drivers of 'Berlin chaises', 'chairs' and 'calashes'. As the scale is dated 1905 these vehicles of the past seem to belong to the present. Now the author passes untolled on a bicycle, wondering whether the tollman would be able to differentiate a calash from a berlin. Motors are ignored on the scale, ranking presumably as 'locomotives'.

North, Sandwich looks over the flats by the ancient Stonar and more ancient Richborough to Ebbsfleet and Thanet; east it looks over sandy levels to where the retreating sea has gone, and all about these level river and shore meadows is now played the royal and ancient game of golf. On approaching Sandwich as we are now doing from the north the way in which all sorts and conditions of people play the great game is at once made strikingly manifest. Girls not yet in their teens are playing here; there is a burly drayman – it is the dinner hour – refreshing himself, with his leather apron tucked up cornerwise to show he is off duty, handling his iron with vigour and precision. We might be in the town of St Andrews, patron saint of golf, by the way in which all ages and all classes follow the game. Out towards the sea are the more notable links. Probably few of those who come hither to indulge in the game are aware that in the sand dunes between here and Deal it was anciently the pleasant custom to bury thieves alive. Women criminals were drowned in the Guestling stream. The Cinque Ports had their own courts and were allowed seemingly to devise their own methods of punishing offenders.

It is said to be a good test of a man's bump of locality if once having visited Sandwich he can find his way through it – say from the Canterbury to the Deal roads – without making a misturning. The thing has been done. Dotted about the town are old houses of Tudor and earlier times, while a portion of worked flint wall – level as bricks – where the old guildhall once stood shows the wonderful way in which some earlier craftsmen did their work. Bits of carved decoration and old doorways and windows are to be seen in many of the streets, while some plain and unsuggestive exteriors hide olden and interesting bits. A one-time wayside inn (now dislicensed) has a fine stone arched room like a bit of an old crypt, and here tradition tells was one of the sleeping places for pilgrims bound for Canterbury. (The curious who go upstairs will find such a contrast between the now and then as may shock them.) On one of the pillars is a rudely incised shield with marks that might be meant for two crescents and a cross.

The chief 'lion' of Sandwich is its plain, modern Guildhall the outside of which scarcely suggests that the inside is well worth a visit. Here is to be seen the ancient woodwork from the older town hall, and here the visitor has an object lesson in the legal phrase 'empanelling' a jury, for the removal of a panel reveals the jury box literally set in the wall. In the upper rooms are portraits of civic worthies and a very interesting series of pictures illustrating a great seventeenth-century seafight between the English and the Dutch, probably that of 1666. On the beams are pikes which were of old carried before the judges at the time of the Assizes. Sandwich has fallen from something of its old estate, and the Assizes are no longer held there, though it is the seat of a Petty Sessions.

Sandwich, raised but a few feet from the surrounding level, was at one time walled partly with stone and partly with high banks of earth. Now these old defences are formed into pleasant promenades. Once the most famous port in the kingdom, then for a time the seat of baize manufacture and market gardening, thanks to the influx of Flemish folk in Elizabeth's time, the town had fallen into a condition of neglect and is said only to have 'wakened up' during the past quarter of a century or so since the great golf revival.

Inland from Sandwich lie many clustering villages but a mile or two apart, approached by roads and lanes largely through unfenced fields. From Little Betteshanger windmill is to be seen a magnificent view backwards to Thanet and eastwards over Deal to the sea; all around us are wide stretching fields of corn, of peas, of beans and of the sainfoin which gives to us so many of our summer scenes in East Kent a touch of unaccustomed colour.

Deal today is a curious mixture of the old and the new, of the fisherman's and sailor's town devoted to the sea, and of the holiday resort depending upon the attractions of the shore. When the Stour channel silted up and the old Roman Rutupiae* became no longer of service as a port, Sandwich rose into prominence, then when the sea retreated further to the east, to Deal fell much of that sea business for which Sandwich had become unfitted. Perhaps in some distant century Deal will have become an inland town and its place be taken by some as

---

* Richborough.

yet undreamed-of town on the Goodwins. Meanwhile, however, the Deal of the holidaymaker enjoys a pleasantly diversified life along its sea front, old, or Upper Deal, being left stranded inland, and to that has been added the attractions of a good beach and one of the most interesting outlooks over the water. It is difficult today, standing on the front and watching a crowd of sunburned children gazing with rapt attention at a Punch and Judy show, to realise the old days when Deal, as a town, was not; when extensive woodlands came probably far nearer to the coast; to realise those days, nearly twenty centuries ago, when Rome, as though prophetically, reached out after this small island destined to an empire greater than her own.

In the 'good old days' – in those days which are, by courtesy, called good – the whole of the coast along here was famous as a smuggling resort, and Deal was a particularly notorious centre. From Deal, all round the coast until our Kentish story merges in that of Sussex, the coast has its traditions of smugglers and their cuteness in running their wares inland; of their bravery in fighting the preventive officers; of the way in which the gentry and squires, aye, and even those who dwelt within the shadow of the old church towers, profited by the illicit transactions of those who spent their lives in support of the saying that stolen fruit is the sweetest. The old Admiralty House, little more than a hundred years ago, is said to have had a room where, within a few feet of the seat of authority, smuggled goods were housed, and here it is said on one occasion the wife of the chief official kept a wounded smuggler *perdu* until he was nursed back to a state of health in which he could make good his escape. The old point of view was taken down a few years ago from a Deal man of eighty-eight: 'Good times then, when a brave man might smuggle honest. Ah, them were grand times, when a man didn't go a-stealing with his gloves on, and weren't afraid to die for his principles!'

When some two centuries ago a great storm swept the country and did more damage than the Great Fire of London of a few years earlier, the townspeople of Deal gained an unenviable notoriety. Hundreds of shipwrecked mariners – a thousand, according to Defoe – had reached the temporary safety of the Goodwin Sands but the Deal boatmen would not be put off to their rescue, contenting themselves with gathering from the waters floating valuables and leaving the men to drown with the next tide. The charge of inhumanity has long since lost any point, and the men of Deal, picturesque loungers about the old capstans along the shore as they seem on a sunny afternoon, are, when roused by storm, ready and daring in their efforts to succour unhappy vessels and launch their boat to the rescue of those in peril on the sea.

*

If the cherry orchards of Kent are places of delight in the spring, their uplifting beauty is soon followed by the green of the growing hops. According to Anne Pratt, a native of our county, 'travellers who have beheld, in other lands, the various scenes of culture – the olive grounds of Spain or Syria, the vineyards of Italy, the cotton plantations of India, or the rose fields of the East – have generally agreed that not one of them all equals in beauty our English hop gardens.' There may be an element of exaggeration in this, but I confess that my first sight of vineyards in Northern Italy was a disappointing one compared with our Kentish hop fields. To be enjoyed properly they should be visited at three stages of their growth: when the bines are partly up their poles and strings, at the end of May; when the growth is completed and topmost aspiring shoots have reached beyond their highest support in July, and again in the autumn when 'hopping' has begun and fields are busy with men, women and children removing the hops from the bines.

Seeing the extent of our hop fields now it is curious to remember that the cultivation of the plant met with considerable opposition at various times. Henry VIII issued an edict against the mixing of hops or sulphur with beer, but not, it would seem, with much result, for in 1552 hop plantations were being formed, and in the time of Elizabeth the plant had come into general use. As a Commonwealth writer on agriculture said, 'it was not many years since the famous City of London petitioned Parliament against two anusancies or offensive commodities which were likely to come into great use and esteem; and that was Newcastle coals, in regard of their stench, etc., and hops, in regard they would spoil the taste of drink and endanger the people.' Opposition notwithstanding, the use of coals and hops went on flourishing and today we may well wonder what we should do without them. Of the fifty and odd thousand acres now grown in England, Kent can boast of (or be reproached with!) having thirty and odd thousand.

A field of well-grown hops is a beautiful place on a hot summer day, the 'hills' placed with such regularity that stand where we may, we see the radiating lines festooned with the handsome plants. Of the various arrangements utilised in different districts it is unnecessary to speak here – of the three-pole hills and the two-pole hills, of the 'umbrella' method of training the bines, the fastening of string from pegs in the ground, to wires criss-crossing from the tops of poles placed at some distance apart, or from lower wires placed from pole to pole at a short distance from the ground. These matters, and the special tools employed in the culture – hop-dogs, and hop-spuds – the incessant work, from the ploughing or digging of the land (hop ground is best hand-dug), belong rather to a technical than a descriptive work.

The hop fields, especially where string is largely employed for the plants to climb, are protected by 'lews' or shelters from the prevailing wind; sometimes these are high, thin hedges of hawthorn or other shrubs, sometimes rows of trees cut down to about twelve or fifteen feet, and allowed to grow laterally, sometimes rows of 'wild' hops on close-set poles, and frequently they are formed of coarse canvas stretched from pole to pole along the whole side of the field.

September, in a season now shortened to something under three weeks, is the great season of hopping, when thousands of poor Londoners invade the quiet country and get a healthful and profitable holiday helping to gather the clusters of delicate catkin-like cones. The aroma is said to be as healthful as it is pleasant, and a hopping holiday has been recommended as a simple-life 'cure'; indeed not long since a novel was published in which the hero (a young nobleman, if I remember rightly) went hopping incognito and met his 'fate' engaged in the same romantic occupation. To those who have joined a hopper's camp for the 'experience' or for the getting of 'copy', there is romance, comedy and tragedy in these gatherings, and a large field for the study of character. The crowds of hoppers scattered about the gardens and surrounded by the ripened crop, take on a picturesqueness which could scarcely be imagined by those who have only seen them massed at the railway termini in London, as they go to catch the early morning hopper trains. There the picture is one of unrelieved greyness and sordidness.

A stranger passing through a hop garden may find himself being honoured by having his shoes wiped with a bundle of hops, on which he is expected to give 'shoe money'; in other words, to pay his footing. The shoe money so collected is supposed to be used by the workers for a small feast of bread and cheese and ale, to be consumed on the ground when the hopping is over.

After being gathered by the hoppers into large bins or baskets, the aromatic harvest is carried off to the cowled oasthouses to have about ten hours of drying over furnaces — in which the weight is reduced by nearly eighty per cent —

before being put up in 'pockets' or a hundredweight and a half each, ready for the market.

In olden times, the early shoots of the hop were cooked and eaten as asparagus, and Anne Pratt recorded nearly seventy years ago, 'Kentish children can tell of pleasant hours spent among the hedges, in searching for the wild hop top, and of wholesome suppers made upon the well-earned treasure, ere they have learned to think their food the better for being rare and costly.' Those who lead the 'simple life' in cottage or in the increasingly popular caravan, please note; and note also that the taking of cultivated hops is a felony!

18

THE LAKE DISTRICT

A. G. Bradley, 1901

Keswick and Derwentwater

The situation of Keswick may in truth, and fairly, I think, be claimed as the most beautiful enjoyed by any town in England. When guide books enunciate in dogmatic fashion that this pass or that valley 'has no equal in Great Britain', thus intruding individual taste or perhaps even local prejudice in the garb of information, one is apt to wax impatient. But Keswick could be proved by mere geography to occupy a site that no other town of several thousand souls in England can offer any parallel to. At any rate if there be such a town I cannot imagine what or where it is. For immediately behind Keswick the noble mass of Skiddaw fills the whole sky upon the north; and Skiddaw, though sneered at by cragsmen, is in outline and dignified independence of position one of the finest as it is almost the highest of northern mountains. Upon the other side, and almost from its doorsteps, the only lake that in beauty is generally thought to rival the head of Ullswater spreads away to the southward, and gleams among its marvellous setting of wood and crag and mountain. To the west the vale of the Derwent spreads a rich green carpet of pasture, wood and meadowland, through which that turbulent river, just released from the upper lake, rolls beneath high and grassy banks to merge itself again in the quiet depths of Bassenthwaite. Keswick itself is a cheery little place of some three or four thousand souls, that in the days before railroads must have enjoyed a great measure of seclusion from the outer world.

Lead pencils are the industry that Keswick chiefly plumes itself on. A hundred or two hundred souls thus make their living amid an aroma of cedar that floats not unpleasantly about the banks of the Greta, whose roaring stream turns their factory wheels. Many hundred tourists, however, deem it incumbent on them to go and see these same pencils being made, and stimulate the industry, no doubt, by buying many contrivances in cedar they do not want, and would not dream of purchasing at home. I was myself several weeks in Keswick, and successfully resisted the still small voice which every wet afternoon tortured me with whispers of the pencil factory, till the very last day, when I weakly yielded. My forebodings were more than justified, and I am supplied with pencils and pen-holders for the rest of my life; to say nothing of some wholly useless cedar boxes, and a monstrosity called a pencil walking stick. All these things I purchased with a deliberation that in the open air afterwards seemed incredible; and the more so as, I am bound to say, no sort of pressure is put upon the intelligent visitor. His craving to support a local industry, beyond the main one he is already supporting, is, I fancy, as spontaneous as it is evanescent.

Having purchased the esteem of the pencil makers I was also entitled to their confidences, which led me to suppose that they do not hold our American cousins in any great regard, declaring that, while their interest in the machinery is greater than that of others, and the questions they ask more numerous, a desire to possess themselves of samples of the work is conspicuously lacking.

As a matter of fact, Americans seem curiously unpopular with all the catering fraternity of the Lake country, except the proprietors of the hotels they actually stop at, which to be sure is an eminently saving clause. One minor cause of complaint is that one of the features of American life is that unnatural craving for cold water, iced if possible, which, stimulated by habit,

amounts almost to a vice. The rosy-faced matron of the Black
Bull or the Dun Cow has practical objections to so untoward
a practice. Carrying out gratuitous glasses of the hostile element not only to young women but to able-bodied men goes
sorely against the grain. Englishmen would not dare thus
much, even supposing they followed the pernicious habit of
drinking cold water between meals. I think the publican who
has enterprise enough to store ice and retail iced water to
American tourists at a penny a glass has a bright future before
him. People who often begin their breakfast with this cheer-
less draught in January will not stick at a penny on a dusty road
in July or August, and there really is no reason why any bad
habit should be indulged in *gratis*. I doubt, however, but that
the question of ice has even yet too unattainable a sound about
it for the rural Englishman.

Various small local industries are pressed upon the attention
of the visitor as he saunters about the pleasant streets and lanes
of Keswick. But it really is so very obvious that its absorbing
industry is entertaining tourists, driving them about, rowing
them on the lake, bedding them, feeding them and supplying
them generally with all the necessaries and such superfluities
as they want. Skiddaw and Derwentwater are much better than
a gold mine to Keswick, which is also a great distributing
centre for notable places around. From May till October chara-
bancs and coaches perambulate the outskirts of the town each
morning in a steady stream, and the eagle eyes of the competition search every cranny of your domicile. You may be shaving
at an upper window, or having breakfast at a lower one, or dis-
cussing household matters in the basement, but they will never
fail to find you out and compel your attention to the fact that
they are about to start for Buttermere or Ambleside.

But Keswick, as I have said, is a cheery place, and should be
a prosperous one. The chief hotel is a very grand establishment,
standing on high ground outside the town and hard by the

station, with a fine outlook. The others are of the old-fashioned description, and, I have no doubt, comfortable, but are mostly in the centre of the town – a situation which does not commend itself to me when touring in a fine country at midsummer. On the side, however, nearest the lake there are terraces of excellent houses facing the mountains and the open country, and commanding beautiful views, where most comfortable quarters can be had at extremely reasonable rates. My experience of this particular class of entertainment in the Lake country leads me to think well of the local landlady. You would not expect it in a country where the Celtic strain is slight, but there is a high average of integrity and sufficiently good manners. With the help of the railway, in addition to coach and cycle, more, I think, can be accomplished without shifting quarters than from any other centre.

I am quite sure that the citizens of no town in all England, to say nothing of the passing sojourner, have such a promenade for the enjoyment of their post-prandial tobacco as have the good folks of Keswick in that leafy walk which borders the Derwentwater boat landings and ends at Friars Crag; whether the sun is still drooping in fiery splendour to the rim of the overhanging hills, or has sunk behind them, leaving its trail of glory and tender afterglow upon land and water, this lower end of Keswick's enchanting lake is not easily surpassed. For boats are then gliding between the wooded islands and promontories, and bright patches of colour flit over waters, here black beneath some upstanding crag, there quivering in the sun's trail like molten gold; and, behind all, the silent mountains, piled up one above the other, yet close at hand, complete a picture that is not given to many English townsmen for contemplation of a summer evening within a gunshot of their doors.

But I really cannot describe Derwentwater. It is more familiar to me than any English lake, and the better one knows it the more futile does such an effort seem. To catalogue the crags and hills and mountains in whose bosom it lies is but a barren business, and brings one no whit nearer to the conception of their infinite beauty and wonderful grouping. To enumerate the leafy islands that seem to float upon the lake's bosom, and descant upon the nature of the woods which in such profusion and with scarcely a break deck the shores, would be an idle waste of words. Let it be mine rather to commend the reader merely to take a boat, if the day be kindly, and paddle leisurely about, and judge for himself if he thinks there can be anything upon earth more fair. And there is no better lake anywhere for boating upon than Derwentwater. It is hardly large enough to often put up seas, in summer time at any rate, that are dangerous. There are no steamers to knock you about, nor yachts to run you down, nor anything like the number of craft that ply on Windermere. It abounds in leafy bays, in snug coves where the water laps against rocky promontories on which pine trees murmur and bilberry bushes covering the ground give completeness to a foreground that carries one's fancy away for a moment to far Canadian lakes. But not in Canada, certainly, nor anywhere overseas, is there that velvety, that mellow perfection of foreground such as only a British atmosphere acting on a British soil seems able to produce. Nor do I know of any other land where mountains of such modest altitude are so boldly fashioned and so assisted by the kind delusions of soft skies as to be well able to challenge comparison with many beside whom they are but pigmies.

There are perch in the lake too in plenty for those who affect this peaceful branch of sport, and one so admirably adapted to family use. There are pike for the more vigorous and unsociable; while for the really serious angler the Derwentwater trout, tolerably numerous, exceedingly capricious, but when captured of most admirable size and quality, afford much scope for skill and patience. I do not think many strangers go to Derwentwater to catch trout, and in this they perhaps exercise a wise discretion. Not but what there are plenty of them; short, thick, lusty well-fed fellows too, the best probably in all the Lake country – though it would not do to say so to a Winder-mere man – and they will average moreover something like a pound apiece. The local enthusiasts, however, are quite numer-ous, and any May day when there is a breeze you will see half a dozen boats at least drifting slowly before it in the upper reaches between the lead mine on the western shore and Lodore upon the other. The Keswick fly fishers, who largely consist of local tradesmen enjoying a well-earned retirement, are as industrious as any company of Waltonians I have ever met. I do not think they ever miss a possible day from the beginning of the season to the end. And when in the first week of June the May-fly puts in an appearance, better results are confidently and with some justice looked for. During that high festival you may see fifteen to twenty boats every morning drifting in slow procession, and in a row, where the wind lis-teth; and in each boat there will be two sportsmen, one standing up at either end, and each sportsman will be armed with a two-handed rod, from fifteen to twenty feet in length. Indeed there will be such an amount of energy and back work going on that a Southerner might well suppose that twenty-pound salmon were the object of pursuit, not one-pound trout. Most people nowadays fish with little ten or eleven feet one-handed rods. But the Keswick angler is a prodigious Tory, and has a belief in his grandfather's weapon that no argument could shake. I have myself both caught and eaten Derwentwa-ter trout, and whether on the end of a line or on a plate want nothing better. It is not easy to have too much of a good thing, and the surroundings of this Keswick lake form a very good thing indeed.

I asked a clear-eyed long-limbed young dalesman who was out with me one day whether he often rowed foreigners about. To which he replied that he took a 'gey few of them' on the lake. I then asked him how he liked Americans. He said he liked them well enough; but countered my query by asking as to the fishing in America, and then went on to say that he supposed the waters there must be either choke full of fish or else that there were none at all.

'What makes you say that?' said I.

'Well, sir, because whenever I take a party of Yankees out they get in a tur'ble way if they don't catch a fish about every two minutes. So I supposed they had either never had a rod in their hands before, or else were accustomed to catching a fish as fast as ever they could haul 'em in.'

I discovered also the interesting fact that only a week or two before, this Hercules had been engaged for several days by a French family straight over from Paris. I asked him if they could speak English.

'Aye,' said the young waterman drily, 'they cud gabble what they ca'd English.'

'Did they talk to you?' said I.

'Aye, they crack'd wi' me a bit.'

A little more encouragement and I was favoured with some of the conversation, which must have been of an entertaining nature, and have given the Parisian matron, her son and daughters who made up the party, a rare notion of Cumbrian amenities.

'There was a young chap, civil enough feller, but jest a little nippity Frencher like, an' he thought he could pull an oar, and was for ever teasin' me to row a race wi' him. Lor, I wasn't goin' to fash myself racin' wi' such as 'im [Hercules, I may remark, is the champion sculler of the lake]; it 'ud be like stannin' up to wrestle wi' a little gal. However, he kept botherin' me, so I said t'last mornin' I'd give 'im a 'alf-mile spin. Lord, it ain't worth talkin' about. I left 'im stannin' still a'corse; an' then I asked 'im if he'd had enough, and told 'im that a Frenchman couldn't no more row than he could fight. All 'e was fit for was to 'oller and make a noise.'

'Well,' said I, 'I shouldn't think you saw much more of your party after that.'

'Oh aye, I did tho'. The very mornin' as they went away, the lady come down to the boat landing, and asked the governor to send for me; and she thanked me for my attention and give me three 'alf crowns.'

I don't think Hercules, who is a really admirable and trustworthy young man, had any notion that he had been discourteous. I think too that the forgiving French lady must have been worth knowing.

19

LEICESTERSHIRE

J. B. Firth, 1926

The Quorn Hunt; Stilton

Here in Leicestershire we are in 'the cream of the Shires' — the exclusive Shires which at one time affected to regard their neighbours as mere 'Provincials'. Leicestershire, Rutland, Northamptonshire and a small fragment of Lincolnshire — these constitute the Shires, the country of the Belvoir, the Quorn, the Cottesmore, the Pytchley and Fernie's. All others — however good — are outside the charmed circle. And it is true that the pleasures of the chase are found in their perfection in Leicestershire, provided that both riders and horses have hearts stout enough to front with confidence the great adventures offered by the broad pastures, by the big fences and streams — more than brooks and less than rivers — which wind through its shallow valleys. A famous sportsman in the early days of the Quorn, Mr Valentine Maher, used to say that he would rather ride to and from covert all his life in Leicestershire than hunt in three parts of the counties of England where hounds were kept. A day in Leicestershire fields is worth a score elsewhere to the true Meltonian.

Nor is this mere local partiality. Mr Apperley, the great 'Nimrod'*, held much the same opinion, and he had ridden

---

* Charles James Apperley (1777–1843), who was born in Denbighshire, wrote hugely popular articles on racing, hunting, and the sporting and society personalities he encountered at various meets around the country. They appeared in *The Sporting Magazine*, amongst other publications, under his pseudonym 'Nimrod'.

with practically every pack of hounds in the land and with Masters who were zealous to show him the best sport that their country afforded. 'It is the only county in the world,' he said, 'that appears to have been intended for fox-hunting and where fox-hunting can be seen in all its glory. The flower of our English youth also (of those at least worth looking at) have always been seen there, and a winter in Leicestershire has ever been found to be, to those who are entitled to it, the *passe-partout* to the best society in the world.' After tasting the joys of Leicestershire, he says, you are spoiled for any other county, for which reason 'no poor man should ever go there'. Second-class horse-flesh will not do at Melton. A superlatively good horse, says Capt. Pennell-Elmhirst[†], is required not only to accomplish the country but to combat the crowd. He should be as nearly thoroughbred as you can get him, or he will not live the pace of jump when he is half beat. Moreover, he must be bold and yet be tractable. 'Leicestershire is the last county over which to rode haphazard, and a Leicestershire horse should possess no common combination of qualities. He must be able to gallop and he must be ready to jump, but he must be handy to turn and easy to stop, willing to creep a bottom, to drop his hind legs at a double, to brush a bullfinch, or to fly an oxer.'

The history of the Quorn is written in books. But a word must be said of its founder, Hugo Meynell, because he is the true Father of English Fox-hunting. The fox, of course, had been hunted for generations in England, but Meynell developed hunting into a system, and well deserved his title of the Hunting Jupiter. No doubt he learnt much from his friend,

---

† Edward Pennell-Elmhirst (1845–1916) was a prominent figure in the Quorn Hunt in the 1870s and 1880s. He wrote for *The Field* under the pseudonym 'Brooksby'.

Prince Boothby, whose sister he had married, for the Booth-bys also were a family of hunters. They started the Quorn together when Meynell took Quorndon Hall in 1754, and there were never more than three or four subscribers to his pack. At first hounds were kept at an inn at Great Bowden, near Market Harborough, but this was soon found inconvenient, as they wished to hunt three days a week, and kennels were trans-ferred to Quorndon. Here Maynell built himself stables 300 feet long, and stalls for thirty horses in a row. 'When I cast my eye upon it,' wrote 'Nimrod' many years later, 'I could not help fancying myself looking at King Solomon's stud, having never seen so many horses in one stall before.'

The Quorn has had its ups and downs, but many of the most famous names in English hunting chronicles are closely associ-ated with it. Those who would read the whole story must study the narrative of Mr Blew, who is the historian of the Hunt. The heroic figures in the catalogue are Thomas Assheton Smith, great cricketer as well as great hunter, and Squire Osbalde-ston, who broke almost every bone in his body. 'I am so unlucky,' he said after a particularly bad smash, 'that I think I shall give up hunting.' But he hunted six days a week to the very end, and always rode his own hack to covert. In his Mastership the subscription to the Quorn amounted to £2,200 a year, and £700 was paid as rent to coverts.

The fame of Melton Mowbray is out of all proportion to its size. It is known, wherever fox-hunting is held in honour, as the capital of fox-hunting Leicestershire. True it has suffered change from the pre-railway days when it set the authentic and exclusive pattern of hunting style and elegance, but Melton is still Melton. During the season it thinks and talks of little else but horses, hounds and hunting, which are indeed the basis of its prosperity. At other times it is an ordinary market town, busy only on market days, rural and agricultural, and its talk of sheep and pigs is varied by talk of Stilton cheeses and pork pies, both of which admirable industries contribute to the volume of its trade.

When the rich hunting set began to resort to Melton, and to be considered a 'Tip-top Meltonian' was to rank as a buck of the first water, new inns soon blossomed forth, and so we find 'Nimrod' writing,

> There is nothing now wanting at Melton for any man's comforts, provided he has the means to pay for them; and there are two hotels, the George and the Harborough Arms, which equal in accommodation and comfort any that I have experience of. Some idea, indeed, may be formed of the style in which the Harborough is fitted by the fact that the very passages, upstairs and down, are entirely covered with carpet.

Such was luxury a century ago.

During this period, say from 1800 to 1830, Melton was mainly a bachelor place; the town was always lively, and occasionally rowdy. Wine flowed freely, and those were the days of 'practical joking', often only a euphemism for sheer brutality. Other times, other manners. The general pace at Melton has never been slow, but some of the 'roaring blades' and 'Corinthian Toms' of the swell hunting set in the days gone by would not be tolerated now. There is a well-known series of engravings illustrating the pranks of the Melton bloods, riding steeplechases at midnight with white nightshirts over their hunting clothes, attacking peaceful citizens, nailing up doors and shutters and the like. The principals engaged in one of these later escapades appeared in the dock at the Derby Assizes

and were fined £100. The Marquess of Waterford was there –
of course.‡ They had wound up a day at the Croxton Park
Races, near Belvoir, with a dinner at Melton and at 2 a.m. sal-
lied forth into the Market Place, where they met a decrepit old
watchman and gallantly challenged him to a fight. Next they
overturned a caravan with a man inside and screwed up a toll-
gate keeper. Then they painted red the face and neck of another
victim and broke open the lock-up and rescued one of their
party. This was too much even for Melton's easy tolerance and
the law was put into motion.

H. Aiken depicted the scene at the toll-gate 'from a sketch
made on the spot'. In a companion picture the revellers are
depicted at work in Melton Market Place, where the White
Swan – which one of the party painted red§ – still looks down
from above the pillared portico of what is now a shop but was
then an inn.

'Larking' has gone; in the 'ragging' which has succeeded
it, the raggers rag one another and do not scour the public
streets for its victims. When in 1890 another midnight
steeplechase was attempted at Melton over a course lit by
railway lamps, the public opinion of the district instantly con-
demned it, and on the Sunday following, an outspoken
sermon was preached in Melton parish church by the rector,
who took for his text: 'Have no fellowship with the unfruit-
ful works of darkness.'

---

‡ Henry Beresford (1811–1859), the 3rd Marquess of Waterford, was a notorious drinker, brawler and vandal, with brutish – some might say psychopathic
– tendencies. Known as 'the Mad Marquess', he often featured in newspaper
headlines during the 1830s. He died in a riding accident in which he broke his
neck.

§ Waterford and his gang daubed other sites in Melton Mowbray with red paint
that night in 1837, and it is from this episode that the saying 'painting the town
red' supposedly originates.

✳

Wartnaby is a pleasant little Wold village with an attractive Hall in a small park and an interesting church of yellow sandstone.[1] But Wartnaby has other interests. The late Sir Rider Haggard came here a quarter of a century ago when he was writing *Rural England*. Desiring to learn at first hand the secret of how to make the best Stilton cheese, he was taken to Mrs Musson of Wartnaby, who was celebrated locally for her skill in the art:

> This is the process of the manufacture of Stilton cheese, as Mrs Musson was so kind as to show and describe it to us. First, the milk that came from Shorthorn cows – which she considered the best for the purpose, although some makers keep other breeds of cattle – was strained or sieved into a big tin vat, where it stood until it had cooled down to 80 deg. At this temperature the rennet is put in, which coagulates the milk and turns it into curd. As to the amount of rennet necessary to this end there seems to be no fixed rule – at least Mrs Musson said that in this matter she was guided by experience. When the curd is ready it is ladled out with a big scoop into straining-cloths, which are placed over a curd-sink, the whey, which is used for pig food, running into a cistern outside the chamber. Here the curd remains to ripen in the surplus whey for a length of time which depends on the weather and other conditions. When the weather is hot it would, I was informed, mature in about 48 hours, the cloths meanwhile being tightened from time to time.
>
> After this the curd was broken up, and salt having been added to the amount of 7 lbs or 8 lbs to 25 lbs of curd, the

---

[1] Henry Rider Haggard (1856–1925), a great lover of Stilton, but better known as the author of adventure novels such as *King Solomon's Mines* and *She*.

whole is put into a hoop with holes in it, but neither top nor bottom, through which the whey drains. In these hoops it stands for seven or eight days, the whole mass being turned each day. Occasionally, also, skewers are driven into the hoops to assist in ridding them of the whey. On the seventh or eighth day it is slipped out of the hoop and invested with a binder or cloth, which is changed every day for another eight days or so, the cheese being turned at the same time. When the binder cloths are found to be quite dry upon the cheese the use of them is discontinued. By this time the cheese should have assumed that wrinkled appearance with which we are familiar in Stilton. It is then moved into a coating room (which must be kept damp and have a cool draught of air passing through it) where, Mrs Musson said, it remains for a week or more, and the surface assumes its light grey colour. After this it is transferred to the storeroom, that should be damp and dark, where it is turned and brushed daily for a period of about six months, during which time it sinks from 18 lbs to 14 lbs or 15 lbs in weight.

Now, if all things have gone right, it should be a perfect Stilton cheese and ready for eating. One of the first qualities of this making of Stilton cheeses – of which Mrs Musson remarked that with the exception that they made no noise they were more trouble than babies – is that all the rooms wherein they stand during their manufacture, and everything that touches them must be kept scrupulously clean. Another is that the temperature must be carefully watched and not allowed to rise too high or fall too low. So far as I could discover, it takes about five quarts of milk to make 1 lb of curd, and 25 lbs of curd to make a ripe Stilton of 15 lbs weight. Mrs Musson continued to make cheeses up to the end of November, but when the frost came the curd began to go back in quality. The finished cheeses she disposes of to factors or at the fairs at Melton Mowbray or Leicester. I gathered that the best price was obtainable from the factors, who, however, made a habit of picking the cheeses and leaving those that were inferior to be disposed of else-where. It should be added that the excellence of the cheese depends greatly on the quality of the grass on which the cows are fed.

From this it will be observed that it takes skill and patience to make a first-class Stilton cheese. It must not be thought, how-ever, that the honour of having invented this delicacy with a rind like the bark of an ash tree, the flavours of the richest pas-turage and the sweet freshness of the most spotless dairy, belongs to Wartnaby. No, that distinction belongs to Wymond-ham, where a certain Mrs Paulet lived, whom let no one rob of the fame that is justly hers. For it was Mrs Paulet and none other who sent the first cheese to Cooper Thornhill, who kept the Bell at Stilton, and laid it before the hungry travellers of the road. *Cui Deus sit propitius.* ‖

‖ 'To whom God is gracious.' (The village of Stilton was an important coach-ing stop on the Great North Road, and it was through being served to travellers that the cheese's fame spread. Although taking its name from the village, the cheese has never been made in Stilton.)

20

LINCOLNSHIRE

Willingham Franklin Rawnsley, 1914

Immingham; Lincoln

At Immingham the most enormous works have long been in progress. A new port has sprung up in the last five years, and to this the Great Central Railway, who so utterly neglect the convenience of passengers with vehicles at the Hull ferry, have given the most enlightened attention, and by using the latest inventions and all the most advanced methods and laying out their docks in a large and forward-looking way to cover an enormous area, have created a dock which can compete successfully with any provincial port in England.

A deep-water channel leads to the lock gates on the north side of what is the deepest dock on the east coast, with forty-five acres of water over thirty feet deep. It runs east and west, and it is about half a mile long. A quay 1,250 feet long projects into the western half of this, leaving room for vessels to load or unload on either side of it, direct from or into the railway trucks. A timber quay occupies the north-west side of the dock, and the grain elevator is at the east end, while all along the whole of the south side runs the coaling quay. There are at least twenty-seven cranes able to lift two, three, five, ten, and even fifty tons on the various quays, and on the coaling quay eight hoists, on to which the trucks are lifted and the coal shot into the vessels, after which the truck returns to the yard by gravitation automatically. Each of these hoists can deal with 700 tons of coal an hour, and as each hoist has eight sidings allotted to it there are 320 wagons ready for each. One of these hoists is moveable so that two holds of a vessel can be worked simultaneously. The means for quick and easy handling of the trucks, full and empty, by hydraulic power, and light for the whole dock also is supplied from a gigantic installation in the power-house, near the north-west corner of the dock; and this quick handling is essential, for the many miles of sidings can hold 11,600 wagons, carrying 116,000 tons of coal or more, besides finding room for empties. The coal is brought from Yorkshire, Derbyshire, Notts and Lincolnshire, and not far short of 3,000,000 tons of coal will be now sent out of England from this port alone.*

It seems to the writer that to send away at this tremendous rate from all our big coaling ports the article on which all our industries virtually depend is a folly which no words are too strong to condemn. With coal England has the means of supplying all her own wants for many generations, but it is not inexhaustible, and when it is gone, where will England be? Will anything that may be found ever take its place? And, unless we are able to reassure ourselves on this point, is this not just a case in which a wise State would step in and prohibit export, and not allow the nation to cut its own throat like a pig swimming?

*

The rate at which the soil of inhabited places rises from the various layers of debris which accumulate on the surface is well shown at Lincoln. In Egypt, where houses are built of mud, every few years an old building falls and the material is trodden down and a new erection made upon it. Stone-built houses

---

* The coal output in the UK in 1913 was 287,411,869 tons, an increase of 27 million on the previous year.

last much longer, but when a fire or demolition after a siege has taken place three or four times, a good deal of rubbish is left spread over the surface and it accumulates with the ages. Hence, in Roman Lincoln or 'Lindum Colonia', pavements may be found whenever the soil is moved, at a depth of seven or eight feet at least, and often more. Thus the Roman West Gate came to light in 1836, after centuries of complete burial, but soon crumbled away; and the whole of the hilltop where Britons, Romans, Danes and Normans successively dwelt is full of remains which can only on rare occasions ever have a chance of seeing the light.

Still there is much for us to see above ground, so we may take a walk through the city, beginning at the top of the hill. Here, as you leave the west end of the cathedral and pass through the Exchequer Gate with its one large and two small arches, under the latter of which may be seen entrances to the little shopstalls where relics, rosaries, etc. were once sold, you pass along the flat south wall of St Mary Magdalen's Church, beyond which the outer Exchequer Gate stood till 1800. The wall in which this and other gates of the cathedral close were inserted was built in the thirteenth or early fourteenth century, to protect the close and the canons. The gateways were all double, except the Potter Gate, which is the only other one now extant.

Passing from the Exchequer Gate you see a very pretty sixteenth-century timbered house, with projecting storey, at the corner of Bailgate, now used as a bank. Hard by on your right is the White Hart Inn, and on your left you have a peep down Steep Street to the House of Aaron the Jew, a money-lender in the reign in Henry II. Looking straight ahead from the Exchequer Gate you see the east gateway of the castle. The West Gate is walled up and the Assize Court within the castle enclosure is near it. The castle was one of eight built by the Conqueror himself, apparently never so massive a building as his castle, which is now being excavated at Old Sarum, the walls of which, built of the flints of the locality, are twelve feet thick and faced with stone. At Lincoln the Roman walls were ten to twelve feet thick and twenty feet high. Massive fragments of this wall still exist in different places, the biggest being near the Newport Arch. Near here too is the Mint Wall, seventy feet long and by thirty feet high, and three and a half feet thick. Most of the fighting in Lincoln used to take place around this spot.

Getting back to the Bail, or open space between the castle gate and the Exchequer Gate, we can go down that bit of the old Ermine Street called Steep Street (and I don't think any street can better deserve its name) and come into the High Street of Lincoln. If we go right down this, we shall see all that is of most interest in the town below the hill. First is the Jew's House, a most interesting specimen of Norman domestic architecture; at the bottom of the street, No. 333, is another charming old structure called White Friar's House with a projecting timbered front. One more bit of old domestic building is the hall of St Mary's Guild, commonly called John O'Gaunt's Stables. In Parker's *Domestic Architecture* it is spoken of as 'probably the most valuable and extensive range of buildings of the twelfth century that we have remaining in England'.

As we pass down the High Street we shall see on our left the Saxon towers of St Mary le Wigford and of 'St Peter's at Gowts'. The 'gowts' or sluices were the two watercourses for taking the waters of the 'Meres' into the Witham; originally there were small bridges on either side over each, with a ford between them for carts. These towers are tall and without buttresses, having the Saxon long and short work and the upper two-light window with the mid-wall jamb, and only small and irregularly placed lights below. They are in style much what you see in Italy, though the Italian are higher, but certainly none in England are so uncompromisingly plain as the towers at

Ravenna and Bologna. Near St Mary le Wigford is the picturesque little remnant of a beautiful but disused church, called
St Benedict's; only the ivy-clad chancel, a side chapel and the
recent low tower are left, a very picturesque and peaceful
object in the busy town. Its original tower held a beautifully
decorated bell called Old Kate. The gift of the Surgeon Barbers
in 1585, it used to ring at 6 a.m. and 7 p.m., to mark the beginning and end of the day's labour. It now hangs in the tower of
St Mark's.

The name of 'le Wigford', Wickford or Wickenford, indicates the suburb south of the river. In the days when kings used
to wear their crowns, an uneasy belief in the saying 'The
crowned head that enters Lincoln walls,/His reign is stormy
and his kingdom falls' made the monarch take it off on passing
from Wickford to the city. It has been supposed that both these
early Lincoln churches were built by a Danish citizen called
Coleswegen, who is mentioned in the Domesday Book as
having thirty-six houses and two churches outside the city. But
though Lincoln has not lost nearly so many churches and religious houses as Winchester has, yet, where she now has a dozen
she once had fifty, so it must be extremely doubtful whether
these two old ones that remain were those of Coleswegen. St
Mary's now has a Perpendicular parapet, some interesting
Early English work, and both churches have some good
modern ironwork in pulpit, screen and rails from the Brant
Broughton forge. The woodwork in St Peter's was done by the
parish clerk, a pleasant feature not nearly so common now as
it used to be.

The 'High bridge' marks the spot where the Ermine Street
forded the Witham. It is the only bridge left in England out of
many which still carries houses on it. The ribbed arch is a very
old one, twenty-two feet wide. The houses are now only on
one side, they are quaintly timbered, and their backs, seen
from below by the waterside, are very picturesque. On the

other side is an obelisk, set up 150 years ago to mark the site of a bridge chapel dedicated to St Thomas of Canterbury. From here you get the most magnificent view that any town can boast, as you look up the steep street to the splendid pile which crowns the height, and see the cathedral in all its beauty.

Two railway stations and the many large iron and agricultural implement works, which have given Lincoln a name all over the world, occupy the lower part of the town, with buildings more useful than beautiful; for this industry has taken the place of the woollen factories which were once the mainstay of Lincoln. But a tall building with small windows, known as the Old Factory, still indicates the place in which the 'Lincoln Stuff' was made, from which the Lincoln 'Stuff Ball' took its name. In order to increase the production and popularise the wear of woollen material for ladies' dresses, it was arranged to have balls at which no lady should be admitted who did not wear a dress of the Lincolnshire Stuff. The first of these was held at the Windmill Inn, Alford, in 1785. The colour selected was orange. But, the room not being large enough for the number of dancers, in 1789 the ball was moved to Lincoln, where it has been held ever since, the lady patroness choosing the colour each year. In 1803 the wearing of this hot material was commuted to an obligation to take so many yards of the stuff. The manufacture has long ago come to an end, but the Stuff Ball survives, and the colours are still selected.

21

LONDON

Mrs E. T. Cook, 1902

Kensington and Chelsea; Shopping

The great highway of Knightsbridge – on the southern side of the Park – leads, as everybody knows, from Hyde Park Corner to Kensington. Kensington, as it is now, is an all-embracing name, a generic term; it comprises not only Old Kensington, but both West Kensington, a new and quickly increasing district of tall flats and 'Queen Anne' houses, as far removed from London proper, for all practical purposes, as St Albans; and South Kensington, a dull and uninteresting quarter, but close to all the big West End museums and collections, and where no self-respecting lady or gentleman of the professional or 'middle classes' can really help living. He, or she, must, nevertheless, beware lest they stray too far from the sacred precincts. For, on the west, South Kensington degenerates into Earl's Court; on the south, a belt of 'mean streets' divides it from equally select Chelsea (and in London, the difference of but one street may divide the green enclosure of the elect from the dusty Sahara of the vulgar); while on the east, its glories fade into the dull, unlovely streets of Pimlico, brighten into the red-brick of the Cadogan Estate, or solidify into the gloomy pomp of Belgravia. These, however, are but Kensington's later excrescences, due to the enormous increase of London's population, and to the consequent building craze of the last century.

The original village of Kensington lies in and about the Kensington High Street, the Gardens and the Palace. It is reached by the Knightsbridge Road, a thoroughfare that, crowded as it is today by the world of fashion, was, only at the end of the eighteenth century, so lonely as to be unsafe from the ravages of thieves and footpads; a road 'along which,' Mr Hare remarks plaintively, 'London has been moving out of town for the last twenty years, but has never succeeded in getting into the country'. So solitary, indeed, was this road that, even at the close of the eighteenth century, a bell used to be rung on Sunday evenings to summon the people returning to London from Kensington Village, and to allow them to set out together under mutual protection.

Some of London's finest mansions are now to be found in this Knightsbridge Road. On the left, as you go towards Kensington, are Kent House, once lived in by Queen Victoria's father, Stratheden House and Alford House. Beyond Kensington Gore (so called from Old Gore House, which once occupied the site of the Albert Hall) is the attractive and strangely rural-looking Lowther Lodge, now so cruelly dominated by tall mansions; and, further still, the vast Albert Hall, a red Colosseum of music. This, in spring, is a delightful drive; indeed, London wears here such a semi-suburban air that it is with almost the feeling of entering a new townlet that we approach the charming High Street of Old Kensington.

But how much, alas, is left of Old Kensington now? Campden Hill is adorned by the aspiring chimneys of waterworks, the peace of quiet Kensington Square is invaded by model lodging-houses, the underground railway defiles the pleasant High Street, and where of old the hawthorn bloomed, tall placards now advertise 'Very Desirable Mansions to be Let on Exceptional Terms'.

Earl's Court — now mainly remarkable for the near neighbourhood of Olympia, the 'Great Wheel' and an endless colony of railway lines — was, some fifty years ago, still a quaint old row of houses, their lattices stuffed with spring flowers, facing a deep cool pond by the roadside, and embowered in orchards. Spots of welcome greenery there still are in the wide area of West and South Kensington; there is a big cemetery to be buried in, and the oval enclosure called The Boltons is a pleasant place to live. But, on the whole, the purlieus of Kensington are depressing. While West Kensington is mainly degraded 'Queen Anne' interspersed with railways, South Kensington has one very general distinguishing mark. It is nearly always stuccoed, and usually also porticoed. Its larger streets, in sun or shine, bear a gloomy likeness to an array of family vaults, awaiting their occupants. The early nineteenth century had, in truth, much to answer for in the way of bricks, mortar and stucco – but principally stucco! Occasionally there is some faint relief to the prevailing mood, and here and there some of the smaller roads are brightened in spring by a few acacias and hawthorns; but in the larger streets there is usually the same saddening uniformity, and, when once you have left the vicinity of Kensington Square, you find nothing in quite the same style until you reach Chelsea and Cheyne Walk.

Picturesque in old days, Chelsea is a picturesque place still, and much beloved of painters, poets and *littérateurs* – the class of Bloomsbury, and yet with a vast difference. Here it is the 'mode' to be select and exclusive. The artistic cliques of Tite Street and Cheyne Walk are nothing if not particular. To use the words of the modest prospectus issued by a recent magazine, they 'will not tolerate mediocrity'. But then no one in Chelsea ever is, or at least allows himself to be, 'mediocre'. Perhaps the fortunate inhabitants feel the important weight of the traditions of their literary past. The spirit of Carlyle, Leigh Hunt, Rossetti, George Eliot, yet give to Chelsea a literary atmosphere that it must at all hazards keep up. A dinner party in its august cliques is not to be lightly undertaken; you feel, as you enter, that this is indeed a holy place.

Yet, already, the seclusion and selectness of Chelsea's sacred circles are being threatened with invasion by the Philistine. On 'the other side of the water' – where a picturesque suspension bridge, the Albert Bridge, throws its graceful chain-curves across Chelsea Reach – lies Battersea Park, surrounded on three sides by myriad red-brick flats of varying cheapness, grown like mushrooms, and still growing. Here is an infant community whose inhabitants can boast, with some truth, that they are 'near the hum of the great city, and yet not of it'. Flats are increasing all over London and its immediate suburbs now to such an extent that they are, indeed, in some danger of being overdone. In Central London, the growth of flats is, perhaps, of little consequence; but in suburban or semi-suburban London, the ubiquitous builder is the great bloodsucker of our day; he wanders perpetually, seeking, like the devil, what he may devour, everlastingly picking up gold and silver.

But the builder has done good work too in Chelsea; for does not Cheyne Walk, of picturesque and venerable aspect, with its well-restored, red-brick, white-casemented houses, and fine old ironwork, lend a dignity to the western end of Chelsea Embankment, to which, lower down, the spacious new red mansions, of ornate yet good style, do no disgrace? And modest Cheyne Row, containing the most famous dwelling in all Chelsea, is built in quiet, unobjectionable style. Carlyle's quiet-looking residence in Cheyne Row is a real 'house of pilgrimage' to the literary world, and is especially the resort of cultured Americans, who have even, it is said, had to be mildly dissuaded from sitting on the Sage's chairs and trying on his headgear. The 'Carlyle House' – desecrated, indeed, to the scandal of its neighbours, for an interregnum of unholy years by a horde of lawless cats – is now entirely restored to its pristine neatness and order.

The fleeting tide of fashion is now at its height in Chelsea; the historic old houses of Cheyne Walk are let at enormous rents, and, year by year, tall, prosaic red-brick edifices spring up like mushrooms all around them. Since Stuart and early Hanoverian days, times have changed for Chelsea and Kensington; they are now – as more distant Hammersmith and Fulham are rapidly becoming, and as Putney and Dulwich soon threaten to be – integral parts of the 'monster London' that, like a great irresistible flood, in spreading absorbs all the peaceful little pools that lie in its path. The squalor and the gloom, as well as the splendour and the riches of the great city, are now their heritage. Never more will the waves lap peacefully at Chelsea along the river's shelving shores; never again will the streets and squares of Old Kensington regain their former seclusion and calm. Instead, a modern, and, let us hope, a yearly more beautiful city will spread, gradually and certainly, over all the available area. Chelsea and Kensington in the past have had many glories; who can say what splendid fortune may yet be theirs? And we who lament the inevitable changes of time, must remember that they are still living cities, hallowed by their past, interesting by their present, but whose greater and more enduring magnificence is yet to come.

*

I am confident that if a million women of all classes could by any possibility be placed in a Palace of Truth, and interrogated straitly as to what they liked best in all London, the vast majority of them would answer 'the Shops'. Indeed, you may easily, and without any undue inquisitiveness, find this out for yourself by simply taking (in May for choice) a morning or afternoon walk down Oxford Street or Regent Street. Every shop of note will have its quota of would-be buyers, trembling on the brink of irrevocable purchase; its treble, nay, quadruple row of admiring females, who appear to find this by far the most attractive mode of getting through the day. I would go further, and say that as regards the more persevering among them, it is difficult to imagine that they ever have any other occupation at all.

The shops of London have wonderfully improved in quite recent years; not perhaps so much in actual quality, as in arrangement and taste. Labels with 'dropsical figures' of shillings and perfectly invisible pence have, as in Dickens's time, still their charm for us; but other things have changed. Everything could, to those who 'knew', always be bought in London; but everything was not always displayed to the best advantage. To dress a shop-front well was in old days hardly considered a British trait. Now, even that Paris boulevard, that Paradise of good Americans, has, except perhaps in the matter of trees and wide streets, little to teach us.

Even the critical American cousin is now beginning to forsake Paris, and to find out the real superiority of London shops. See how he – she, I mean – helps, in her numbers, to swell the shop-gazing crowds in Oxford Circus. Tramping from Bloomsbury boarding-houses – or, more aristocratic, from Northumberland Avenue hotels – the Americans have discovered, and are in a fair way to dominate, London; the London, that is, of July and August.

What are the special qualities that constitute 'a good shopper'? They would appear to be as follows: endurance, patience, strength, coolness, self-control, amiability, mental arithmetic, and, lastly, an eye to a bargain. All these cardinal virtues are, for the average shopper, considered as generally necessary for salvation: but yet there are other qualifications. For instance, the intense delight that most women (and a few men) feel in obtaining an article at 1s. 11?d., that has once been marked with the magic 3s. 6?d., is of distinct value in this connection. How many women have delightedly bought a thing that is not of the slightest value to themselves or anyone else, simply because it is thus reduced in price!

Caveat Emptor! It is the object of the seller merely to sell; and in his behalf it may be urged that there is no gauging the absurd vagaries of the public taste. Some shops have taken to the inauguration of strange fashions. Lately a well-known West End emporium started that blue cat with pink eyes, wearing a yellow riband, tied in an enormous bow round its neck. It was an aesthetic, Burne-Jonesian* cat; indeed, it was hardly like a cat at all; but, nevertheless, it sat in rows in that shop window, and the line 'took', and forthwith no home was complete without a cat. Then a little, muzzled, foolish-looking china puppy became the Regent Street rage, and was forthwith attached as an ornament to every suburban house door. Whose is the great mind who set these fashions, before whom every household bows? It would be interesting to know.

Everything can be got in London, if you know where to go for it. Old timber, for instance, can be bought not only at the Westminster wharves, but also in the Euston Road; old silver may be had in the now spoiled Hanway Street, and Holborn; old furniture and antiques in Wardour Street and its neighbourhood; new furniture in Tottenham Court Road; livestock in and about Seven Dials; artists' materials in Soho, and so on [. . .]

Sales, however tempting, should be avoided by the unwary shopper, for they are dangerous as spiders' webs. They vary in honesty. Some of them are really held in order to clear out, at a sacrifice, the old stock; some, especially in the smaller shops, are simply quick sales of cheap lines bought in on purpose. Sale days are truly terrible experiences to the uninitiated. If you happened, unwittingly, to go to some familiar shop on one of these yearly occasions, the mass of crowded, struggling, gasping humanity, nearly all pushing, and nearly all fat, would lead

---

* Sir Edward Burne-Jones (1833–1898), eminent Pre-Raphaelite artist.

you to imagine that life and death, at least, were intimately concerned in the tussle.

The shopping of the rich, however, is one thing, and the shopping of the poor is another. Most interesting, to those who care to study the book of human nature, are the 'street markets' of the people, those rows of noisy booths and barrows which have stood from time immemorial, by traditional right, in certain streets, and where jets of brilliant, flaring naphtha-lights display the kaleidoscopic stock-in-trade. Among such streets are Goodge Street, Tottenham Court Road, Leather Lane in Holborn or, to descend to a yet lower social depth, Brick Lane in Spitalfields. In Goodge Street fruit and vegetables are mainly sold; in Leather Lane, tools, appliances, pedlars' wares, butchers' meat, everything, in fact, in infinite variety; in Spitalfields, birds and livestock, together with old clothes and second-hand goods generally. In such street markets, from eight to ten on Saturday night is the gala time for business. In Brick Lane – not the Jewish 'Ghetto' but the purely English quarter – there is, moreover, a Sunday morning 'poor man's market'. It is usually, in more select London highways, more or less difficult to make purchases, be they never so necessary, on Sunday morning. I remember, indeed, a despairing search for food on such an occasion (necessitated by the arrival of unexpected visitors), which ended in the obtaining, almost by force, of boiled chickens from a small Italian restaurant, with the added injunction to 'keep them well hidden' from the eye of the law on the homeward journey. In the East End, however, it is very different. Brick Lane, an unsavoury region, described by the late Mr Montagu Williams as 'a land of beer and blood', presents on Sunday morning a strange sight to the uninitiated.

The barrow-men, who pay small rates as compared to shop-owners, give good value in return for their money, with much homely wit and caustic joking thrown in. Of course, when dealing with barrows, the buyer must have as many eyes as possible [. . .]

For those London visitors who do not appreciate the slums, yet whose olfactory organs are not too fastidious, the big London markets – Covent Garden, Smithfield, Billingsgate – will perhaps afford a sufficient experience in that line. Billingsgate is the most perilous excursion of the three. Its aroma is strong and lasting, and the stranger in its diverging courts and alleys runs considerable danger of having winkle-barrels or fish crates descend on his devoted head, as they are lowered from the wharves on to their respective carts. Yes, a little of Billingsgate will go a very long way. The language of Billingsgate fishwives and porters is proverbial, yet it is perhaps hardly worse than in many other less fishy quarters of London.

But, though a visit to Billingsgate is only faintly suggested, and the delights of the great central meat market of Smithfield are, it is fair to say, only capable of thorough appreciation by farmers and connoisseurs, every visitor to London ought to be enjoined to go and see Covent Garden Market, and preferably in the early hours of the spring morning, the time of its highest activity. Covent Garden is still faithful to its fruit and vegetables, though these, alas! are no longer to be seen *growing* there, but are transported thither from the rich gardens of England, as well as from colonies and nations overseas. Here, within this small enclosure, can be got, it is said, all that skill can grow, care can transport, and money can buy. Here can be obtained, at any time, and at short notice, the roses of a Heliodorus, or the orchids of a Vanderbilt; together with priceless fruits in mid-winter, new vegetables in February frosts, and tropical produce all the year round. The middle avenue of Covent Garden is expensive, but it can produce anything wished for in the fruit and flower line. Riches in such places are as the magic wand of an Aladdin. The central avenue of the market is refined and polite; outside its limits, however, the manners of the locality are original and peculiar, a kind of 'law unto themselves'. The Covent Garden porters and market-women are rough diamonds; the men, especially, full of good-natured horseplay, seem alarming on a first introduction, but harmless when you are used to them. Yet I have known timid ladies who have shrunk from a walk through 'the Garden', imagining its denizens to be robbers and cut-throats, or, at least, revolutionary citizens of a supposed Reign of Terror!

The subject of shops and markets would lead us naturally to that of restaurants. These, at the present day, are many and excellent. While the more ancient taverns of Covent Garden and the City have largely lost their fashionable vogue, the general improvement in restaurants and modern hotels has been rapid. The art, even the poetry, of dining may be thoroughly studied in London at the present day. Every passing mood may be consulted, every gastronomic fancy indulged. If the lady whom you honour be frivolous by nature, you can take her to the smart restaurant of the Hotel Bristol, and to a comedy adapted 'from the French'; if she be serious, to the Grand Hotel, and then to Shakespeare; if crude, to Frascati's and to melodrama. But, whether you choose expensive dining places or cheap ones, and in whatever manner you may elect to spend your long London day, one thing is certain, that at its close you will generally find yourself to have spent a considerable sum.

2 2

MIDDLESEX

———◆———

Walter Jerrold, 1909

Harrow and environs;
the Northern Suburbs

In his various verses, inspired by recollections of Harrow, Lord Byron was thinking of the great school which is perched on the point where the London Clay rises to an apparently high elevation above the surrounding levels, and it is of the school that the majority of people, including those who have not been Harrovians, first think on any mention of Harrow. The fact that it has become an extensive residential neighbourhood does not make us think of it, without a distinct mental effort, as such. But Harrow, with its ever growing modern additions, is in parts taking on some of the unloveliness of suburbia – it is but ten miles from the Marble Arch by road. Its rows of villas, large and small, are eating into the pastures, yet also it remains unspoiled, and still from its high churchyard is to be obtained the extensive view which delighted the poet. Though the hill on which Harrow is situated, and round the base of which it is spreading, is not lofty, its more or less abrupt rising from the surrounding level country gives something of the impression of height, and makes it, with the famous spire of its church, a notable landmark from Willesden and other places. From the church the view from south-east to south-west includes the clump of Knockholt Beeches and the glitter of Crystal Palace on the one hand, and Windsor Castle, with Berkshire and Buckinghamshire woodland, on the other. That the beauty and

extent of the view are well appreciated is made plain by the
seats provided for visitors, and by the fact that such visitors
are almost constant. From the church tower it is claimed that
thirteen counties are visible in favourable weather.

The growth of London towards Harrow in recent years has
become great. And indeed there is not much open country left
now between the Metropolis and Harrow, though there are yet
tree-grown fields about the lane towards Wembley, and
between Wembley and Harrow, and some rural bits along the
Brent valley. Wembley Park itself is a beautiful extent of
between two and three hundred acres of well-timbered
ground, overlooking the Brent valley towards Willesden. Here
was started the Watkin Tower, designed to be a rival of, and 175
feet loftier than, the famous Eiffel Tower of Paris, but its building had not proceeded beyond the first stage when it was
abandoned, and for long it remained something of a blot on the
landscape, until it was finally demolished a year or two ago.
Wembley Park, however, it is said, is still to be maintained as
a place of resort, and in the neighbourhood is to be laid out a
residential 'garden city'. Further west, at Sudbury, another
garden city is planned. To the south of Sudbury rises Hors-
endon Hill, a conspicuous landmark from the further side of
the valley, within recent years a place on which cowslips flour-
ished in profusion. A mile or so to the west, to be reached by
footpath, is the hamlet of Greenford Green, on the Grand
Junction Canal, notable for its chemical works. It is not in itself
an attractive spot – the neighbourhood of chemical works
rarely is – but it is a point from which some delightful footpath walks, some of the longest and most varied so near to
London, may be taken. From here we may choose these pleasantest of byways to Wood End and the Roxeth suburb of
Harrow, or to Northolt, West End and Yeading, with its
brickfields, and so out to Uxbridge road and its trams between
Southall and Hayes. Northolt is a very small, attractive village,

scattered about a green, and beyond, on rising ground, a small old church.

The country immediately to the east and north-east of Harrow is another district in which the follower of footpaths is particularly well favoured; possibly in some instances the right of way has been established by successive generations of schoolboys. One of these paths, starting near the school, may be followed to Preston, whence another goes by Woodcock Hill to Kenton, while from there yet another will take us across the fields to Edgware – a delightfully rural walk of about five miles, nearly the whole of it by footpath, and entirely within a nine-mile radius of the Marble Arch. These footpaths are generally short cuts from place to place, in protest, as it were, against the curious curves and angles made by twisting roads. And some of the roads about here turn and twist in an almost unaccountable fashion.

From many vantage points, notably towards Pinner, we get fresh and delightful views to which Byron's memory turned. Pinner again, with its two railway stations, is expanding into a new villadom, but around it still is much of rural attractiveness in open fields and tree-shaded lanes, while its wide village street, rising gently to the flint and stone church, with its old-fashioned shops and irregular houses, its picturesque Queen Anne inn (1705), has about it an air of old-world comfort and prosperity. Long before its development as one of the outer residential suburbs, the district was noted for the comfortable houses in which, at various times, men of note lived. At Pinner Place, long his residence, died Governor Holwell, one of the few survivors of the indescribable horrors of the Black Hole of Calcutta, and historian of that awful tragedy. Pinner is an admirable centre for country walks. To the north-west is Northwood, another of the developing 'centres' in which those who like to live away from, yet within easy reach of, London are establishing new villadoms, with the woodlands and parks of the Hertfordshire border just beyond; to the west is the well-wooded tract about the great reservoir; while to the south-west Ruislip is within easy reach, by a delightful walk through Eastcote.

The long, straight road which runs north-westerly from the Marble Arch – part of the great Watling Street of the Romans – is known by many names along its different parts; at its London end, however, it is Edgware Road, from the fact that, after leaving suburban villages of a few years ago – the suburban districts of today – the village of Edgware, between eight and nine miles away, was the first considerable place that was reached. Now, with electric tramcars running for some miles along the old way of the Roman legions, Edgware itself is within measurable distance of being, is perhaps already, reckoned as part of suburbia. Though here, as elsewhere in our county, the coming of the trams has meant at some points the widening of the road, the pulling down of houses, or the slicing off of picturesque old fronts to be replaced by ugly substitutions, yet the loss in one respect has been a gain in another; and much of the old-world Edgware is yet to be seen in the gabled houses and small-windowed shops, especially in the old inn, the Chandos Arms, in the garret of which is an ornate carved fireplace, brought hither from the dismantled mansion of Canons. The coming of the tramcars may have tended to the sophistication of an old-world village, but it has made the country around that village newly accessible to many people. Both highways and byways have much to offer in the near neighbourhood – to the immediate north the old Watling Street, rising over two hundred feet in a couple of miles, takes us to Brockley Hill, from whose slope is to be had a grand far-extending view to the south and east. On the road across the summit is a fine avenue of limes, with on one side beyond the trees a sheltered footway, suggesting that when our roads are remoulded nearer to the motorist's desire, this plan might be followed for the preservation of pedestrians.

We may cross the main street of Edgware and follow a winding way to Mill Hill, with inviting lanes turning off to the left. At about a mile or so from Edgware, having crossed the Dean's Brook by a ford, we reach the hamlet of Hale, and so by Mill Hill Station (Midland Railway) come to the straggling village of Mill Hill itself, a growing place scattered along a broad highway and about several byroads. It is a delightful village of large institutions and scattered 'lumber' cottages and shops straggling along elevated ground, with many trees and pleasant grassy-margined roads.

Highwood Hill – to be reached also directly from Hale by taking the left turning as you reach it from Edgware – a little to the north-west of Mill Hill, from which it is divided by a sudden dip on one bank of which is a rambling old wooden inn, is a hamlet from which we get fine views, and about which the names of several celebrated residents may be recalled. Here Mrs Mary Porter, one of the famous actresses of the eighteenth century – the vehemence of whose rage in tragedy Dr Johnson never saw equalled – lived for many years. Mrs Porter was in the habit of journeying home, after her performances at the theatre, alone in a one-horse chaise, with a book and a pair of pistols. That the pistols were necessary in those days of foot-padding and highway robbing might well be imagined, and the time came (about 1730) when the tragedian had to threaten to use them. Stopped by a robber, she levelled her pistols at him, and cowed him into confessing that he was but an amateur at the game, being a man rendered desperate by affliction. Instead of firing her pistols, the tender-hearted actress gave him ten pounds. When starting to continue her homeward journey the horse bolted, the chaise was overthrown, and Mrs Porter had her thigh dislocated, so that she was compelled to be absent from the stage for a couple of years, and subsequently always to walk with a stick. At Highwood House Sir Thomas Stamford Raffles lived the last year or two of his life. He had recently returned from the East, from the founding of Singapore, saddened by the loss by fire on board his ship of all the notes, maps, and natural history and botanical specimens which he had collected for years. It was while here that he set about founding the Zoological Society, though he did not live to see the famous Gardens established. In June 1826, he wrote, 'Wilberforce takes possession tomorrow, so that we are to be next-door neighbours, and divide the hill between us.' Within three weeks of welcoming so congenial a neighbour as William Wilberforce the philanthropist, Raffles died suddenly in the very prime of life.

*

Taking the next of our radiating highways, we pass from one-time 'merry' Islington through Barnsbury, Canonbury, Highbury, Holloway and Stoke Newington; all these crowded districts – the salubrious suburbs of a few generations ago – are now part of the great congeries of towns known as London. At Finsbury Park we step out into Middlesex proper again, but the Great City is to all intents and purposes still with us, far along towards Enfield. In Finsbury Park itself, the northern suburbs have a recreation ground of about a hundred and twenty acres. Well planned and planted, this is one of the most attractive of London's suburban open spaces, with its broad stretches of turf and its hilltop lake, on which boating is indulged in. Here are public tennis courts and cricket pitches, and capital gymnasia for children and adults, so that it forms a valuable, as well as a beautiful, playground for the people.

The road beyond Finsbury Park, the 'Green Lanes' of our grandparents, with its ever-humming succession of electric tramcars bound for Enfield and New Southgate, affords a seemingly endless succession of houses and shops; but few patches of open land are left near the road, though here and there we may leave the main thoroughfare, and after an interval of villa-lined byways attain the comparative rusticity of open fields, beyond Wood Green.

Between Southgate and the Great North Road about Finchley are still bits of open fields and woodland, though after but a few months of absence change is to be noticed. In this district a conspicuous landmark is the Alexandra Palace, standing on the high ground of Muswell Hill. About this and the opposite hillside new streets are rapidly forming, though there is still a stretch of greenery given up to games in the valley between this and Shepherd's Hill, running to North Hill and Highgate.

Crouch End, Muswell Hill, Fortis Green and part of Highgate are all comprised within the old bounds of Harringay or Hornsey. Here in olden times the Great Black Forest of Middlesex stretched, and there may be seen some of the best bits of woodland left within easy reach of the metropolis. Highgate Woods became public property over twenty years ago, when they were dedicated to the public by the City of London. Linking up, more or less closely, with Parliament Hill and Hampstead Heath, they help to make this north-western the most favoured of suburban districts. From their higher parts wide views are to be had, and London is to be considered lucky, for their old-time celebrity for healthfulness might well have led to their being among the parts first built upon. Given a clear atmosphere, from the summit of Parliament Hill, beyond London's wilderness of houses, may be seen the Surrey hills.

Apart from its happily preserved woodlands, and some of the 'fair houses' in large grounds, the Highgate district has become a populous suburb about the boundary between the old county of Middlesex and the new County of London – the actual division between the two here runs along the road, which is carried high above the Great North Road on Highgate Hill by the famous Archway. The ancient North Road ran through more wiry ways to avoid the height, but it is now several centuries since the newer was cut through Highgate Hill.

Beyond the modern Archway – a recent successor to a clumsier erection of 1813 – houses and shops line the way to the county limits beyond Whetstone, but there are many points of interest all about this bit of London that lies around the fine irregular tract of woods and commons stretching from Highgate to Hampstead, and from near Kentish Town to near Golders Green. Beyond the metropolitan limits here and there, the open bits of country that are left are intersected by footpaths, and starting from bleak Hampstead's swarthy moor, we may yet get some measure of rusticity. It is, however, but an urbanised rusticity that we get, for on either hand the march of progress is being accelerated by tramrails, more potent than seven-league boots.

23

NORTHAMPTONSHIRE AND RUTLAND

———◆◆◆———

Herbert A. Evans, 1918

Rockingham Forest and King's Cliffe; Weedon, Ashby St Ledgers and the Gunpowder Plot

As late as the early part of the fourteenth century Rockingham Forest stretched from Northampton to Stamford and from the Welland to the Nene. From this time onward its area gradually diminished till at the close of the eighteenth century what was left of it consisted of three detached territories, called bailiwicks, from two to four miles apart. These were the bailiwicks of Rockingham, Brigstock and King's Cliffe, each being divided into smaller areas, called lawns or walks. The Forest Commission issued its report on Rockingham Forest in 1792. By this time almost the whole of the forest had passed from the Crown into the hands of the great landowners, subject to certain royal rights over the timber. The Commissioners, however, did not consider that it was to the public interest that these rights should be preserved and they reported that:

A forest in a situation so distant from any residence of the royal family, with an establishment of offices, either granted in perpetuity or esteemed of little value by those who possess them, and in which so little of the right timber has been reserved, can neither contribute much to the amusement of the king, the dignity or profit of the crown, or the advantage of the public.

And though the ancient forest laws, and the courts, when regularly held, have been found by experience to conduce very much to the increase and preservation of timber in forests thinly inhabited . . . yet in Rockingham Forest, where the crown has little property left, where a considerable part of the land is already in tillage or pasture, and the country pretty fully inhabited, it cannot be desirable that those laws should be continued.

Rockingham Forest accordingly ceased to be a forest in the technical sense, and the Crown rights were purchased by the several landowners. But under the new system the woods were regarded chiefly from the point of view of the game preserver, and it was hardly to be expected that the timber profits, apart from the sale of coppice-wood, should be very great. With the revival of wood-craft as a national industry they may recover something of their economical importance.

That at King's Cliffe we are well within the forest boundaries is evident enough from some of the neighbouring place names, if for no other reason. Such names as Westhay, Morehay and Sulehay recall the old *hays* or enclosures into which the deer were driven for the purpose of easier capture; they differed, in fact, little from a park, which was also a part of a forest fenced off from the rest, as, for example, Flitteris Park in Rutland Forest, and Windsor Park in Berkshire, enclosed out of Windsor Forest. As for parks belonging to private individuals, which may or may not have originated in connection with a royal forest, and which the word now usually connotes, they had been confined to great nobles and bishops in medieval times and did not become general till the time of the late Tudors.

From our comfortable rooms at the Cross Keys we look across the street to the fine cruciform church of King's Cliffe and are struck at once by the curiously stunted appearance of the spire, due to clumsy repairs. When we climb the opposite hill we get a bird's-eye view of the village with its long lines of houses stretching for some distance along the valley and the graceful curve of the railway on its northern slopes. The valley is watered by a small stream, the Willow Brook, out of which fishponds have been formed, and higher up at Blatherwick and Deene actual lakes; after a devious journey it finally unites with the Nene below Fotheringay; I have called King's Cliffe a village, but in point of fact it is a 'decayed' market town, which at one time boasted a three days' fair as well as its market. The latter has long vanished, but people still living can remember the fair, though it was only a single day's festival, and will tell you that on that occasion, and on that only, any man who chose to set a green bough before his door became a licensed publican for the day. Good wine, the proverb says, needs no bush, from which the inference is that bad wine does, and so the people of King's Cliffe seem to have thought, for they took care to appoint ale tasters on the day before the fair to test the quality of the liquor. Particulars as to their visitations have not been preserved, but the fact is well ascertained that other commodities besides beer were bought and sold at this annual merrymaking. These included linen and cheese, and above all the products of the turner's lathe, for which the place was famous quite down to recent times. The dexterity acquired in this trade was so great that it is said that on one occasion a single worker for a wager turned out 417 egg-cups in eight hours. But here as elsewhere the dumping of cheap stuff 'made in Germany' has proved the ruin of the industry.

*

As everybody knows, Weedon ever since the year 1803 has been the seat of a Royal Military Depot; in other words, its chief title to fame is the possession of a magazine and extensive barracks. Therefore, as we shall see presently, the stranger, at any rate in war time, will do well to walk warily, and to put himself right with the powers that be. This settled, he will find a hospitable welcome, good cuisine, and comfortable quarters with Landlord Tuck at the Globe, and he may spend three or four days in the exploration of the surrounding country.

Now it happened to be the third month of the war when I was staying at Weedon. The place was beginning to ruffle its feathers, and strangers, especially if armed with maps and other paraphernalia, were looked at askance. Indeed, I am afraid that I was the occasion of certain qualms to my agreeable messmates at the Globe, the newly arrived colonel in charge and one of his captains, and when a certain pocket compass I had the misfortune to leave upon a gatepost out Everdon way fell into the hands of the police, matters began to look serious, and the worthy colonel had some trouble over the telephone on my account. Of course it was gratifying to find that the authorities were so wide awake, but had I not been able to refer them to a name well known in that county I might have found myself in an awkward predicament. However, I had not much longer to spend at Weedon; in another couple of days I was to finish my programme. Ashby St Ledgers I was determined to visit as the home of the Catesbys.

A fresh morning takes me to Welton station, and now I traverse the couple of miles through the leafy lanes westward which separate me from Ashby St Ledgers, one of the most delectable spots in Northamptonshire. I hardly know which to praise first, manor house or church, but they lie, as the custom is, close together, and you have the church on your right as you pass through the flat-topped archway beneath the 'plot room' into the manor precincts. Skirting the garden wall on the right, you are soon face to face with the venerable gabled front of Tudor times, at right angles to which runs a range of kitchens and offices of earlier date and lower elevation. You may long for a sight of the interior promised by such a fascinating survey, but in the absence of the owner, Lord Wimborne, this is impossible. This morning, however, permission to walk through the gardens and view the south and east sides of the house is courteously extended. The south front is now a rich jumble of turrets and oriels, all worked in the deep orange stone of the district, and in the centre is the wide open door of the hall. Attached to the northern end of the east front is a charming black and white building transported hither a few years ago from the Eastern counties and still feeling rather puzzled by the change. The gardens are delightfully arranged with an expanse of water below, and the elevation being nearly 500 feet they command an extensive view northwards towards Kilsby and Crick across a verdant and well-timbered country characteristically English.

But it is of Catesby and the Gunpowder Treason that those of my readers to whom the name of Ashby St Ledgers is familiar will be thinking, and indeed it is with his head full of bonfires and fireworks that many a visitor must have made his way here. 'Ashby', like 'Catesby', smacks of the Danes, and neither place is very far from Watling Street. It was from Catesby, some half a dozen miles to the south, out by the head waters of the Leam, that the family took its name, and hence came the progenitor of John Catesby of Ladbroke, Warwickshire, who in Edward III's time married the heiress of Ashby. From him, Robert, the conspirator, was the eighth in descent. 'He was,' says Dr S. R. Gardiner in the *History of England*,

a man capable of becoming the leader in any action requiring clearness of head and strength of will. He was a born leader of men, and had the rare gift of a mind which drew after it all wills in voluntary submission . . . As Catesby brooded over the wrongs of his Church – wrongs which were made the more palpable to him by the fact that so many of his kinsmen and friends were suffering by those evil laws – the idea arose within him . . . of righting the grievous wrongs by destroying both the King and Parliament by means of gunpowder, and of establishing a Catholic Government in their place.

His mother, now living at Ashby, was a Throckmorton of Coughton, between Warwick and Worcester, and all round about were scattered the houses of many other Catholic families, all more or less intimate with the Catesbys. A persistent tradition points to the room in the gatehouse at Ashby as the place where the plot was hatched.

It was about 6 o'clock on the evening of Tuesday, November 5, 1605, that Catesby and four of his friends, John Wright, Christopher Wright, Thomas Percy and Ambrose Rookwood, galloped into the west end of the village about a quarter of a mile from the manor house. Guy Fawkes and his powder magazine had been surprised late on the previous night, and in the morning when the news reached them they saw that their only chance lay in flight. London is nearly eighty miles from Ashby, and the route was along the great north-west road through Barnet, St Albans, Dunstable, Stony Stratford, Towcester, Weedon and Daventry. Horse and man were thoroughly tired out by the time that they came in sight of Ashby, and Lady Catesby, Robert's mother, was just sitting down to supper in the wainscoted hall with* Robert Winter of Huddington,

---

* The author adds a footnote here: 'I am told that this hall has undergone drastic changes in the recent "improvements". Till then it had remained as it was in the Plot year.'

The house continued to be owned by the Wimbornes, although it fell into further neglect throughout the twentieth century. In 2005 – with a whiff of irony – it was bought by the Crown Estate.

another of the plotters, when a message was brought to Winter that Catesby wanted to speak with him 'hard by the town's end'. Hurrying thither, he learnt the news of the discovery of the plot, and advised instant surrender. He was, however, over-ruled by Catesby, and the whole party, fatigued as they were, rode on to Dunsmore Heath by Dunchurch, where, under the pretext of a great hunting match, a large number of Catholics had assembled, ready to act on the arrival of news of the success of the conspiracy. Catesby's idea was now to make for Wales, where he expected to be joined by a large number of malcontents. Accompanied by all those of the hunting party who could be induced to share his fortunes, he reached Winter's house at Huddington, near Droitwich, on the sixth, and on the next day he rode on to a house of the Littleton family at Holbeche, across the Staffordshire border. This was the last scene of the plot as far as Catesby was concerned; the officers of justice came up, and in the struggle that ensued he was killed.

24
NORTHUMBRIA

P. Anderson Graham, 1920

Newcastle upon Tyne; Hadrian's Wall

Newcastle's paramount claim to attention is that in the whole world there is not a more stirring monument to human energy than is presented by the town and its river, the Tyne. It has been shown that distinction has been achieved at a price, but the price has not been too great. To say otherwise would be to reverse the highest praise bestowed on 'Men, my brothers, men, the workers.' The fitting eulogy of Newcastle would be a recital of the names of the great shipbuilding and other works on the Tyne, the array of inventions and discoveries which trod hot on the heels of Stephenson's first locomotive, and the bulk of goods manufactured by those armies of labour which man the innumerable works. To do that adequately would necessitate the production of statistics easily accessible and not very suitable for these pages.

Newcastle is not a creation of yesterday. Its merchant princes were famous in the Middle Ages, only its advance was enormously accelerated during the latter half of the nineteenth century. It was not until 1850 that the River Tyne Commission was formed as an outcome of a feeling that improvement was possible and indeed imperative. Until 1850 or thereabouts the Tyne retained much of its ancient character. Wilderness and moorland had given place to agricultural land on its banks, but the stream itself was shallow and in other respects unfit for navigation. The magnificent harbour of Tynemouth with its Black Middens remained as dangerous as it was when, according to

Bede, Cuthbert performed the miracle of saving the men on a sinking ship. The North Pier was begun in 1854, completed in 1893, destroyed in 1897 and since rebuilt. During the same period the channel was deepened, the banks straightened, docks built, and the difficult, dangerous river mouth was transformed into a magnificent harbour in which a navy could ride in safety. 'Men, my brothers, men, the workers' had conquered the apparently insurmountable obstacles to progress. It was regrettable but inevitable that much of historic value should be swept aside in the process. Many traces of the Roman Wall and even of the City Wall disappeared. Yet much remains to recall the city's dramatic and stirring history.

Newcastle is a pleasant town for a ramble. Long ago when I used to go there from the country it impressed me only as a welter of streets full of people in a hurry. Then during a prolonged visit there came an understanding of the reason why the inhabitants are so proud of it. I must be content to record a few personal impressions. One of them is that the manners of the place have changed much and for the better since the time of John Wesley. In his journal he says of the population of the Sandgate: 'So much drunkenness, cursing and swearing even from the mouths of little children do I never remember to have seen or heard before in so short a compass of time.' It is getting on for two hundred years since that was written, and it holds no longer. North country people have not the polite manners of the south. They do not 'sir' you or touch their caps. With them the bob and curtsey have long gone out of fashion. But they make up for it in genuine kindness and intelligence. I remember once asking a Lincolnshire rustic if Oliver Cromwell had not fought a battle near Somersby, and his answer was that he 'did not know the name – it must have been afore my time'. But along the Roman Wall, any day, labourers can talk to the point about the Romans in Britain, and in the slummiest part of Newcastle I have been astonished at the

knowledge of local history. Once, indeed, a tatterdemalion*
showed me to the old stone steps leading to the upper storey
of the Guildhall in the Sandhill, and spoke of John Wesley's
visits to Newcastle. Nor did he hang about afterwards for a tip.

Nothing is pleasanter than to hang about the old streets near
the quay and river and peer up the narrow entries called
'chares'. If their glory has departed it has left no melancholy
behind, any more than there is in the modest villa which a man
advancing in the way of prosperity forsakes for a mansion. Up
to a hundred years ago the notabilities still lingered by the Tyne
and had private residencies and public offices there. They left
only because quickening trade made demands on the shore.

Two heritages from antiquity tower above all others in Newcastle. It owes its name to one of them, the Castle, the
fortification put up by the Conqueror's son Robert Curthose
in 1080. But probably nothing remains of this structure.
William Rufus began the building of the great Norman Keep,
and the work was concluded by Henry II between the years
1172 and 1177.

The Castle occupied an area of three acres, enclosed by a
curtain wall through which the chief entrance was by the Black
Gate. The upper portion, most of which was Roman and from
the Wall, was restored by the Newcastle Society of Antiquaries.

In a county so full of historical associations as Northumberland it would make a notable advance in education if a museum
exclusively devoted to local antiquities were established in
each local centre. There are already many museums in the
smaller towns, but they are too miscellaneous, and often
contain articles brought home by travellers that would find a
more appropriate habitation in a great central museum.

---

* Ragamuffin.

Northumbrians are born antiquarians, and young people especially delight in that kind of history which enables them to compare the village or town in which they live with the same place as it was in the days of their forefathers.

It must be very difficult for a stranger to get into the atmosphere or recognise the true spirit of Newcastle. The first barrier in the way is dialect, and the dialect is more formidable in print than in speech. The late Mr Swinburne gave up all hope of writing poems in it, and used the braid Scots tongue for his Northumbrian ballads. But for this difficulty, any stranger could learn much about the manners and traditions, habits and humours of Newcastle by reading *Tyneside Songs*. They take you into what may be called low company, but it is a company of real men and women. Though they are closely akin to the dramatis personae of the Jolly Beggars of Robert Burns, a very considerable portion of the poets were ne'er-do-wells, eccentrics, wastrels of one kind or another; and here a peculiarity of Northumberland in general and Newcastle in particular may be noted. In other parts of the kingdom the rich are the leisured class who find time to write verses, and the poor are the horny-handed who have no leisure. But in Northumberland these conditions are reversed. The city merchants have always been too much immersed in the great projects of their generation to cultivate the Muses. But the poor sprang largely from the raiders of Reedsdale who, like a good canny man, depended for their livelihood on lifting cattle. There is something of the outlaw lingering still in the families of those who form the 'characters' of Newcastle. One consequence is that they break into rhyme very easily and the rhyme is steeped in local tradition and expressed in the local dialect. Although only one or two of these rhymers touch the high-water mark of poetry, they are homely and friendly, they are full of spirit and they reproduce with good humour the prize fights and cock fights, the drinking habits, the racing, the practical jokes and quips of the tap and bar. In this way they make themselves essential to a sympathetic understanding of that old Newcastle out of which the present one came.

We cannot take leave of them in terms more fitting than are to be found in William Watson's 'Thumping Luck to yon Town':

> *Here's thumping luck to yon town,*
> *Let's have a hearty drink upon't*
> *O the days I've spent in yon town,*
> *My heart still warms to think upon't*

*

There is no ancient relic in Northumberland to compare with the Roman Wall. Yet imagination is needed to realise its full impressiveness. The remains have in many cases to be sought for diligently, and nowhere do they arrest attention by gigantic proportions or towering heights. The Wall stretched from the mouth of the Tyne to the Solway, passing over a rich variety of scenery – rivers and rich meadows, wild craggy moorland, farms and woods – with Roman directness and Roman disregard of obstacles, dipping into the hollows and climbing heights of the rugged whinstone. But in the centuries elapsed since its building, so many changes, wars, movements have surged over the country that, in times of desperate fighting and amid revolutions that shook old faiths as well as governments, its origin and purpose have been forgotten.

An ancient 'Hindenburg line' may serve as a rough description. The reader will readily make a liberal allowance for the differences in fortification rendered necessary by the substitution of poisonous gas and high explosives for the arrows, catapults, balistae and other engines employed by the Roman legions.

It may be regarded as a series of fortifications linked

together so as to enable the occupants to assemble promptly at any given point either for attack or defence. Those wishing to explore it cannot do better than take Dr Collingwood Bruce as a mentor. His famous handbook has, since his death, been edited and kept up to date by a most competent successor, the well-known archaeologist, Mr Robert Blair, one of the secretaries of the Newcastle Society of Antiquaries. There are few more agreeable ways of spending a Northumbrian holiday than with his book for company, exploring the Wall from start to finish. 'Perhaps I am the first man who ever travelled the whole length of the Wall and probably the last who will ever attempt it,' wrote William Hutton, of Birmingham, in 1801, giving an eloquent testimony to the great difficulties of travel a hundred years ago. The journey is an easy one today. Between Wallsend and Solway is rather less than seventy-four miles, so that the pilgrimage along it presents no formidable task to a moderate pedestrian who is able to take his ease at his inn when fatigued with the rough going.

Where the first three stations of the Wall were, you see today the busy industrious side of Northumbrian life. But the Wall has a long way to go, and presently there will be unfolded to the pilgrim who perseveres all the wild beauty of the Northumbrian moors. And the wilder the region the more complete and interesting become the remains of the Wall. Where the scenery is tame, the Wall was an accessible quarry. Roman workers had hewn the stones at a time when the building art had undergone temporary oblivion in Great Britain. Few things are more startling in history than the completeness with which ancient civilisations have passed away. Northumberland is rich in prehistoric forts that had been erected with skill and judgement by races inhabiting land that now is little better than desert. But there had been a great retrogression, and in troublesome times old arts had been forgotten.

Where the Wall has been preserved, its completeness is

amazing. Where it has been practically destroyed it is strange
to note to what a variety of uses the stones have been put. Here
as elsewhere the imperturbable husbandman has been the
greatest sinner. He has mended his roads, patched his dry stone
dykes, built his farmhouse and mended his byre with stones
from the Wall. Let him not be called Hun or Philistine on that
account. He has only acted in the same way as those agricul-
turists and others (clergy included) who, further south, have
built pigsties with materials torn from Tudor masonry, turned
old stone coffins into cattle troughs, and laid paths through the
farmyard with historical tombstones. Reverence for the past
was not a striking characteristic of the eighteenth and early
nineteenth centuries.

When wandering about the Wall during the World War[†] and
observing the myriad proofs it supplied of organised government and organised labour, of intelligence and enlight-
enment, it was impossible not to muse over the chance that
human progress might possibly have reached its culminating
point in the twentieth century and be followed by a Dark Age.
I did not think it would come from the victory of one side or
another, but from the break-up of nations into warring divi-
sions. The worst law is better than anarchy, but it is at least
imaginable that no fraction would remain united. Subdivision
into groups would go on ever growing smaller like the family.
The individual would become the unit. Then it would be 'wolf
to wolf's throat'. No longer would there be property, no
longer education, every generation growing more ignorant
than its predecessor until any ancient who told of a people who
could navigate the air and travel under the sea, who could chain
the lightning and converse a thousand miles apart, would
be regarded as a dotard. A gloomy vision, but not altogether

---

† i.e. the First World War.

fantastic! Some such process must have checked human progress more than once.

But the clouds have lifted and the sun is again shining.

25

NOTTINGHAMSHIRE

J. B. Firth, 1916

Nottingham; Newark

Nottingham! Few towns or cities in England are better known or better liked than Nottingham. It challenges goodwill from a score of different approaches. It is associated through Robin Hood with the fables of childhood; it is linked through a long succession of heroes of the ring, the cricket field and the football arena with the sports of youth and manhood. 'The famous town of Nottingham', as the old song had it, was honoured for the strength of its ale, for the size of its great Market Place, for the mystery of its caves and cave-dwellers, for the splendour of its Castle, for the untamed spirit of its Lambs, for the cheerful riot of Goose Fair, for the surplusage and good looks of its daughters.

Moreover, it was also long renowned for the remarkable beauty of its situation. In the old days the traveller approaching Nottingham from the south along the London road used to catch his first glorious view of the Trent valley from the top of Ruddington Hill. He saw spread below him a spacious plain through which the Trent pursued its rapid and capricious way, spanned by the many-arched Trent Bridge. But for a mile on the other side of the river, right up to the foot of the hill crowned by the square tower of St Mary's Church, the meadows stretched unbroken. They were mostly the common lands of the burgesses, and the high causeways bore witness to the fact that they were subject in winter to encroaching floods. Now the river has been tamed, and the railways have come, and streets and factories cover the meadows, and the rare beauty of the scene has departed, though even today the view from Ruddington Hill can hardly fail to impart its thrill. But Nottingham has now become an industrial centre, instead of being what it was for so many centuries, just the capital of a county and an important market town.

The Market Place is the largest of its kind in England, having at one end the Exchange or Town Hall – an unpretentious and uninteresting building, which is likely to be replaced before long by another more consonant with the dignity of the City. The Long Row, on the north side, is still the principal shopping centre of Nottingham and a few of the old gables and pillared projections, which used to offer a dry passage in all weathers, still remain. The South Parade on the other side, once known as Timber Hill, had a row of trees in front of it in the eighteenth century, and where Queen Victoria's statue now stands was the Malt Cross, a relic of the days when Nottingham was full of crosses, such as Week Day Cross, Hen Cross and many others. The broad streets leading out of Long Row are of quite recent date; in the olden days only narrow lanes broke its uniform lines.

Nottingham Market Place is a scene of cheerful bustle on Wednesdays and Saturdays, when the whole great square is covered with booths, and for three days every October it is given over to the jovial riot of Goose Fair – a festival known far and wide throughout England. This is of very respectable antiquity, for the earliest reference to it is dated 1541, and in those spacious Tudor times the fair lasted for fifteen days. But Goose Fair was then a serious market as well as a holiday, and even as late as 1766 a riot started in the cheese section because the dairymen asked 28s. to 30s. per cwt. for their produce – to the just indignation of the citizens. The Mayor was felled to the ground by a cheese, and the 15th Light Dragoons had to be called upon to restore order. Now there is no pretence of business at the Fair. It is simply a carnival of amusement, and the square is filled with travelling roundabouts, shows, menageries and boxing booths. The din is indescribable, the pandemonium appalling. For three whole days and nights, the Market Place is given up to jostling, pushing, shouting throngs. There is plenty of horseplay and 'mafficking'* but the merry-makers enjoy it, and the fastidious can keep away. Goose Fair is not a very cred-itable example of English manners; the blatant, raucous voice of the steam organ gives the note of the whole assembly; but it is a highly cherished institution in Nottingham, and it will die hard.

There is another place to which a word must be devoted. That is Trent Bridge. Not the bridge itself, which is an iron affair, and a dull substitute for the old stone bridge of many arches, itself the descendant of the mysterious Heth-Beth bridge, the name of which still puzzles the local antiquaries and defied a standardised spelling for centuries. Trent Bridge stands for something else. It stands for Notts cricket and for Notts football. But there is not much sentiment about bygone football, and the ghosts which haunt the big ground beyond the river are flannelled. What a company they make! There is the older generation – William Clarke†, the great lob bowler; Redgate the giant hitter; the Oscrofts of Arnold who could put a whole eleven into the field, and the incomparable George Parr, hero alike with bat and ball, who made the mighty soar-ing hit out of the ground over the elm tree which bears his name to this very day. They and their faithful followers are long

---

* Riotous celebration. The word derives from the celebration following the relief of the British garrison besieged at Mafeking, now Mafikeng, in South Africa in May 1900.
† Clarke founded the cricket club in 1838 in a meadow behind the Trent Bridge Inn, having married the landlady.

since gone, but Dean Hole‡ has pictured in a vivid sentence or two the scenes in which they took part.

> That dear old field with its long line of booths and stands, with Clarke the captain having a few confidential words with the Rector of Gedling, a devoted lover and learned judge of cricket, and with Johnson, the secretary, smiling at everybody through his spectacles, and the fruit merchant inviting us to buy his pears at six a penny, and the dealers in correct cards announcing, 'The order, gentlemen, the order – Nottingham goes in.'

Long since, indeed, it must have been if pears were six a penny.

The writer knew Trent Bridge best and wasted many a summer day there, when a later but equally splendid generation had succeeded, when Arthur Shrewsbury and William Gunn used to open the Notts innings – and glad the enemy were to break *that* partnership – when Barnes was in his prime, and Wilfrid Flowers' broad smile embraced the whole ground, and Mordecai Sherwin played his cheerful antics behind the wickets but 'kept' with the best of them, and the lions of the visiting team were George Ulyett and blithe Tom Emmett, and Hornby and Barlow – the run-stealers who 'flickered to and fro' – and the bearded giant 'W.G.' was at his prime, and Long Tom bowled for Surrey, and no one was quite sure whether Peel was better than Briggs, or whether Abel or Shrewsbury held the first place in the averages. To every cricketer in the wide world the name of Trent Bridge is only less well known than that of Lord's and the Oval, and the proud boast of Notts cricket has always been that no man plays for Notts unless he be a Notts man. Kent and Yorkshire have the same fine tradition.

---

‡ Samuel Reynolds Hole (1819–1904), Dean of Rochester, famous horticulturalist and the author of three volumes of memoirs.

Southerners may talk of the Hambleden men, and Canterbury is a rare ground when the bells are pealing on a summer afternoon in the Harry Tower of the great cathedral, and Lord's is superbly metropolitan on a big day, and the Oval is cheerfully cockney, and the Red Roses and the White bloom gaily enough on their native heaths. But Trent Bridge has memories as fine as any of them, and a list of names that equals the very best. Long may the correct cards go round! 'The order gentlemen, the order – Nottingham goes in.' [. . .]

Where the main road to Derby crosses the Leen and the Nottingham canal, stands the entrance lodge to Wollaton Park. This is a picturesque building with round angle turrets on either side of the gateway, and a flat lead roof. Wollaton Hall is the family mansion of the Willoughbys, ennobled in 1711, and is one of the most imposing Renaissance mansions in the kingdom. The chief beauty of the Park, which is nearly eight hundred acres in extent and is enclosed by a fine brick wall, is a magnificent avenue of limes, through which the Hall is approached from Lenton. The gardens, still of great beauty, once had the reputation of being the finest in England, and the first glasshouse for the protection of plants is said to have been built at Wollaton at the end of the seventeenth century. Wollaton has never been a show place. Even in the eighteenth century the artist-tourist, Bray, complained that permission to see the mansion was refused him – 'a piece of pride, or gloomy inhospitality,' he comments, 'which for the credit of the county is rare'. But in these days by writing in advance, permission may sometimes be obtained. Wollaton is perilously near Nottingham, and the tide of advancing bricks and mortar, which has already in recent years rolled down the steep hill from the city, will not long be stayed by the Leen and the canal. The family is very rarely in residence, and there is little doubt that sooner or later Wollaton Park will share the fate – and it has been an entirely honourable fate – of the park which once was the pleasaunce of Nottingham Castle. Then will come such chance of making a new suburb as does not occur once in a century. But let Nottingham take care that the speculative estate-knacker is kept out at all hazards! This is a work worthy of the City herself.

*

Fortunate, indeed, is the county which includes Newark within its borders. For Newark, which John Wesley described in 1786 as one of the most elegant towns in England, is favoured in almost every respect wherein an inland town can be favoured. It is small, yet big enough to have a real character of its own and to possess industries which bring occupation to many and wealth to a few, but still is not so big to tempt it to adventures and large schemes of improvement or to ambition to be called a city, and other vainglory of that sort. You can walk right through Newark from end to end and be out in the fields again without growing tired of its streets. Moreover, Newark has a castle and a glorious history, and a church with a spire that is a joy to look upon, and a market place where you can be brisk if you choose, and plenty of old inns where you can dawdle away an idle hour, in sight of the printing shop where Byron printed his 'Hours of Idleness', and many old buildings and quaint courtyards. Then it has a good stretch of Roman road, not to mention the Great North Road along which you can whisk away to Scotland and scarcely encounter a stone to jar your rolling progress. And finally, it has not one river only, but two. No wonder, then, that Newark has a place in English history, and no wonder she has found worthy and loving historians to trace back her ancient chronicles to incredibly mythical days.

Here then is the Castle, looking pleasantly down upon the stream, 'slighted' with gunpowder and now a mere shell, yet still wearing a brave look on this side at least and with a single graceful oriel window in the great hall which suggests not war but gaiety. At its side the massive Norman gatehouse and south-west tower still stand in fair preservation. The rest has gone.

No one thinks of leaving Newark without a visit to its famous parish church, the pride of the town, as its beautiful spire is the pride of the surrounding country. What affection these famous spires excite! The tapering spire of Salisbury Cathedral, the Three Sisters of Lichfield Cathedral, the spire of Ashover, the Pride of the Peak, or that of Grantham, Newark's near rival; people grow to love them who have little interest in or love for the churches themselves. The spire of St Mary's Newark, 252 feet high, is not quite so tall as that of Grantham, and about a century ago it lost ten feet of its final taper, but its beauty is unchallenged. The same masons were at work here as at Grantham, completing it by about the year 1330, just before the Black Death of 1349, which brought the rebuilding of the body of the church to a sudden standstill. For nearly six centuries, therefore, this exquisite spire has delighted the eyes of the thousands of travellers who have passed along one of the busiest thoroughfares of England.

Newark contains several old inns interesting alike for themselves and for their associations. The principal ones stand, as they should, in the Market Place, where the tide of activity flows fastest and fullest, and the Saracen's Head and Clinton Arms between them take up no inconsiderable portion of one side of the square. The Saracen's Head is the older, and there has been an inn of that name in Newark from the year 1341. Tradition says that Charles I stayed a night beneath its roof, and Sir Walter Scott frequently passed under its arch on his way to and from London. The Clinton Arms, next door, has memories of Byron. It was called the Kingston Arms at the beginning of the nineteenth century, when the poet used to ride over from Southwell, in order to see the proofs of the verses which

Ridge, the bookseller at the corner of the square, was publishing for him. 'The Kingston Arms is my house,' wrote Byron.

The same inn was also the headquarters of Mr Gladstone in 1832, when he was contesting Newark as the nominee of the Duke of Newcastle, and by that time it had taken its present name. While Gladstone was speaking from one of its windows, a man hurled a stone which broke a pane within a foot of his head, but the culprit was caught and let off on promise of his vote the following day.

Dr Warburton, whose name is prominent among the famous sons of Newark, was a son of the Town Clerk. Warburton studied law but entered the Church. Once on the ladder, he mounted high, rising to be Bishop of Gloucester. The Bishop was a famous controversialist, whether in politics, theology or literature. He carried a big stick and brandished it violently. Gibbon called him 'the dictator and tyrant of world literature'. Bolingbroke, in excusing himself from controversy, said that he had 'no desire to wrestle with a chimney sweep'; Bentley said that Warburton had 'a monstrous appetite with a bad digestion'. It was characteristic of him that he considered his abilities inadequately recompensed. To the end of his days, though, he spoke of Newark with affection. He wrote: 'I now enjoy little pleasure compared to what I formerly had in an autumn morning, when I used, with book in hand, to traverse the delightful lawns and hedgerows round about the town of Newark, the unthinking place of my nativity.' Why 'unthinking'? The epithet has caused the Newarkers of later generations some searching of heart. Probably it meant no more than an episcopal rebuke – rather in sorrow than in anger – at the want of appreciation which Newark had shown of his genius while he lived in his birthplace. But it is an old story that a prophet has no honour in his own country.

26

OXFORD AND
THE COTSWOLDS

Herbert A. Evans, 1905

[**Editor's note:** those parts of the Cotswolds dealt with by Evans in this volume are chiefly the Gloucestershire Cotswolds, which, naturally enough, also appear in the *Gloucestershire* volume in the series. The selection here, therefore, is wholly concerned with Oxford.]

Oxford (Term and Vacation; Merton College; Boating)

The great difference between Oxford in Term and Oxford in Vacation cannot fail to strike the most hurried visitor. Three times a year the streets leading from the railway station to the academic quarters of the town are crowded with vehicles bearing the undergraduate and his fortunes to pass a brief eight weeks in the bosom of Alma Mater, and three times a year the same vehicles may be seen bearing him away. In the interval he reads, rows, runs, rides – and is examined. The splendid palace, dedicated to the goddess of Examinations, richly dight with sculptures, frescoes, marble mosaics, electric lights and electric clocks, occupies a commanding position in the High Street, and will be one of the first wonders to be visited by the stranger. As for the ceremonies here conducted, and the previous course of probation required, these are high matters on which he must seek for information elsewhere. How the future examinee spends his days he may partly guess from the gowned figures, each provided with its notebook, which he will see flitting along the pavement from college to college, or later on from the spectacle of the same figures, now clad in the airy costume of the athlete, wending their way to the river and the running grounds. If the crews are in training for the boat-races, he will do wisely to make for the towing-path, and he will there understand how the virtues of fortitude and endurance are still taught at Oxford.

It is not, however, only members of the University who are to be met thronging the streets on their way to lecture; troops of the other sex, whom the magnanimity of professors has admitted to the privilege of discipleship, will be seen hastening either on foot or on cycle to the same fountains of knowledge: like the men, you may know them by their notebooks, the pages of which, I suspect, are less often desecrated by sketches and caricatures; such follies they leave to their brothers, and I should not be surprised to hear that the lecturer often finds among them the most appreciative as well as the most critical part of his audience. The woman student hails from the great suburb known as North Oxford, which owes its existence to the great feminine invasion of the last thirty years. This invasion has been threefold: first, there are the families unconnected with the University who have settled here in Oxford, as a pleasant centre for concerts, lectures, libraries, museums and tea parties; formerly they would have chosen Cheltenham or Leamington. Secondly, there is the married fellow, now a very numerous species, but in the old times a *rara avis*; and lastly there are the colonies of women students. Hence, whereas the town used to come to an end just beyond St Giles's Church, it now spreads over nearly the whole space between the canal and the Cherwell, and extends northwards for two miles till it includes the once rural hamlet of Summertown.

Should the visitor be less curious to see Oxford life than Oxford itself, and should he long to revel undisturbed in the silence that broods over college quads and college gardens, he will of course choose the Vacation. Then, indeed, like Elia, he can 'play the gentleman and enact the student. In moods of humility he can be a Sizar, or a Servitor. When the peacock vein rises he can strut a gentleman commoner, in graver moments

proceed Master of Arts, and in Christ Church reverend quadrangle be content to pass for nothing short of a Seraphic
Doctor.'* Should he mount the broad and easy staircase that
leads to the reading room of the Bodleian, he will no longer
see any signs of vacation: to all appearances it is still the height
of full term; beneath the painted roof of Duke Humphrey, and
amidst the laden shelves of Sir Thomas, such merely pedagogic
distinctions of times and seasons are unknown. The librarians
are at their posts, the clerks are hurrying up and down with
their armfuls of books, the readers are hunting in the catalogue, or immersed in their researches at the desks. And
nowhere in the world can researches be prosecuted with such
readiness and comfort. Within easy reach of his chair the student has all the books of reference he most frequently wishes
to consult, while by the simple process of turning up an entry
in the catalogue and writing the pressmark, or title, on a slip,
he may command the use of some 600,000 volumes of printed
books, and 30,000 volumes of MSS. Any guidance or information he may require is promptly and courteously afforded him
by the staff, and any complaints or suggestions he may have to
make he is invited to enter in a book kept for the purpose, for
the inspection and consideration of the librarian.

But the charms of the Bodleian must not detain us now;
fascinated though we are, we must leave the happy scholars
to their books and sally forth.

As the oldest of the Oxford colleges, Merton must always
have an especial claim upon the stranger, and if he hails from
a distant land, in which the college system is unknown, he
may care to dwell for a few moments on its meaning and
significance.

Before the coming of Walter de Merton the Oxford students

---

* Charles Lamb, 'Oxford in the Vacation', *Essays of Elia* (1823).

had lived in private houses — whether called halls, inns, or hotels, it makes little difference. The discipline and supervision to which they were liable were merely such as could be supplied by the rather remote agency of the university officers. Under these conditions there was little beyond the uncertain and precarious influence of some prominent teacher to form a centre round which any company of scholars could rally. A field for competition was thus opened, and the Friars were not slow to enter it. Nor can we blame them if the interests of the Order were their first consideration, and the widening of its sphere of influence their ultimate aim. This however was something quite distinct from the true aims and the true ideals of a university; these might best be served in quite another fashion, and to Walter de Merton is due the credit of devising an expedient which solved the question. It was he who saw the gain which would result from the formation of a society bound together by the domestic bond of a common habitation and a common discipline — a society the whole aim and purpose of which should be the advancement of learning and the training of citizens qualified to serve God in church and state. To this end order and discipline were the first essentials for seniors and juniors alike, and in 1264 he drew up the code of statutes to which Merton College owes its inception.

It was for the benefit of the secular clergy that his foundation was designed. Not that he had any quarrel with the regulars, but he saw that their position was sufficiently secure, while the ground they were gaining in Oxford was actually being won at the expense of the seculars. He therefore provided that membership of any religious order whatever should be a disqualification for enrolment in his new society. The very buildings which he designed for its use proclaimed its non-monastic character. Like the religious houses they included a common church and a common refectory, but they were plainly marked off from them by the absence of that distinctive feature of the convent, the cloister. The members of a college had their private chambers, and the cloister became superfluous.

The buildings adjoining Merton chapel have a unique interest. To the south is the most ancient quad in Oxford, dignified, no one knows why, by the name of Mob Quad. In the north-eastern corner is the singular building called the Treasury, remarkable for its high-pitched roof of solid stone flags. So steep is the slope from the roof-tree, and such is the weight of the flags, that as a piece of constructive masonry it has excited the wonder of every generation; it has stood as it now stands for six centuries, and yet no Merton scholar has ever felt it 'tremble o'er his head'. To the fourteenth century also belong the four sides of the quad; nor do they show any signs of decay. They are in fact for the most part built, not of the perishable Headington sandstone, but of the hard and durable oolite from the quarries of Taynton, a pretty village on the Oxfordshire flanks of the Cotswold. The far-sighted architects were not to be deterred by the twenty miles or more of haulage – a serious consideration in those days – and posterity has had good reason to be grateful to them.

To pass from the solemn seclusion of Mob Quad into the spacious ease of the Fellows' Quadrangle is to pass in a moment from the rigour of medievalism into the amenities of modern life. Built at a time when, in another Midland town less than forty miles away, *Cymbeline*, *The Tempest*, and *A Winter's Tale* were being written, the Fellows' Quad at Merton is, like those immortal dramas, redolent of romance. It may rank with the beautiful buildings of Wadham, the unrivalled garden front at St John's, and the glorious staircase of Christ Church as the last expression of the romantic feeling in Oxford architecture before the advancing wave of Puritanism swept all such sentiments away. Did it not form part of a college it might easily be mistaken for the courtyard of a Jacobean mansion of the first rank. It is the most delightful habitation in Oxford, and we cannot wonder that the queens 'of either Charles's days' chose it as their abode. It was in this quad that in 1661 the first Common Room in Oxford was opened, and here it still remains. Access from the hall is easy, and on a winter's night, when the mist lies thick on Christ Church meadow, or the storm comes driving across the valley from the Cumnor Hills, when the dark-panelled walls are glowing in the firelight, and the candles in their silver sconces are reflected in the vistaed depths of the polished table, when the fellows and their guests are assembled, and the college port goes round, it would be hard to find a pleasanter fireside in Oxford.

Each college has its barge or house-boat, which is to the river what the pavilion is to the cricket field. Cross the river in a punt and stroll down the towing-path, and you will have a good view of the practising eights and fours, as well as of sundry smaller craft. This will give you a good idea of Oxford 'form' in its various stages of efficiency, but if you want to see it at its best, you must wait for the bumping races in February and May. The towing-path is then a less desirable point of observation, for it is crowded by an excited multitude, tearing along to keep pace with the competing boats, and cheering their crews not merely vocally but by all such sounds of harmony as may be produced by rattles of large size, megaphones and even pistol shots; while if a bump be imminent, the air is rent by shouts that may be heard half a mile away. But I must not assume that the reader is initiated into the mysteries of Oxford boating, and he may very naturally wonder what a bump might be. I hasten therefore to explain that the river is not wide enough for more than two boats to start abreast, and that arrangements have to be made for at least a score. Each college has its own boat, and some colleges have two. Under these circumstances the problem is solved as follows: the several boats are posted in a long line at equal distances apart, the tail boat being close to Iffley Lock. On the first day of the races, which last a week, the order of precedence is that of the final order resulting from the races of the previous year. At a given signal the boats start simultaneously, and it is the object of each to foul with its bows the stern of the one immediately ahead of it. This manoeuvre is the bump, and the next day the bumping boat takes precedence of the bumped. The February races are those of the junior crews or 'Torpids'; the May races those of the senior crews or 'Eights'. The Eights are recruited from the Torpids, and the University Eight from the college Eights.

The May races are the great Oxford carnival: mothers, sisters, cousins, aunts come flocking in their hundreds; picnics, promenades, teas, dinners are the order of the day; even dances – long supposed the peculiar privilege of Commemoration week – have been heard of, and both entertainers and entertained may boast with Lord Foppington that life is an eternal round O of delights. But Eights' week or not Eights' week, summer term is the time for 'the Joys of Oxford Living', the time for Panama hats and loose attire, the time for lounging in punts, or flirting in 'Canaders'. It may be that presently when we turn out of Mesopotamia into the Parks and saunter along the willowed margin of the 'Cher', we may chance to spy Youth on the prow, and Pleasure at the helm gliding softly up towards distant Islip, babbling of many things, but not unmindful of luncheon and of a descent upon the ripening meadow of some long-suffering Marston farmer. Or it may be, we shall see made fast beneath the shadow of some overhanging poplar the cushioned punt, where 'Some on earnest business bent / Their murmuring labours ply', for even in summer term the victim of 'Exams' cannot ever play regardless of his doom. Even in summer term the paths of Oxford lead but to the Schools.

27

SHAKESPEARE'S
COUNTRY

W. H. Hutton, 1914

Stratford-upon-Avon

We are come to the centre of our shire – the goal of our quest. Say what you will, Stratford is the heart of Warwickshire, even of England, for all who visit it today; and the small stream of Avon is the most famous of all English rivers.

The poet and the river are certainly the two governing factors in the life of Stratford. Shakespeare is to be seen and heard everywhere. The river, which half encircles the town, is more easily forgotten, yet it gives the setting which bestows on the place its only distinction of beauty, and it no doubt founded the prosperity which has never wholly deserted it.

In the eighteenth century the town began to have a special fame because it was Shakespeare's town; and it was Garrick, one may fairly say, who made it famous. *The Beauties of England and Wales*, 1814, contains such a delightful description of the occasion, and what it seemed to the Georgian folk to mean, that I cannot forbear to quote it:

> Until the early part of the eighteenth century polite literature was confined to so few that the national love of Shakespeare was not sufficiently ardent to lead numerous pilgrims to Stratford, for the purpose of poetical devotion. But with the spread of letters inevitably kept pace the progress of Shakespeare's fame. His readers must needs become innoxious idolists; and for very many years, Stratford has witnessed throngs of visitors, anxious to tread the

ground which Shakespeare's feet had pressed in boyhood; and to express, by mournful contemplation over the spot hallowed by his ashes, their gratitude for the banquet of intellectual joys afforded by his all but superhuman talents. The public inclination to visit this favoured neighbourhood was promoted by the man who, perhaps of all others, was best able to appreciate the poet's merits – the celebrated Garrick. In the year 1769, he instituted at Stratford a festival in honour of Shakespeare, the Jubilee. This interesting celebration commenced on the morning of Sept. 6, 1769, and terminated with the evening of the following Friday. An octagonal amphitheatre was erected on the Bankcroft, close to the river Avon, which was capable of holding more than 1,000 persons. The amusements consisted of a public breakfast at the Town Hall; the performance of the Oratorio of Judith in the church of Stratford; a public ordinary at the amphitheatre; and assembly; a masquerade; the recitation, by Garrick, of an ode and oration in praise of Shakespeare; and exhibition of fireworks; and a horse race for a silver cup. The town was illuminated; cannon were fired; and bands of music paraded the streets. The concourse of persons of rank to assist in this poetical festival was so great that many were not able to procure beds in the town, and are said to have been constrained to sleep in their carriages.

Shakespeare's birthplace (so believed) was bought by national subscription in 1847, the New Place estate (which he had bought in 1597) in 1862, in 1891 the Birthplace Trust was incorporated by Act of Parliament, and in the following year Anne Hathaway's cottage was acquired. The two houses to the south of the birthplace were given by Mr Andrew Carnegie in 1903; they are now used as the offices of the Trust.

Thus the ages left their marks on Stratford, from the Domesday of William Conqueror to the generosity of an American millionaire. Much that is truly ancient survives in this town of restoration and, one must admit, of occasional impostures. Let us take one example of survival. Stratford still preserves its ancient fair or 'mop'. How few are left of these historic festivals; and how keenly those that remain are enjoyed! Stratford Mop is fed from all the neighbouring villages and by excursion trains from distant towns. A description in journalese, of the scene of October 13, 1909, is worth preserving:

Stratford-upon-Avon rose to the occasion in gallant style, and for a few hours the old-world town ran riot with frolic in which young and old joined with happy disregard for age or decorum. The seriousness of work and wages is brushed on one side, and the thoughts uppermost in the minds of the rural element is how to get the maximum amount of enjoyment in the minimum time.

To assist them in carrying out this intention there is no lack of means, provided they have the wherewithal. First and foremost, there were eight prime oxen and close upon a dozen porkers to be consumed, and the work of turning the beasts, which were impaled upon great spits, before blazing wood fires, and the basting of the same by cooks in white garb, was followed with interest by the crowd.

Then there was sightseeing. 'Cheap Jacks' with varying supplies of Birmingham jewellery were in old haunts in the High Street, and it was astonishing the value for the money here offered. Imagine a gold watch, with two or three sovereigns into the bargain, for one sovereign! Vendors of pirated music were here, there and everywhere, and visitors were reminded not to forget the little ones at home, for whose delectation wonderful creations in the form of the 'Dying Duck' or golliwog, 'all alive', were to be had for a copper or so.

No doubt Shakespeare saw a 'mop' very like this. It is certainly worth seeing Stratford on mop day; but it is not a day to choose if one wants to meditate upon the scenes of the poet's life.

Such is the history – how shall we begin to visit it? The first thing a traveller may be expected to want is an inn, though I am inclined to believe that it is almost the last thing he thinks of. Stratford is well stocked with hostelries.* Across Clopton Bridge the first thing he sees on the right is the unpretentious but pleasing Unicorn, where he may feel quite modern unless he happens to occupy a large room which has actually no window, and no light at all except from a skylight. But everybody who goes to Stratford ought to remember that Washington Irving made one inn famous:

> To a homeless man, who has no spot on this wide world which he can truly call his own, there is a momentary feeling of something like independence and territorial consequence when, after a day's travel, he kicks off his boots, thrusts his feet into slippers and stretches himself before an inn fire . . . The armchair is his throne, the poker his sceptre, and the little parlour, some twelve feet square, his undisputed empire . . . 'Shall I not take mine ease in mine inn?' thought I, as I gave the fire a stir, lolled back in my elbow-chair, and cast a complacent look about the little parlour of the Red Horse, at Stratford.

In spite of this description which has made the inn one of the famous sights of the town, it is not spoilt. Washington Irving's room is kept as he described it, with the poker, guarded as a relic. There is still an old-world air about the Red Horse, per-

---

* It had been well stocked for centuries; Shakespeare's father, John, was for a short while an ale-taster in Stratford, at which time the town had thirty taverns.

haps due to the fact that from its position in the middle of
Bridge Street it cannot be indefinitely enlarged, except at the
back where it extends to Guild Street. It remains an eigh-
teenth- or early nineteenth-century inn, not an Elizabethan
hostelry or a modern hotel. Of such there are plenty in Stratford. There is the Shakespeare Hotel in Chapel Street with
many pleasing old features. There is the Falcon at the corner of
Scholar's Lane, looking on Chapel Street and almost exactly
opposite to New Place. If you find this house very full – it is a
very pleasant one, and they will even tell you that Shakespeare
visited it often (which is not at all unlikely) – you may even
have the chance to be given a bedroom not far off in the
restored and redecorated Tudor House, and the bedroom will
be panelled entirely with old dark oak up to its fine plaster ceiling. The town has also many smaller inns and many good
lodgings. It certainly 'lays itself out' for visitors.

New Place, or the site and foundation of it, must certainly
be examined by every visitor to Stratford. It stood from 1483,
when it was built by Sir Hugh Clopton. Between 1597 and his
death, Shakespeare had been its owner. There he died on April
23, 1616. He left it to his daughter, Susanna Hall, who lived
there till 1649, succeeded by her daughter who lived till 1670.
Rebuilt by Sir John Clopton in 1702, it was demolished in 1759
by the Rev. Francis Gastrell, Vicar of Frodsham, Cheshire, who
had bought it three years before. This testy personage was
vexed by continual requests to see the house of Shakespeare,
and with equal vandalism he cut down a fine mulberry tree
which the poet was said to have planted. A visitor to Stratford
in 1760 gives, I think, our earliest record of this:

> There stood here till lately the house in which Shakespeare
> lived, and a mulberry tree of his planting; the house was
> large, strong and handsome . . . As the curiosity of this house
> and tree brought much fame, and more company and profit,

to the town, a certain man, on some disgust, has pulled the house down, so as not to leave one stone upon another, and cut down the tree, and piled it as a stack of firewood, to the great vexation, loss, and disappointment of the inhabitants.

Only the foundations of this house are now visible, covered over by wire. The great garden, at the back of this site, is now a public garden, and in it, on the central lawn, is a mulberry descended from the poet's own tree.

If Shakespeare's house is destroyed, that of his grandson, Thomas Nash, survives. It has been completely altered. A while ago it was an eighteenth-century house to look at, within and without, but a thorough 'restoration' has given it something of the appearance it had in Shakespeare's day. Following the notice of the Birthplace Trust, on which it is difficult to improve, one may observe that after Nash's death in 1647, the house, 'portions of which are four hundred years old', was left

to his wife for life; at her death in 1670 it passed to his cousin Edward Nash. In the course of the next two centuries the house was tenanted by a succession of private owners, and underwent from time to time much structural change and disfigurement. In 1862 it was purchased for the nation as part of the New Place estate, the whole of which was con-veyed in 1891 to the Trustees [who] in 1912 re-adapted the house to public uses. Surviving features of the sixteenth century were freed of modern accretions and the fabric was restored in all essentials to its early condition.

The transformation is certainly wonderful to those who remember it only a few years ago. It now contains a very inter-esting collection of 'relics of the Poet's demolished Residence, of Garrick and of the Shakespeare Jubilee of 1769, his letter to the Corporation when he was given the freedom of the town, and some boxes made from the mulberry tree'.

From New Place, where Shakespeare certainly died, it is not far to the house where he was probably born. It may be well to remember that, as a place of pilgrimage, what is now called the Birthplace has a much shorter record than New Place. Apparently not till after 1760 was this double house in Henley Street regarded, or made famous, as that in which Shakespeare was born. Even the sexton who showed the house to Washington Irving, years after that, insinuated a doubt as to the house. But John Shakespeare had property in Henley Street, for certain, as early as 1552, when he was fined for having a dungheap in front of his house. In 1556 he bought a freehold house in the street; in 1575 he bought the house now called the Birthplace. They are to all intents one house. William Shakespeare was born in April 1564. From these facts one may draw what conclusion one can.

Early in the seventeenth century the eastern part of the house was let separately as an inn. During the eighteenth century the western part was used as a butcher's shop. When Nathaniel Hawthorne saw it, there was still trace of the base uses to which it had come. Both houses were then bought by Thomas Court, whose widow's death in 1847 caused them to be sold by auction, when they were bought for the nation.

A tradition has grown up which, we see, the trustees sanction, that the true birth-room is that at the front on the first floor. The ceiling, the walls, the windows, are covered with names of visitors, highly distinguished persons some of them – I regret to say that Walter Scott is among the number – who ought to have known better than perpetrate such an offence. There is an amusing story about this. A virago of a caretaker was once dismissed from her post; she spent her last night in whitewashing the walls, thinking to destroy these records of interest, but she forgot to size her work and it was easily removed. Was this the person whom Washington Irving saw and immortalised?

'A garrulous old lady,' Irving wrote,

> in a frosty red face, lighted up by a cold blue anxious eye, and garnished with artificial locks of flaxen hair, curling from under an exceedingly dirty cap . . . was particularly assiduous in exhibiting the relics with which this, like all other celebrated shrines, abounds. There was the shattered stock of the very matchlock with which Shakespeare shot the deer on his poaching exploits. There, too, was his tobacco box, which proves that he was a rival smoker to Sir Walter Raleigh; the sword also with which he played Hamlet; and the identical lantern with which Friar Laurence discovered Romeo and Juliet at the tomb! There was an ample supply also of Shakespeare's mulberry tree, which seems to have as extraordinary powers of self-multiplication as the wood of the true Cross.

Whatever its authentic history there is nothing in Stratford quite like the Birthplace. It has at least the 'aura' of many centuries of devotion. It stands alone among the Stratford houses.

In a few minutes you can be away from all the noise and bustle of tourists; you can lie down under the shadow of the riverbank, and ponder over the old days, wonder at the memories that have brought you so far, then fall asleep and dream of Shakespeare, in whose country, the very heart of England, you have found yourself.

28

SOMERSET

Edward Hutton, 1912

Bath

As you discern the long lines of her terraces, so orderly for England, about the vast amphitheatre of her hills, you might think Bath, even from the railway, the capital of some Italian province, a Latin city, full of Roman traditions and memories of the south.

Florence in England you might say indeed, as you make your way about those beautiful hillsides that everywhere look down upon the city, through which, not the tawny Arno, but the crystal Avon flows; and more especially perhaps if you come to her first along the road from London or through Widcombe from that truly Italian palace Prior Park, under Combe Down, or, better still, from Charlcombe on the shoulder of Lansdown between white villas and garden walls hung with stone-crop and geraniums and battlemented with roses as though Charlcombe were Settignano.

Nevertheless on a nearer view something pleasantly and even characteristically English in those sober streets and quiet crescents obscures your first impression until you are ready to discern, and above all in the grey towers and pinnacles, the lean buttresses and traceried windows of the great church of the place something peculiarly your own. And yet little by little, even there too you find something – how shall I say? – alien, strange. That great church you note, stands not in any green close as you might expect, but in a paved piazza in the very midst of the city; while the street which was at first sight most unmistakeably English, proves on closer acquaintance to be in truth a way older far than any English town.

And so at evening in the twilight as you loiter perhaps on Beechen Cliff for the sake of the view, or pass down one of those great silent terraces on Lansdown, or linger in the windy piazza by the church, your first impression returns to you, and you remember the Roman city that lies buried at the roots of that you now see; and in a moment you understand that this alone of all English cities has by some fortune or some miracle remembered her origins, that those ruins on which she stands have in a very real way passed into her life, involved her in their beauty, and given her, as a free gift, something of her nobility; that indeed they have attained to this much immortality, that they live again in her.

That Roman note which so many have found in Bath becomes ever more dominant as you linger with her; nor is it only to be explained by the fact that the Latin ruins upon which she stands are so considerable and so haunting in their fascination and interest. Bath, in fact, mainly, as we see her, a creation of the eighteenth century, added to and modified but not altogether spoilt in the nineteenth century, seems, if we compare her with her rivals in the South of England, Canterbury and Winchester, for instance, scarcely English at all, to be, as we might think, out of our tradition.

Those cities of rosy brick, lovelier by far than Bath with the loveliness of the Middle Age of which they are full, and as English as the meadows in which they stand, fill with their fame the history of our country; but Bath has almost no memories of the Dark Age which brought St Austin to Canterbury and established Winchester as the capital of England, and but few of medieval times. Founded by the Romans for the sake of her hot springs, she was ruined by the fall of the Empire and for over a thousand years she remained little more than a village clustered about a monastery, Roman still in this if you will, that the Church held what the Empire had abandoned, but of little or no national importance till her marvellous resurrection in that great classical period of English life, the eighteenth century, when once more, as in Roman times, and for the same reason, the city became the focus of fashionable life, and the baths, after how much more than a millennium, were rediscovered and rebuilt; and for a brief hundred years, from the visit of Queen Anne in 1702, this city of western England became as it were the epitome of English social life, the school of manners of a new civilisation, the home and perhaps the inspiration of a new art which we regard as classical and look back upon, amid all the confusion of today, with reverence and regret.

Thus Bath, which had almost no part, certainly no great part, in the history of England till then, suddenly in the eighteenth century comes to fill a great role, and what we see inevitably is not the creation of anything new, but the resurrection of the old Roman city with its beautiful classical buildings, its temples, as one might think, its palaces, certainly, and its Thermae, so strange and so delightful in England, which give the city a unique splendour, built as they are of enduring stone and in so fortunate a moment.

That stately eighteenth-century city, shining upon the western hills, full of a beautiful dignity that seems to draw its life, as it certainly does its beauty, from something older and greater than England, is the gate of Somerset; and since all western England, with its isolated hills and enclosed valleys, has everywhere something Roman about it, it is well that it should be held by so noble and so Roman a port.

It has always been known that there were Roman baths at Bath, but we knew nothing definite concerning them till a century and a half ago, and it is only with the last twenty-five years that our knowledge can be called systematic. To this day we do not know who built and owned the baths, nor whether they were in public or private hands.

All this is little enough, but even this we should probably not know if early in the eighteenth century Bath had not suddenly become popular as a watering place among the wealthier classes. The first discovery of Roman remains was made in 1727; exactly what was then found we do not know. In 1755, in the course of pulling down a house to make room for the Duke of Kingston's baths, a large swimming basin was found, and traces of the Great Bath were discovered; but little more was done till, in 1878, the Corporation employed the late Major Davis, then the city architect, to conduct extensive excavations.

Really, I suppose the Bath of the eighteenth century was the unconscious creation of the *malade imaginaire*. The gradual amelioration of the world at the beginning of the eighteenth century, the recovery of Britain from the economic disaster of the Reformation, and the revolution in manners then just beginning, consequent upon that recovery, gave Bath a new opportunity which was, in fact, in some sort a reproduction of Roman conditions. It was due to two men, Allen and Nash, that Bath was able to seize that opportunity and to make the utmost of those conditions.

'At this time,' says Goldsmith, by far the best authority,

London was the only theatre in England for pleasure and intrigue. A spirit of gaming had been introduced in the licentious age of Charles II, and had by this time thriven surprisingly. Yet all its devastations were confined to London alone . . . people of fashion had no agreeable summer retreat from the town . . . they wanted some place where they might have each other's company and win each other's money . . . Probably upon this distinction and by the arrival of Queen Anne there for her health, about the year 1703, the city of Bath became in some measure frequented by people of distinction . . . Still, however, the amusements of the place were neither elegant nor conducted with delicacy. The nobility still preserved a tincture of Gothic haughtiness and refused to keep company with the gentry . . . gentlemen and ladies appeared in a disrespectful manner at public entertainments in aprons and boots. With an eagerness common to those whose pleasures come but seldom, they generally continued them too long; and thus they were rendered disgusting by too free an enjoyment.

Thus Goldsmith shows us the extraordinary difference in culture and civilisation that separated the upper and middle classes at that time in England; it was the social reconciliation of these classes, in culture and manners, that was achieved at Bath and by 'Beau' Nash.

He arrived in the midst of the hurly-burly of barbarism and horseplay described by Goldsmith, he organised the entertainment of this crowd of ill-assorted people, was apparently at once recognised as the necessary leader and 'the sovereignty of the city was decreed to him by every rank of people'. As 'King of Bath' he presently drew up a set of 'Rules to be observed at Bath' and posted them in the Pump Room. These rules, written by himself, seem to us both insolent and stupid, but they were then regarded as witty, and as such they were accepted and obeyed, and Goldsmith tells us that even the royal family themselves had not influence enough to make him change them. One day when, breaking his rules, the Duchess of Queensberry appeared on a ball night in a white apron, he 'stript it off and threw it at one of the hinder benches among the ladies' women', observing that none but Abigails appeared in white aprons. 'This,' says Goldsmith, 'from another would be an insult; in him it was considered a just reprimand, and the good-natured duchess acquiesced in his censure.'

But if Bath owes much to Beau Nash, she owes more to Ralph Allen, without whose noble and attractive character the eighteenth century over which Nash ruled with so frivolous a despotism would have lacked both its charm and its permanence. He had become proprietor of the Combe Down quarries, and having invented a means of conveying the great blocks of hewn stone from the quarries to the canal, he did a huge business in stone. He became thus the great capitalist in Bath, and though only once mayor, in 1742, as a fact he always ruled the city. His true memorial is the city of Bath, as we see it, with its noble buildings, its squares and terraces and parades, that give it so classic an air. His architect was John Wood, a Yorkshireman, born in 1704, probably introduced to Bath by Allen, first displaying his powers of design in the North and South Parades. By the end of 1725 he had at the suggestion of Allen formed a noble plan, really for the rebuilding of the city, its tremendous enlargement upon the hillsides. In this plan there was to be, we are told, 'a grand place of assembly', to be called the 'Royal Forum of Bath'; another, for the exhibition of games and sports, to be called 'the Grand Circus', and in 1727 these noble and grand ideas for the transformation of a city, the greatest that had appeared in England since the Reformation, began to be carried out. Queen's Square, Gay Street, the Circus, finished by the younger Wood in 1785, the Parades, the old Assembly Rooms were built. And when Wood died in 1754, his work was continued by his son, John Wood junior. To him we owe the Royal Crescent, the Upper Assembly Rooms, the Hot Bath and the Royal Private Bath in Hot Bath Street, the York House Hotel, and, indeed, all York Buildings, Brook Street, St Margaret's Chapel (now a skating rink), Edgar Buildings, Princess Buildings, Alfred Street, Russell Street, Belmont and Nelson Park.

But Bath was not only the birthplace of the new civilisation, of the new architecture, it was the mother or at any rate the patron of the new school of painting which was to place England in this, too, beside the very greatest the world had known.

Gainsborough, at the suggestion of Philip Thicknesse, came to Bath in 1760, and thereby took his first step to fame and fortune. He occupied an apartment in the new-built Circus, for which he paid £50 a year. He began to paint portraits there for five guineas, but his success was so great that he quickly raised his price to eight, and before long was able to obtain forty guineas for a half length, and as much as a hundred for a full length. He remained in Bath for fourteen years, and painted there some of his best works, among them, according to Sir William Armstrong, the *Blue Boy*.

The authors whose genius has, as Macaulay declared, 'made it classic ground', brings us to the last and not the least important set of people who have helped to make the eighteenth century famous in Bath. There Rochester wrote his fine historic dialogue 'Alexis and Strephon'. There Wycherley and Congreve and Defoe went to recruit, Addison took the waters, and Steele found material for his satire. Fielding and Pope were often there as the guests of Ralph Allen, and from Anstey to Dickens, through Smollett, Frances Burney, and Miss Austen, the three literary pillars of Bath society, there is scarcely a great name in literature that has not its connection with Bath: Bolingbroke, Arbuthnot, Gay, Butler and Berkeley, Smollett who wrote a treatise on the Bath waters and filled *Roderick Random* and *Peregrine Pickle* with his reminiscences of the town; Young, Hume and Goldsmith, whose *Life of Beau Nash* was the result of his visit, Sterne who was there painted by Gainsborough in 1765, Scott and Southey, Johnson and the faithful Boswell, Gibbon, Coleridge and Hazlitt and Carlyle and Landor they are all in the picture, and helped to make Bath what in their day she was, the epitome of England, the polite metropolis of our civilisation.

And now that Bath has become, in any superficial view of her, almost as any other town in England, though at least to the seeing eye still that stately and beautiful city which the Woods made her, it is with these great ghosts of the eighteenth century we people her, as idling about her terraces and squares we pass the languid days in so great a quietness. If you will but have patience and day it may chance you will see Burke steal out of his door on the North Parade. In Pierpoint Street you shall meet little Lord Nelson with his empty sleeve and it is lovely Miss Linley herself who will drop you a curtsey and make you happy for a whole day on her way to the Assembly Rooms.

And yet the Romans are not more dead than they. Nay in Bath it is, amid all the ghosts, only Rome that continually endures, that does not pass away, that cannot be denied. Akemanceaster, the great Norman Abbey, the medieval city, where shall we find a stone of them or anything to remind us they ever were? Yet that which was the root of them all, out of which they were created, and because of which they had a being, remains, astonishing and even tremendous, something that even time has not been able to destroy or to erase from the memory of men.

29

SURREY

Eric Parker, 1908

Guildford; Epsom

To arrive at Guildford by train is like walking into a garden over a rubbish heap. In the grace of its building, the charm of its colour, the fascination of the prospects of its hillside High Street, no town in Surrey, and perhaps only Oxford in England, is comparable with it. But between the railway station and the High Street it is desolation and blank walls. A few pretty old cottages jut out over a narrow pavement; beyond a huddled roof or two rises the tower of St Nicholas's Church, umber and solid; nearly all else is tumbled down ugliness, broken brickwork, mud and shaggy grass. A clear space, a level green, a bed of flowers – what an introduction that might be to Guildford. But, doubtless, the rubbish heap is, or some day will be, valuable as building land.

Beyond the turn of the road is the most delightful street in the south of England. It rises from the bridge crossing the Wey steep into the blue air over the hill. Each side of it is a stairway of roofs up the slope, a medley of facades, a jumble of architecture astonishing in sheer extravagance and variety. Gabled houses red-tiled and gay with rough-cast and fresh paint; dull, sad houses with sleepy windows like half-shut eyes; square, solid Georgian houses for doctors with white chokers and snuff-boxes, and prim old ladies with mittened wrists; low, little dolls' houses, red brick neatly pointed; tall slim houses graceful with slender casements and light shafts of wood; casements nobly elaborate in wood-carving and heavy with leaded panes; bay windows which should light a library, delicately fastened with wrought iron; painted pillars supporting window seats for cats and demure young ladies; broad-stepped entrances to hotel halls, and archways under which barrels roll to bursting cellars; Guildford High Street is a model of what the High Street of an English town should be. Has it a single dominating feature, or is its air of distinction merely compact of the grace and old-worldliness of its shops and houses? Perhaps the single extreme impression left by the High Street is its clock, swung far out over the road.

Guildford's history, until comparatively recent times, has been the history of the wool trade and cloth manufacture. The beginnings of the industry go back to the settlement in the south of England, in the reign of Edward III, of Flemish weavers and dyers. Before the end of the fourteenth century the cloth industry had come to the dignity of legislation. Nobody might buy cloth before it had been 'fulled and fully performed in its nature'; this was to prevent dishonest people from stretching the cloth and so giving the public short measure. It was highly illegal to stretch cloth in any way. So important a part of Guildford's life had clothmaking become under Elizabeth that the Corporation required special acknowledgement of the fact from the innkeepers, doubtless because prosperity in the town meant full tankards emptied at the inns. Every alehouse keeper had to have a signboard hung above his door with a woolsack painted on it, under a fine of six-and-eightpence; he had to buy the sign from the hall warden at the Town Hall, and pay two shillings for it.

Guildford's inns have been famous for centuries. Guildford is the only town in Surrey which Camden* mentions in his *Britannia* as having good inns; John Aubrey† remarks that they are

---

* William Camden (1551–1623). His *Britannia* (1586) was the first historical and topographical survey of Britain.

† 1626–1697.

'the best perhaps in England; the Red Lion particularly can make fifty beds, the White Hart is not so big, but has more noble rooms.' John Taylor‡, the Water Poet, in his *Catalogue of Taverns in Ten Shires near London*, made in 1636, goes out of his way to mention particularly that Guildford 'hath very faire Innes and good entertainment at the Tavernes, the Angell, the Crowne, the White Hart, and the Lyon'; and Guildford only, of all the towns he mentions, has all its inns either still standing or represented under the same names, wholly or partially rebuilt. The Angel has kept more of what is old than the others, including a panelled hall with a seventeenth-century clock, and some fine timber and brickwork best seen from the inn yard.

The Red Lion was the best inn, according to Pepys. It was at the Red Lion that he 'lay in the room the King lately lay in', which would have pleased Pepys; and it was with the drawers of the inn, one Saturday night, that he and Mr Creed made merry over the minister of the town, who had a girdle as red as his face, but preached next day a better sermon than Pepys had looked for. The inn had a garden, out of which on another occasion the gossiping little Admiralty official cut 'sparagus for supper – the best that I ever ate'. Doubtless the host of the Red Lion liked Pepys's recommendation, but Pepys and his wife must have occasionally been rather noisy guests. It was in the same inn garden that he and Mr Creed 'played the fool a great while, trying who could go best over the edge of an old fountain well; and I won a quart of sack§ of him.' Afterwards, at supper, 'my wife and I did talk high, she against and I for Mrs Pierce (that she was a beauty) till we were both angry.' Pepys's journeys to Portsmouth, where his Admiralty business took

---

‡ 1578–1653.
§ A general name for a class of white wine from Spain and the Canaries, common in taverns in the seventeenth century.

him, seem generally to have been broken at Guildford, which was the first stopping place after leaving 'Fox Hall', as he calls Vauxhall.

A gentler traveller through Guildford used to drive along the Hog's Back in the early morning, breakfast at the Lion or the Angel, and reach Sloane Street at half-past six or so in the evening, when she was glad to get to bed early. That was when Jane Austen was writing at Chawton. One of her letters, very typical of her in its regard for the pleasant little minutiae of a day's business, describes a drive from Chawton up to London. At Guildford she was 'very lucky in my gloves – got them at the first shop I went to, though I went into it rather because it was near than because it looked like a shop, and gave only four shillings for them; after which everybody at Chawton will be hoping and predicting that they cannot be good for anything.'

Guildford once had nine 'gates'; eight have disappeared. The charm of the chief buildings remains, but here and there modern needs have spoiled the smaller houses. In the High Street, for instance, Number 25, not much more than a hundred years ago, must have been a quite perfect little house, with its large casements and their curious iron fastenings, its noble staircase, and its delightful doorway. One building has altered very little. That is the old town hall, whose clock swings out over the road, and has been sketched more often, perhaps, than any clock in Surrey. The original town hall belongs to the time of Elizabeth, and was probably built into the present structure, which dates from 1683. It is in some ways the chief feature of the High Street, with its heavy balcony, supported by monstrous black oak brackets, and its cupola and bell-turret. The clock has a separate history. Massive, black and gilt, and fastened to the face of the old Town Hall with an ingenious structure of steel stays, it has told Guildford the time for two centuries and a quarter. In the year when the town hall was built, one John Aylward, a clockmaker, came to Guildford and asked leave to set up in business. He was a 'foreigner', that is, he came from another part of England, and the Gild merchant refused permission. Undaunted, he retired and set up his shop outside the borough, made a great clock, presented it to the governing body, and so obtained the freedom of the town.

*

Epsom is the centre of the country between the great railway lines. It has its own railway, but is midway between the lines that run express trains to Brighton and Southampton; Epsom's own expresses only run for two weeks in the year, when the races come round. For the other fifty weeks Epsom is a quiet town of villas, once a village, now nearly a suburb like Esher or Weybridge. Lord Rosebery sometimes lives near the town, at Durdans, and deplores the large numbers of lunatics who are brought to live near the town always. But Epsom is only occasionally ruffled by the lunatics, and has developed a dangerously good train service.

The story of Epsom, until the two great races that belong to its downs were founded over Lord Derby's wine, is the story of its wells. Before Epsom Salts there was hardly an Epsom to give them a name. Then, one hot summer day in 1618, the lucky thing happened. Henry Wicker, trying to water his cattle on the common, found a small hole with a spring in it; he enlarged it, and took the cattle to the water, but could not make them drink. Then the doctors were told about it. They used it first, as Pownall the local historian tells you, 'as a vulnerary and abstersive', and healed wounds with it; then some labourers accidentally drank it, and Epsom's fortune was made. The doctors agreed; Epsom salts were bitter, diluent, absorbent, soluble, cathartic – everything that salts should be. In two years the wells were enclosed with a wall; in twenty years France and Germany had heard of Epsom, and distinguished foreigners obediently paced the common. But the great days were still to come. As yet few buildings had grown up close to the wells, merely 'a shed to shelter the sickly visitors'. Then came the year 1670, when Charles II gave Barbara Villiers his palace of Nonsuch two miles away. She, as careless of a king's gift and as avaricious as a king's mistress should be, turned the palace into cash, and out of its demolished walls the local builder piled up houses by Epsom Wells.

One of Epsom's inns was already built, the King's Head. Pepys was there in 1667, and gives us a glimpse of Nell Gwynne, though she was at Epsom to amuse herself, and was not one of Pepys's party. Pepys went on July 14: he got up at four in the morning, and talked to Mrs Turner downstairs while his wife dressed, and got angry with Mrs Pepys because she was so long about it. They were off in the coach by five, with bottles of wine and beer and a cold fowl, Pepys writes, and so came 'to Epsom, by eight o'clock, to the well; where much company, and I drank the water: they did not, but I did drink four pints.'

When Nonsuch was built up again into Durdans and other houses near the wells, then came full tide. Epsom was completed. Pownall dates the climax about the year 1690: 'Taverns at that time reputed to be the largest in England were opened; there was a public breakfast, with dancing and music every morning at the wells . . . and we may add that neither Bath nor Tunbridge ever boasted of more noble visitors than Epsom, or exceeded it in splendour, at the time we are describing.' In the days when the city aldermen brought their wives to show off their finery, and the young sparks threw their money about at Epsom, what a bustling, handsome, pursy, turtle-soup sort of place the wells must have been.

And in 1715 it had all come to an end. Epsom's glories tumbled, like a pack of cards. It was the fault of one man: Pownall has gibbeted the rascal; Epsom fell through the 'knavery of Mr

John Livingstone, an apothecary'. Mr Livingstone may have been a knave, but he was also evidently a fool. He began admirably, as a doctor with a speculative eye should do, by building a large house with an assembly room for dancing and music, 'and other rooms for raffling, dicing, fairchance and all sorts of gaming'. He was quite a heathen, for he planted a grove, and he made a bowling green, and then spoiled it all by sinking a well, putting a pump to it, and calling the place the New Wells. The new water was neither diluent, nor absorbent, nor cathartic, nor anything else that water at a watering-place should be, and the visitors found out the difference. But the end was the maddest thing of all. Somehow or other, Livingstone got a lease of the old wells, the real, genuine spring. Then he locked up the old wells, and tried to make money with the new. It killed the watering-place.

Water ended Epsom in 1715; wine began Epsom again in 1780. A party of gentlemen, drinking at Lord Derby's table at Lambert's Oaks, a house on high ground above the town, lifted their glasses to the glories of horse racing. They founded two races, one, in 1779, for three-year-old fillies; another, in 1780, for three-year-old colts and fillies. They named the races after their host and the house where they drank, and Epsom was made again. The Derby and the Oaks became national institutions. The watering-place has become a circus. The race week brings down all London. The road must have been the thing to see; not as we see it today, when motor cars start for the course before lunch instead of before breakfast, and luxurious railway trains draw decadent racegoers to Tattenham Corner. In the real Derby days all racing men that were men drove to Epsom, early in the morning, by road. Four-in-hand coaches travelled level in the pack and the dust by costermongers' donkeys; at every inn there were touts and tipsters, haunting creatures with secrets of betting – you merely had to pay for the knowledge. Wayside strips of green were turned into coconut shies, wherever a man might wish to shy at nuts; clowns on stilts stalked in chequered blue. They still drive four-in-hand coaches up the hill; but the motor-horn follows the coach-horn.

But the crowd itself, and what the crowd does, and what it sees and feels – that, surely, has changed hardly at all. The gipsies still swarm; the bookmakers, bedizened with belts of silver coin, and outlandish hats, and flaring assertions of personal integrity, still clamour by their blackboards; still, down a course cleared empty, distracted dogs rush madly; still, before the start for the great race, there broods over that huge concourse an intense, almost a dreadful silence; still there is the shout as the jackets flash from the starting gate, still the hum as they sweep down the bend, the roar as they rush for the straight, the yell as the leader drops back, shoots out, thunders past the judge. All that remains, and will remain. But two changes are insistent. One is the motor cars. The other is the advertisements on the kites. In the old days the downs lay under blue sky and white clouds. Now they lie, on Derby day, under strings of kites. You may go to Epsom to see horse racing, but you will not escape soap, mustard, or pills.

30
SUSSEX

———◆———

E. V. Lucas, 1935 (Revised Edition)

The Downs; Winchelsea and Rye

The Downs are the symbol of Sussex. The sea, the Weald, the heather hills of her great forest district, she shares with other counties; but the Downs are her own. Wiltshire, Berkshire, Kent and Hampshire, it is true, have also their turf-covered chalk hills, but the Sussex Downs are vaster, more remarkable, and more beautiful than these, with more individuality and charm. At first they have been known to disappoint the traveller, but one only has to live among them or near them, within the influence of their varying moods, and they surely conquer. They are the smoothest things in England, gigantic, rotund, easy; the eye rests upon their gentle contours and is at peace. They have no sublimity, no grandeur, only the most spacious repose. Perhaps it is due to this quality that the Wealden folk, accustomed to be overshadowed by this unruffled range, are so deliberate in their mental processes and so averse from speculation or experiment. There is a hypnotism of form: a rugged peak will alarm the mind where a soft green undulation will lull it. The Downs change their complexion, but are never other than soothing and still: no stress of weather produces in them any of that sense of fatality that one is conscious of in Westmorland. Thunder-clouds empurple the turf and blacken the hangers, but they cannot break the imperturbable equanimity of the line; rain throws over the range a gauze veil of added softness; a mist makes them more wonderful, unreal, romantic; snow brings them to one's doors. At sunrise they are magical, a background for Malory; at sunset they are the lovely home of the serenest thoughts, a spectacle for Marcus Aurelius. Their combes, or hollows, are then filled with purple shadow cast by the sinking sun, while the summits and shoulders are gold.

In *The Spirit of the Downs*, by Arthur Beckett, is this tribute to their fragrance and their apartness:

The Downland air is always fresh and pure. It has a quality which elevates the spirits and braces the physical frame. Here you may always find a breeze; even on the hottest day soft, sighing zephyrs fan the face. Pleasant winds on the levels below are here boisterous breezes, and breezes are wild hurricanes.

I know nothing more stimulating than a walk on the Downs when a brisk breeze is blowing. Your strong swimmer may sing of the delights of the sea, but for invigorating enjoyment grant me a tussle with the wild winter wind, or the impudent autumn breeze on the hilltops of high Sussex. Go there on an autumn day, when the clouds are racing across the sky, and run with them. Throw off your starched dignity, put your cap in your pocket and bound across the brow of the hill and down the declivity to the next. Often have I in this fashion drawn the stare of the solitary shepherd moving slowly by the side of his browsing sheep; but no man encouraged by the Spirit of the Downs will mind how mad others may think him when engaged in such joy-giving exercise. As a nation we do not run enough; to this all will agree who have experienced the exhilaration of a chase across the springy turf of the Downs.

In walking through the Sussex Downs from end to end the pedestrian is at once struck with a sense of loneliness. The sensation is akin to the awe that descends upon those who enter a vast, empty cathedral at twilight . . . No noise comes from the plain but the occasional lowing of kine, the shout of a shepherd commanding his dog, the song of the lark. I have walked for days on the Downs without meeting a human being; the builder has been scared away from them, and except for an occasional farmstead in a hollow, or a village at the foot, the habitations of men are hard to find.

Chanctonbury Ring enjoys the distinction of being visible from longer distances than any height in the range; but for the best panoramic views I commend Ashdown Forest, between Wych Cross and West Hoathly and elsewhere, the southern slopes of Crowborough, Chailey windmill, the West Hoathly church public park, Waldron churchyard and Dallington.

Since so many of the great estates date from a time when it was the mode to dwell on low ground, the best views in Sussex are by no means for the rich. There are cottagers on the various ridges who have the whole range of the Downs before their eyes, while everyone occupying that ignominious hamlet called Punnett's Town can feast on the Vale of Heathfield as it slopes greenly down to the marshes and the sea.

The Downs have a human and historic as well as scenic interest. On many of their highest points are the barrows or graves of our British ancestors, who, could they revisit the glimpses of the moon, would find little change. After the Briton came the Roman, to whose orderly military mind such a chain of hills seemed a series of heaven-sent earthworks. Every point in a favourable position was at once fortified by the legionaries. Standing upon these ramparts today, one may imagine one's self a Caesarian soldier and see in fancy the hinds running below for safety.

After the Romans came the Saxons, who did not, however, use the heights as their predecessors had. Yet they left even more intimate traces, for the language of the Sussex labourer is still largely theirs, the farms themselves often follow their original Saxon disposition, the filed names are unaltered, and the character of the people is of the yellow-haired parent stock. Sussex, in many respects, is still Saxon.

*

In the opinion of many good judges Sussex has nothing to offer so fascinating as Winchelsea and Rye; and in certain reposeful moods, when the past seems to be more than the present or future, I can agree with them. We see many ancient towns in our progress through the county – Chichester around her cathedral spire, Arundel beneath her grey castle, Lewes among her hills – but all have modern blood in their veins. Winchelsea and Rye seem almost wholly of the past.

Rye approached from the railway is the suddenest thing in the world. The traveller leaves Ashford, in a South-Eastern train, amid all the circumstances of ordinary travel; he passes through the ordinary scenery of Kent; the porters call 'Rye' and in a moment he is in the Middle Ages.

Rye is only a few yards from the station; Winchelsea, on the other hand, is a mile from the line, and one has time on the road to understand one's surroundings. It is important that the traveller who wishes to experience the right medieval thrill should come to Winchelsea either at dusk or at night. To make acquaintance with any new town by night is to double one's pleasure; for there is a first joy in the curious half-seen strangeness of the streets and houses, and a further joy in correcting by the morrow's light the distorted impression gathered in the dark.

To come for the first time upon Winchelsea at dusk, whether from the station on from Rye, is to receive an impression almost if not quite unique in England; since there is no other town throned like this upon a green hill, to be gained only through massive gateways. From the station one would enter at Pipewell Gate, from Rye, by the Land Gate. The Land approach is perhaps a shade finer and more romantically unreal.

Winchelsea and Rye are remarkable in being not only perched each upon a solitary hillock in a vast level or marsh, but in being hillocks themselves. In the case of Winchelsea there are trees and green spaces to boot, but Rye and its hillock are one; every inch is given over to red brick and grey stone. They are true cities of the plain. Between them are three miles of flat meadow, where, among thousands of sheep, stands the grey rotundity of Camber Castle.

The light above the sheep levels changes continually: at one hour Rye seems but a stone's throw from Winchelsea; at another she is miles distant; at a third she looms twice her size through the haze, and Camber is seen as a fortress of old romance.

Rye stands where it always stood: but the original Winchelsea is no more. It was built two miles south-south-east of Rye, on a spot covered by the sea but now again dry land. At Old Winchelsea William the Conqueror landed in 1067 after a visit to Normandy; in 1138 Henry II landed there, while the French landed often, sometimes disastrously and some-times not. In those days Winchelsea had seven hundred householders and fifty inns. In 1250, however, her downfall began. Holinshed* writes:

On the first day of October (1250), the moon, upon her change, appearing exceeding red and swelled, began to show tokens of the great tempest of wind that followed,

---

* Raphael Holinshed (died c.1580). He compiled *The Chronicles of England, Scotland and Ireland* (2 vols, 1577), the second edition of which (1587) Shakespeare used as the source for many of his plays.

which was so huge and mightie, both by land and sea, that the like had not been lightlie known, and seldome, or rather never heard of by men then alive. The sea forced contrarie to his natural course, flowed twice without ebbing, yielding such a roaring that the same was heard (not without great wonder) a far distance from the shore. Moreover, the same sea appeared in the darke of the night to burne, as it had been on fire . . . At Winchelsey, besides other hurte that was done, in bridges, mills, breakes and banks, there were 300 houses and some churches drowned.

On 4 February, 1287, during another storm the town was practically drowned, all the flat land between Pett and Hythe being inundated. New Winchelsea, the Winchelsea of today, was forthwith begun under royal patronage on a rock near Icklesham, the north and east sides of which were washed by the sea. A castle was set there, and gates, of which three still stand – Pipewell, Land and New – rose from the earth. In 1448 the French came for the last time, the sea having become very shallow; and a little later the sea receded altogether, Henry VIII suppressed the religious houses, and Winchelsea's heyday was over.

She is now a quiet, aloof settlement of pleasant houses and gardens, prosperous and idle. Rye might be called a city of trade, Winchelsea of repose. She spreads her hands to the sun and is content.

Rye, like Winchelsea, has had a richer history than I can cope with. She was an important seaport from the earliest times; and among other of our enemies who knew her value were the Danes, 250 of whose vessels entered the harbour in the year 893. Later the French continually menaced her, hardly less than her sister Cinque Port, but Rye bore so little malice that during the persecutions in France in the sixteenth century she received hundreds of Huguenot refugees, whose descendants still live in the town.

The church, the largest in Sussex, dominates Rye from every point, and so tightly are the houses compressed that from the plain the spire seems to be the completion not only of the church but of the town too. The building stands in what is perhaps the quietest and quaintest church square in England, possessing beyond all question the discreetest of pawnbroker's shops, marked by three brass balls that positively have charm. Externally Rye church is magnificent, but the pity of it is that its encroaching square deprives one of the power to study it as a whole. The clock over the beautiful north window, which is said to have been given to the town by Queen Elizabeth, is remarkable for the two golden cherubs that strike the hours, and for the pendulum that swings in the central tower of the church, very nigh the preacher's head.

Hardly less interesting than the church are the bystreets of Rye, so old and simple and quiet and right; particularly perhaps Mermaid Street, with its beautiful hospital. In the High Street, which is busier, is the George Inn, the rare possessor of a large assembly room with a musician's gallery. One only of Rye's gates is standing – the Landgate; but on the south rampart of the town is the Ypres Tower (called Wipers by the prosaic inhabitants), a relic of the twelfth century, guarding Rye once from perils by sea and now from perils by land. Standing by the tower one may hear below shipbuilders busy at work and observe all the low-pulsed life of the river. A mile or so away is Rye harbour, and beyond it the sea; across the intervening space runs a little train with its freight of golf players.

It is true that Rye has cinemas and is a mark for the charabanger; but after business hours it is an abode of peace and antiquity and the most foreign town in England. It is also the most compressed town in England, and the one which puts up the most determined defence to the builder, who must inevitably pull down something before he can erect anything new. Not an inch to spare is there.

3 1

NORTH WALES

A. G. Bradley, 1898

Snowdon

The view from Llyn Padarn from one part of its banks of Snowdon and the Glydyrs piled up in the sky ahead is very fine. In
the days when the Welsh princes hunted through this country,
and had a lodge at Dinorwig yonder across the lake, it was
beyond a doubt in keeping and sympathy with the grandeur of
the still unspoiled wilderness into which it leads. Now, however, there is too much traffic about it. The tourist even where
thickest does not damage nature so much as is supposed. But
the capitalist is another matter. There were mines working in
Llanberis over a hundred and forty years ago at any rate, but
now the quarrying industry is altogether too much in evidence,
and along the treeless shores of a lake, which in absolute solitude would be impressive, a railroad rumbles with great
commotion, while there is a hum and stir in the atmosphere
generally, and an upheaval and interference with nature that
discount even the majestic and silent background.

Llyn Peris like Llyn Padarn, though for a shorter distance,
fills the narrow valley and must have once been a beautiful
enough spot, grand and solitary. Even now I am not sure if from
one point of view, it is not one of the weirdest scenes in Wales.
Certainly it is one of the strangest. For the whole face of the
mountain for hundreds of feet sheer up from the long smothered and buried banks of the gradually narrowing lake is one
gigantic quarry. The summit of Elidyr Fawr lies back, serene
and quiet, amid the clouds. Nothing is visible here, however,

but its lacerated shoulder, rising to a prodigious height in jagged terraces laid bare by half a century's ceaseless work. It seems as if puny man were determined to expose the very entrails of this great mountain, and one might well fancy it groaning in its agony, for all the ceaseless and horrid din, the rattle of trucks, the shout of countless men, who swarm like ants along the giddy heights, the crash of falling rocks, the creaking of machinery, the roar of blasting, and when a brief interval of silence admits it, the dull splash of some avalanche of loosened debris toppling into the lake.

But now, as we leave the roaring slate quarries and the deep dark water behind us, and pass through the hamlet of old Llanberis, the wild bleak pass that for grandeur travellers hold even above Nant Ffrancon begins to open out. The eastern shoulders of Snowdon are pressing upon our right. Upon our left the western slopes of the Glydyrs rise bare and almost verdureless. The road, which winds for three miles up the narrow gorge to its summit, is admirable, but the wise man will dismount and walk much of the distance, not only for the sake of his interior machinery, but that he may absorb and properly attune himself to the sublimity of the scene. I had known Wales well, for many years, before making the acquaintance of the passes of Llanberis and Nant Ffrancon, and thought I had at least gauged its limitations. But I was mistaken. For here, after losing sight of the lakes and the sound of quarries, and getting fairly into the narrow glen, and breasting the long ascent was a scene more savage, and more awe-inspiring, than I could have deemed possible, in a mountain group so limited in area and in altitude.

It is the great saddleback, the long ridge which Snowdon flings to the north, and up which the main path and also the new railroad travels, that towers such a formidable height above us. The further side is comparatively smooth, but this one is a tumultuous chaos of rock and crag, as if Titans in some burst of fury had been rending cliffs and flinging their fragments far and wide over miles of a slope that is just sufficiently off the perpendicular to lend them a precarious lodgement. The sun on this north-eastern aspect is chary of his beams, and rocks and precipices that under a noonday blaze in a south aspect look stern enough, gather here some additional terror, if I may use the word, from the dark shadows that begin so early in the day to brood over their face. What lends much charm to these wild scenes is the brilliant colouring that fills every space and crevice between the blacks and the greys of rock and precipice. Heather and ferns, sweet turf glittering with the dew of mists and rains, and spouting springs, bog grasses, and the varied fauna of the Welsh mountains bloom and blaze where they can, as if in vain efforts to soften the terrors of the landscape.

It is an hour's steady climb to the top of the pass. The Wyddfa, the main peak of Snowdon, shows from time to time, and a faint white puff stealing along what looks from here like the edge of a mighty precipice, marks the approach of Sir Edward Watkin's little train to its aerial terminus. People talk in somewhat exaggerated fashion, it seems to me, about these mountain railways, and indeed, about all railways in their connection with scenery. By one's fireside the size of a mountain is apt to dwindle, and that of a locomotive to be magnified. But when it comes to the reality, what a tiny speck is this diminutive train on the wide waste of Snowdon, passing in and out of one's vision three or four times in the course of a long summer's day, in its tortuous journey of an hour and a half from Llanberis to the summit. There is a vague impression abroad, and I must confess to having once felt something of the kind myself, that the Snowdon railway would in some sort spoil the mountain, that its solitudes would be desecrated and shaken by the perpetual roar and clutter of a noisy locomotive. If the main line of the South-Western with four tracks, and trains following one another every ten minutes along each, ran over the top of Snowdon it would be another matter. As for this little midget, it seems to me a trifle scarcely worth considering, except for the pleasure it gives to innumerable people who are still possessed of all their faculties, have eyes and brains and every necessary qualification to enable them to enjoy the noblest view on Britain, but may perchance no longer be able to climb 3,560 feet without injury or discomfort.

Even river valleys, the most beautiful of them, such as one has known and loved from childhood, survive the invading railroad. It does not seem to me that the railroad, whether in Wales or the West of England, is in truth the hideous despoiler of nature's charms that it gets credit for. Saving only for a few brief minutes in each day, the old music of the stream still fills the air. The willows flicker on the shining shallows as effectually as when the faint and fitful note of the coach horn was the only sound that spoke of it. The period of construction is, I admit, a lamentable one, but nature after all soon clothes and screens and mellows the new-laid railway track and renders it almost as inoffensive as an average turnpike.

We are now not, however, in a Welsh valley, but on the shoulder of the greatest of Welsh mountains. Crib Goch, the sharpest of its four outlying peaks, a pile of naked rock, springs high above us close at hand. The Wyddfa itself fills the sky upon the south-west, and when the summit of the pass, Gorphwysfa, or 'the resting place', marked by a lonely and homely inn, is at length reached, if rest and refreshment could ever be earned it would surely be here. But this indulgence it would be well to postpone, seeing that a mile's run down, with a drop of 500 feet and a few minutes of back-pedalling, lands the traveller at the equally lonely but more capacious, and in its modern fashion quite historic hostelry of Pen-y-gwryd. Though universally patronised by passing coaches in the season, it still belongs to the order of the snug and friendly Welsh inn as opposed to the caravansary under 'English enterprise' where you become a number and are at the mercy of a young woman from Manchester, dressed in the height of second-class fashion, to whom the neighbourhood of Snowdon is an intolerable exile to be counted by days.

For my part I love these old Welsh inns. It takes a vast deal to spoil them. There are not many left, it is true, in the Snowdon mountains, but Pen-y-gwryd, if not precisely a type of those I am thinking of, has, hitherto at any rate, been of the genus. But I know them well, from Aberdovey to Flint and from Aberdaron to Montgomery. Now I do not like your chilly and pretentious coffee room, where you ring the bell for your modest requirements, and sit upon an anti-Macassared chair looking at a print of Her Majesty's Coronation till a waiter in a white tie brings your change on a silver tray. Give to me, ever and always, the snug parlour behind the bar, where the landlady, in the interval of her manifold duties, takes fitful snatches at her needlework, and the local gossips foregather. And Welsh landladies, I may remark, are generally bright and often very clever matrons indeed, and the best of company. Here let me eat my noonday crust and crack my bottle of Wrexham ale, while the metal horse that wants neither ostler, nor food, nor water waits patiently in the passage.

The inn at Pen-y-gwryd, with its half dozen windswept trees before the door, is an oasis in an indescribably fine wilderness of mountain and moorland. It rests upon the very apex of the ridge that parts the waters going northward by way of the Conway valley, from those that are falling and trickling in every direction from mountain fastnesses towards the west and Cardigan Bay. Backwards we may look down between the long sweeps of Moel Siabod, and the rocky breast of the Glydyrs, to the lakes of Capel Curig glittering in the sun. Ahead of us, and to the west, and far below us, lies glowing in its summer dress the most lovely of the Snowdon valleys, Nant Gwynant. Here as elsewhere, the road is perfect, and a steady downward slope

of three miles might offer much temptation for rapid move-
ment. But to yield in this case would be a scandal and a crime.
Of all views of Snowdon this is the grandest. You really feel on
intimate terms here with the mighty mass for the first time.
You can follow the great bastions it flings so far out to east and
south and west, and from their isolated outstanding peaks trace
the craggy ridges as they climb upwards along the skyline, to
where the Wyddfa lifts far above aught else its shining
precipice.

Beneath us, fed by the stream that like a silver thread winds
through the meadows, sleeps the bright and beautiful lake
Gwynant. Woods blow all around its shores, while the great
spurs of Snowdon rise above to Lliewedd, which is close upon
3,000 feet. For nearly a mile we skirt its shores, longing but
fearing to dally. Two or three boats are drifting with the light
breeze, and patient anglers are absorbed in the no simple task
of capturing short-rising trout on a July afternoon. The stream
breaks out again at the foot of the lake, and hurries on its way
rejoicing down a lovely and fertile glen, and we after it close
beside its banks. A small hamlet, a few farms and well-wooded
country houses squeezed between the hills, and the road
emerges on the shores of Llyn-y-Dinas, a smaller and not quite
so beautiful a lake as the other.

Still following the brawling brook once more released, and
on a highway smothered somewhat in woods, and overhanging
verdure of all kinds, we skim rapidly down towards far-famed
Beddgelert. Upon the right rises a lofty, insulated and wooded
rock. Let us salute it with due awe. It is Dinas Emrys, whither
Vortigern, in despair of making further head against the Saxons
whom he had invited to Britain, retired to brood upon his folly
and his sorrows, and the remains of the ramparts and walls he
raised are still to be seen upon the summit.

The way out of Beddgelert lies along the crystal and foaming waters of the Glaslyn. The deep-cut gorge through which

the Glaslyn and the highway, one of the very smoothest bits of road by the way in Wales, escape from the basin to the great sea levels known as the Traeth Mawr, is held to be one of the sights of Snowdonia. As a geological freak the precipitous cliffs, seven or eight hundred feet in height, have no equal in the country. It is in fact a little bit of Switzerland pure and simple, except that the charming river which resounds in the narrow gorge is happily no foul mud-coloured glacier stream, but of a crystal quality even above, if that were possible, the quality of Welsh streams.

Once out of the gorge, we are clear of the Snowdon mountains, and a great expanse of lush meadows spreads out towards the sea, distant now some half a dozen miles. On our left the great low ground sweeps southward to the oak ridges, beyond which the Dwryd spreads its pleasant streams. All this in the last century was covered with seawater and shifting sands. There was here a famous and royal salmon weir in olden days. Welsh princes held it jealously for their own use, and the English kings as their successors took careful toll of its revenues.

The rod fisher alone now takes toll of the king of fishes, and not a very heavy toll at that. This, however, is taking no account of what wild work is done on winter and autumn nights upon the spawning fish as they lie in the mountain brooks beneath the shadow of Snowdon. For the Welsh peasant is the most inveterate fish poacher in all of Britain, and being greatly encouraged by the sympathy he too often meets with at the hands of the magistrates, and the nominal fines inflicted, he has played sad havoc with many once prolific streams.

3²
SOUTH WALES

A. G. Bradley, 1903

Fishguard and Goodwick; Knappan

It is a prodigious drop from the sea-coast ledge down to Fishguard harbour, and as violent a change of climate as of outlook. Here, in the narrow valley, down which the Gwayne pours its limpid streams through miles of hanging woodlands, flowers and shrubs of southern climes, myrtles, hydrangeas and fuchsias luxuriate in the mellow air. A country house, notable as having been a century ago the abode of Fenton, the well-known historian of Pembrokeshire, with its charming grounds and plantations, embellishes still further the seaward outlet of a glen that for many miles inland is well worth exploring, and may readily be followed on a passable road.

The town of Fishguard crowns the summit of the steep hill beyond. Down here the scene is essentially Cornish – a mountain stream tumbling out of a gorge almost into the sea; a long narrow harbour of green water, walled in by precipitous rocks and overhung by lofty hills; a single long row of old-fashioned cottages with slate-stone roofs and whitewashed walls lining the wharf, while a dozen small sailing craft and a score of boats ride at their moorings.

Such is Fishguard harbour where Napoleon's soldiers intended to land in 1797, but did not, as we shall see. A steep climb of many hundred feet brings one to Fishguard itself, an old-fashioned and somewhat tight-packed little town, with an open space in its centre and various narrow and devious ways leading out of it. Fishguard, however, has witnessed what no other place in England or Wales has seen in modern times, namely the surrender and parade of a French Corps as prisoners of war, and the Black Bull Inn, which was the headquarters of the British force and witnessed the signing of this notable surrender, is still standing.

An outstanding and rocky headland divides Fishguard harbour from Goodwick bay, the last presenting a beautiful picture, as we drop down the long descent on to the only strip of sandy, sheltered beach that all this inhospitable coast can show. It is half a mile long, and is coming into some repute among bathers with the help of recent enterprise on the part of the Great Western Railway. It was on these very sands that General Tate and his fifteen hundred Frenchmen laid down their arms with such cheerful alacrity. It was on the hill to the left, as we descend from Fishguard, that the Welshwomen in their red shawls played that unintentional (or as some say cunningly devised) practical joke on the French, and made them think that the British army was coming up in force.

Goodwick is really a beautiful bay. On the east side a rocky promontory, with an ancient fort upon its point, shoots out a mile into the sea. Upon the west there leaps out seaward the headland of Penainglass, a rugged lofty mass of wood and heather and shining light grey cliff, to whose steep slopes the pretty little watering-place clings.

Of all these modest bathing resorts on the south-west coast of Wales, Goodwick seems to me to be very easily the most attractive. Nor is it any drawback that you can get there by train with reasonable patience; the Great Western having quite recently extended thus far a branch line from Clynderwen, on their main route. The same company are building stone wharves here on a considerable scale, with a view to bringing sea traffic into connection with their line, and rumour says, a new route to Ireland.

These same improvements include also the only modern

hotel of the first class on the whole coast south of Aberystwith. This has been placed, too, in the most romantic situation, at the far extremity of the village, on a ledge in the wooded cliff looking down upon the sea and across the bay, and is already the chosen resort of many Welsh people of taste and discrimination. Newer Goodwick, with its not as yet very numerous residences and villas, runs pleasantly along the terraced way leading to the hotel. Right over Fishguard is the dark mass of Llanllawer mountain, and away to the right, on the horizon, the humpy forms of the Precelly hills, the one really extensive bit of wild mountainous upland in Pembrokeshire.

But Goodwick and its immediate neighbourhood for the moment must claim our whole attention, and above all that French invasion, which is still, after the lapse of a century, such a burning memory.

It is just twelve years since an old woman, one Nelly Phillips, died near Fishguard aged 103. She was nine years old at the time of the great event, and was driving the cows home when she remembered seeing the French frigates first appear off Fishguard bay. I am afraid those fifteen hundred French soldiers who landed on the rocky point of Carregwasted were not very reputable ones, or very formidable warriors. They were under the command of a General Tate, an American, supposed to be a man of enterprise, and a fire-eater. Some of the officers were Irishmen. Some of the men were selected dare-devils, others were released convicts, whose character and situation would make them useful allies for their more respectable and disciplined comrades. Some cynics have affirmed that this expedition was planned by the French Government for the purpose of getting fifteen hundred incorrigible ruffians boarded and lodged at the expense of the British. This would have been a really excellent and profitable joke to have played on a country with which you were at war, and surely a quite legitimate one. But it is to be feared this humorous conception of the affair is not accurate, and indeed it would not do to hint that it was so in South-West Wales, and rob the Pembrokeshire yeomen and the Cardiganshire militiamen of their glory, for the former still carry 'Fishguard' on their standard, and are rightly proud of it.

It was on February 22, 1797, in fine weather, that three frigates and a lugger were observed sailing northwards off St David's, and so close to shore that Mr Williams of Trelethin, who first observed them, and was a retired sea-captain, knew them to be French. They carried, however, the English colours, and would have deceived any other local eyes but those of this agriculturally minded seadog. St David's was aroused, and a considerable body of people headed for Fishguard. The natives living on the cliff-lands were so persuaded that an English flag meant an English ship that the good Mr Mortimer of Trehow-ell actually prepared a supper for the officers, which the French eventually ate. The character and intentions of the visitors were no longer doubtful when the British flag was lowered, and that of the French Republic hauled up in its place. Great then was the confusion and terror of these simple people.

General Tate, his six hundred regulars and nine hundred convicts, known officially as the 'second legion of France', got themselves on shore with the loss only of their guns, on that very evening of February 22nd. Fifty men posted on cliffs above could have made the attempt hopeless. But the fifty men were not there, for the natives were flying inland as hard as they could travel, laden with spoons and bedding and such house-hold goods as carts, horses, and backs stiffened by terror could carry.

General Tate, who seems to have been rather a good fellow, sent his men out the following morning to prospect among the twenty or thirty homesteads that, cut off from the interior by a wild, craggy mountain ridge, lie between the latter and the coast. There were few people left, but plenty of food, and the general took up his quarters at Trehowell, where there was a good supply of claret in addition. A certain amount of looting of a not very baleful character, though rich in humorous and almost bloodless incident, was perpetrated. The main body of the French force were strongly entrenched on a rocky hill above Llanwnda church, and almost within sight of Fishguard across the bay, three miles away.

In the meantime the great news had spread inland like wildfire. By noon the next day, Lord Cawdor, acting for the Lord Lieutenant, was at Fishguard with the Castle Martin yeomanry, some militia and a few volunteers, numbering in all 750. An officer with some experience of war was present, one Captain Davies, and he was entrusted with the task of so drawing up the small British force as to give it the most imposing appearance possible. This the gallant captain did with much success; but the hills around were now crowded with country people. Legend is very positive that Lord Cawdor and Captain Davies utilised the crowds of North Pembrokeshire women in their scarlet cloaks, or 'wittles', and tall beaver hats in their dispositions, and even goes so far as to maintain that they marched a file of them round and round the hill to give the impression of an abundant supply of British infantry coming up to their support. To the amazement of the spectators of this scene, so unforgettable in the annals of Pembrokeshire, and apparently to that of the French themselves, the three frigates were seen to spread their sails and take wing. History has never cleared up this somewhat mysterious abandonment of General Tate and his motley corps, but it has informed us that two of the ships were captured before reaching port, and that one of them, very appropriately rechristened *The Fishguard*, did duty in the British Navy.

*

Reading that quaint and delightful account of his native county by George Owen*, of Henllys, gives us a picture of pasture and corn lands, farms and markets, land tenure and labour, the amount and distribution of game, the comparative scarcity of deer and the extraordinary abundance of 'seeley hares'. But it is on the ancient south Welsh game of Knappan he expands himself at greatest length and with the greatest effect. Those who like to hunt up a radical cause for everything might find perhaps in the pages of George Owen the clue to the problem of why the pick of a handful of south Welshmen, not for the most part educated at public schools, have for years routed the pick of all England at Rugby football.

Knappan was even in our author's time a very ancient game. It was regarded as the best training for war, and was chiefly played, or at any rate survived longest, in Welsh Pembrokeshire and South Cardigan. The game takes its name from the ball used, which was of some hard wood, and well greased for each occasion, and just small enough to be grasped in one hand. The distance between the goals was several miles, running with the ball the chief method, the number of players reaching on occasions the formidable number of two thousand.

There were two classes of these fearsome contests in southwest Wales – 'Standing Knappans', that is to say, regular annual matches on Church holidays between particular districts, and impromptu games promoted by private gentlemen. Nevern and Pembroke, for instance, met every Shrove Tuesday, but the great contest must have been Kemes or virtually North Pembrokeshire against Cardiganshire, which was a regular fixture for Corpus Christi Day. 'At these two plays have often been esteemed two thousand footmen besides horsemen,' the latter an addition which will cause the modern athlete to open his

* 1552–1613; Owen was a lawyer, naturalist and antiquarian.

eyes. But even in the private games the numbers appear to have been quite as formidable, for when two gentlemen had made a match, they proceeded to whip up whole parishes and hundreds upon the principle of 'the more the merrier'. In addition to the multitude of players came 'great store of victuallers with meat, drinks and wine of all sorts, also merchants, mercers and pedlars would provide stalls and booths'.

The fun began at 'one or two of the clock'. And while the two thousand or so players are stripping themselves of everything but 'a light pair of breeches', the author himself, a frequent spectator and former player, reads a little homily on the thoroughly sporting spirit which animates the crowd.

> They contend not for any wager or valuable thing, but only for glory and renown, first for the fame of their country in general, next every particular [individual] to win praise for his activity and prowess, which two considerations ardently inflameth the minds of ye youthful people to strive to the death for glory and fame, which they esteem dearer unto them than worldly wealth.

No actual goal seems to have been requisite in these colossal contests. The ball was thrown off at some central spot, and whichever side carried it furthest into their opponents' country and kept it there till nightfall had the honours.

Running with the ball and hurling it when tackled was the simple principle of this rough and hearty sport. The author somewhat deplores the extreme roughness which had begun to characterise the game within his memory. 'You shall see gamesters return home with broken heads, black faces, bruised bodies and lame legs, yet laughing and merrily jesting at their harms.' Now, he says, 'at this play private grudges are revenged, so that for every small occasion they fall by the ears, which being once kindled all persons on both sides become parties, so that you shall see five or six hundred naked men beating in a cluster together as fast as the fist can go – brother against brother, man against master, friend against friend. Nowadays, too,' laments Owen, 'they will not scruple to pick up stones and use them in their fist.' Then a still greater terror is added to the pandemonium of this 'truly warlike exercise', for the horsemen with their cudgels ride pell mell into the struggling infantry, trampling on their naked feet and dealing blows 'that would fell an ox or a horse', particularly if they see a man to whom they owe a grudge, regardless of whether he have the Knappan or not.

George Owen concludes his description with a 'merry jest touching the same sport', related to the year 1588, when the Spaniards were off the coast with their 'not truly termed invincible Navy'. A great match of Knappan was going on in view of the sea, and a mariner sailing by asked how peace would be restored, and was surprised when he heard it was all a pastime. 'If this be play,' he said, 'I wish the Spaniards were here to see; certainly they would be in bodily fear of our war!'

33

THE WELSH MARCHES

S. P. B. Mais, 1939

Talgarth and the Brecon Beacons

I first came to Brecon by way of Talgarth, a very happy accident. I had never heard of Talgarth. I couldn't even pronounce the name properly. The accent is on the first syllable. I had intended to spend the night nearer Lord Hereford's Bluff, but I was instantly ensnared by Talgarth's complete unpretentiousness. I was surprised to find so large a hotel as the Tower, where I was looked after much better than I should have been in one of those hotels where they charge about five times as much. There is a stream running through the village to join the Afon Llynfi a little beyond the station. The houses are of solid grey stone, and cluster together under the foot of the hills. I found a thirteenth-century tower near the bridge, and in the church, which was a fortified tower once used as a prison, I saw a memorial to Howell Harris, the founder of Welsh Methodism. I was told that Jane Williams, the authoress, was born here, but as her work is unknown to me, I was less interested in that than in the advertisement in a shop window announcing a Gala Week, and asking for help on the Publicity Committee. There was, I gathered, to be a Beauty Queen. The competition for that honour must be pretty severe, for I saw coming in and out of the schoolroom dance-hall bevies of remarkably good-looking girls, all in the highest spirits. There is a fortnightly fair, and pleasure fairs are going on all the time. The inhabitants of Talgarth have no need to use their railway station or bus services to seek entertainment elsewhere. They draw other men and women to them. As soon as I had unpacked, I asked the chemist for the nearest profitable hill, and he directed me to Mynydd Troed. I can recall no hill that provides greater reward for so little effort.

I left the southern hill road after a mile or two, and after reaching a farm at the end of the lane, found myself on the lower slopes of a bracken-covered, steep, open slope which rose to 1,997 feet in about half a mile. I zig-zagged about among the black-faced sheep and found myself going over the right-hand edge, where I suddenly looked down on a secret valley between hills, the presence of which I had never suspected. It was marked on the map as Cwm Sorgwm, and in a patch of green in the hollow stood the solitary, whitewashed farm of Sorgwm. If you want a holiday completely out of the world, you should go there. There must be a track to it, but I could see no road.

I climbed down to the summit over the boulders and stood on top of the world. First I was struck by the amount of water that I saw below. There was the wide sheet of Llangorse Lake, the largest natural lake in Wales after Bala, being five miles round. It is shallow and reedy, but very popular among anglers. Then I looked down the Valley of the Usk, and there were flashes of distant waters showing where the reservoirs had been damned in the hills. Next I discovered that the Black Mountains, which look so grim and black seen from the English side, are in point of fact sepia-coloured. The stone is old red sandstone, and not in the least grim.

Probably the mountains look their best from Mynydd Troed, which is an isolated, elephantine hump standing a little apart, providing an excellent idea of the wild, open moorland of Waun Fach (2,660 feet) and Pen-y-Gader-Fawr (2,624 feet), the highest points of the Black Mountains.

The actual Border runs farther east, almost along the top of the steep, rocky escarpment to the east of the Vale of Ewyas above Llanthony. For a good walking holiday it looked to me as if the Black Mountains would be very hard to beat, but my mind was set westwards on the much grander peaks of the Brecon Beacons, and it was there I decided to go on the morrow.

When I got down to Talgarth, the village boys were sitting on the steps under the ancient tower. There were two girl hikers walking through, and on a distant radio some crooner was telling Talgarth that four blonde women were making him wild.

Next morning I watched the elder children catch the train to school in Brecon and the younger ones in spotless frocks capering up the road to the village school. And after breakfast I went on my way Brecon-wards.

I shall not forget my first near view of the Brecon Beacons. I came on them quite suddenly from a bend in the road. There outstretched before me over the hedge was the great, wild panorama over the intervening, gracious green valley of the Usk. The vivid lush green stopped suddenly at the foot of the hills, and the deep bracken that followed was in its turn succeeded by slopes of greyer hue where the rocks peeped through the worn green, and the shadows formed by the great peaks in the distance were black.

I had no eyes for Brecon itself on this first visit. I was so eager to get on and climb the Beacons that I didn't even see where the cathedral stood. In point of fact it is the only cathedral I know that does not overshadow the city that it controls.

I only spent enough time to telegraph to Weston-super-Mare for the sixteen-guinea Zeiss binoculars that I had regarded as too extravagant when they were under my nose, to buy an inch-to-the-mile ordnance map, and to ask the best way up from the very knowledgeable young man who was knocking two-penn'orth of nails into my boots. He recommended the way of Cwm-Ilwch, so by way of Cwm-Ilwch we went.

That meant crossing the Usk and taking the third turning to the left and later, at a fork of three roads, choosing the middle one. There then followed a most attractive, narrow, high-hedged green lane running alongside a long copse with a stream running through it. This lane got more knobbly and rutty, and eventually petered out into a walled green track of huge boulders. And at the shepherd's cottage at Cwm-Ilwch we parted from the ways of men altogether.

It was a very hot July day, and we pined for milk. Eventually a young woman's face appeared from an upper window. She explained to us that the baby at her breast was only ten days old, that it weighed ten pounds, that the shepherd, her husband, was out at the shearing, and that Gwendolen Jane was looking after the house, cooking, buying the food and so on. As Gwendolen Jane was only six, we could hardly blame her for an absence of milk.

We went on our way thirsty, but fortified by the sight of many cascades in the narrow ravine that led to the very heart of the mountain. One of our number decided on that as the way up for him, on the ground that it was the most direct, the steepest and the wettest.

'I'll have six bathes and beat you to the top,' he said. He did.

I elected to take a more leisurely, circuitous route. I have learnt wisdom in climbing hills. All pleasure goes if you overexert yourself to the extent of not being able to enjoy the reward of the view at the top. So I wandered breast-high through the bracken, beating off as well as I could the onslaught of flies that buzzed round my head.

In shape the hill looks like Snowdon, with great shoulders culminating in a peak above a sheer drop to two little black tarns. There were red screes below the summit. My way was first along a soft green track, then right-handed over a wide, low shoulder of coarse grass, then came a long, diagonal climb along a faintly marked track to a high plateau where the ordnance map masks an obelisk.

This obelisk marks the spot where the body of five-year-old Tommy Jones was found after a search of twenty-nine days. Tommy Jones was the son of the shepherd at Cwm-Ilwch, and had gone out with his father to the shearing on the evening of 4 August, 1900. He wandered away playing happily, presumably through that high bracken. He may just have gone on wandering higher and higher.

As I stood looking up at the summit from the spot where the boy died, I saw it gradually assume the likeness of two faces, an ancient sphinx-like god and a more benign goddess. Both seemed to me to be yearning with outstretched arms towards the earth below. Perhaps, I thought, they were childless immortals, and to appease their want took to their bosoms the small lost child. I felt his presence very strongly as I walked on up the last steeper edge of the corrie. The bather stood proudly on the summit waving his huge alpenstock. He had, of course, missed the obelisk.

The view from Corn Dhu, the first of the Beacons, which stands at 2,863 feet, was tremendous, embracing on one side all the sweet, soft loveliness of the Brecon pasture-lands, with their infrequent, whitewashed farmsteads, and on the other side range upon range of wild moorlands stretching as far as Carmarthen-fan.

Below, on the southern side, in a great gully between the hills, lay the long chain of reservoirs that supply Cardiff and Swansea with their water. A smear of grey smoke stood over the colliery valleys to remind me of the happy fact that work had in some small degree come back to the distressed valleys of the Rhondda and Ebbw.

We lay in a crevice of the rocks out of the wind and ate our luncheon, with our legs dangling over a great precipice. There were whortleberry bushes, but no fruit, and some white flowers that were unknown to me. I was surprised to see some quite wet bogs shining on the southern slopes. My path had been bone dry all that way. I ran on over the little saddleback that separates the two peaks to the slightly higher one of Pen-y-fan, where I encountered several swifts and two other walkers. In all I was there about half an hour, and in that time eleven people passed, so you must not think of the Brecon Beacons as unvisited.

I have a strong feeling that I saw both Plinlimmon and Cader Idris that day. It was a day of exceptional clarity. What clouds there were, were well above the tops of the hills. I lamented all the more the false economy that had made me resist the temptation to buy those Zeiss glasses in Weston. Probably I should never climb the Beacons again, and, if I did, never on such a clear day.

When we got down to the tarn below the red screes, we unanimously decided on a bathe. The two other walkers who had decided on the same project kindly affected to ignore our presence as we dived into the icy, black waters with no clothes on, only to find it crawling with leeches. The bathe was short, sudden, but not brutish. It was ecstatic. It is very curious how infinitely more exhilarating bathing is in absolute nakedness. We had six more bathes in the little pools below the waterfalls in the gully before we got back to Cwm-Ilwch.

That night I went up to see Talgarth church, which has the usual stout Border belfry capable of holding all the villagers during a raid and defending them. On my way back I saw a pleasing scene in the fading light. An egg-tester with a powerful electric torch was submitting each of a thousand or so eggs to the X-ray of his arc lamp. Nearly all the insides of the eggs looked rosy and clean. If they were cloudy or deep red, the eggs were bad.

Then at the bottom of the village I found a very well-patronised flannel dance in progress. I longed to join in. The band was advertised as the Imperial Dance Band, 'recently successful in BBC audition test'. I could have kicked myself for my shyness in not daring to join them, and even when I got to bed I nearly got up again to join in the jollity.

34
HARDY'S WESSEX

Hermann Lea, 1913

[**Editor's note:** in this volume of the series, Hermann Lea assumes the role of literary detective by deducing, where possible, the real places in Wessex that appear (renamed) in Hardy's novels and poetry. Hardy's fictional place names are given in italics for clarity, except in those instances where they form part of a quote from the novel, where they remain in roman type. That style is retained here.]

Tess of the d'Urbervilles

The action takes place over a wide stretch of country – from Salisbury Plain in the north to Dorchester in the south; from the New Forest in the east to Beaminster in the west. In leading my readers over the ground covered by the different scenes, and in pointing out certain towns, villages, houses and natural landmarks, it must be clearly understood that these are merely originals which approximate to the imaginative backgrounds set up by our author. In the volume with which we are now dealing such features have been rendered more realistically than in some others, and accordingly we find little difficulty in reconciling the actual with the ideal.

The story opens by introducing us to John Durbeyfield as he journeys homewards to *Marlott* from *Shaston*, and the meeting with Parson Tringham, which reveals to him that the name of Durbeyfield is synonymous with d'Urberville – obviously a close imitation of the real name of a family now extinct in the county.

We will precede Durbeyfield and enter the village of *Marlott* (Marnhull, more or less). The 'Forest of the White Hart' is an alternative name for the valley which our author occasionally employs. Marnhull would seem to be a corruption of its original name of Marnhill, a more significant title, referring apparently to the white clay or marl which crops up there and which, after exposure to the air, hardens into a freestone. The church and many of the houses are built of it. Marnhull was once quite a considerable place; the remains of many streets may be traced where the houses have entirely disappeared. The dwellings now are curiously disconnected, but new buildings are rapidly springing up, and the village bids fair to assume its old size at no very distant date. Its old notoriety for drunkenness and general debauchery has now passed away, and it is no longer known as 'the booziest place in Dorset'.

Here we meet Tess for the first time, making her way with the other village maidens to the field where the May-dance was to take place. Towards them came Durbeyfield, driving in a vehicle belonging to the *Pure Drop Inn*. This inn figures many times in the book, and may, by its position in the village, be recognised as the Crown. *Rolliver's*, the other inn mentioned, would seem to be suggestive of the Blackmoor Vale Inn on the western and lower side of the straggling village.

The only other feature with which we have to deal at the moment is the old cottage in which Tess was imagined to have been born, but this, alas, appears to have been swept away. From the description of its situation we may assume that it stood at the end of the village nearest to Shaftesbury. At this village, too, Angel Clare comes on stage; and we are made acquainted with Mrs Durbeyfield and the younger children.

The next background in Tess's history with which we are concerned is exhibited when she starts for *Casterbridge* (Dorchester) very early in the morning to deliver the load of beehives. After passing the little town of *Stourcastle* (approximately Sturminster Newton) the road rises steadily towards Hazelbury Bryan – a village we shall visit later.

A few miles beyond *Stourcastle*, Tess and Abraham came in sight of Bulbarrow, rising high on their left hand. It is the second highest point in Dorset. From its summit extends on all sides a magnificent view, the eyes of the beholder penetrating far over Dorset into the adjoining counties. Many places interesting to Hardy readers can be identified from here with the aid of a glass, and amongst others is 'the hill-town called Shaston'.

It is to this place that Tess walks when she goes to visit her reputed relative; and from here she rides in the carrier's van which travelled to *Chaseborough* (nearly Cranborne) and passed near *Trantridge* (suggesting Pentridge – 'the parish in which the vague and mysterious Mrs d'Urberville had her residence'. We may regard this house as purely imaginary, or at least as having been drawn from a model in some other district, for there is no house here answering to the description, though there is one near Wimborne.

We are now brought to the environment of the first real tragedy in Tess's career – when she found herself at the mercy of Alec d'Urberville. *The Chase* (Cranborne Chase) was a chase proper, and must not be confused with a forest – a prerogative of kingly right. It embraces an area of some 800,000 acres and is 'the oldest wood in England'. One may readily wander for mile after mile in this ancient Chase without meeting a single human being; and although certain tracts have been brought under cultivation, there is a tendency for these to revert again to forest. No fitter scene could have been chosen for such an episode.

Subsequently we follow Tess back to *Marlott*, when she meets the text-writer – an individual who is by no means extinct at the present day. On many a gate and stile in the Wessex lanes and byways we may discover evidences of his industry in quotations more or less apt, but nearly all of gloomy, Calvinistic significance.* It is here, at *Marlott*, that her baby is born, and here that it dies and is buried 'in that shabby corner of God's

---

* A real-life example of philosophical, rural graffiti in the early twentieth century is given on this page in the original edition – a photograph, taken by the author, shows an old field gate, on the top bar of which an anonymous Dorset 'text-writer' has written **'HOW SHALL WE ESCAPE?'**

allotment where He lets the nettles grow'. There is no stone to mark the place of burial, and as the churchyard today is scrupulously neat and well cared for, its appearance at the date of the story can only be imagined. Down to the third quarter of the last century, however, such corners were often reserved in country churchyards for that reprobate class of person designated.

Our next scene is at the dairy at *Talbothays*, the location of which has evoked considerable controversy amongst those who have attempted to identify the places mentioned in the Wessex Novels. The description in the novel of the position occupied by the dairy in relation to other landmarks would seem to indicate that, in the writer's fancy, the spot lay at no great distance from the junction of the Dorchester–Tincleton and Puddletown–Ilsington roads, on the southern margin of *Egdon Heath*.

The Froom Valley sweeps through Dorset from above Maiden Newton, till the river empties itself into the tidal estuary at Wareham, and contains the most fertile and valuable land of its kind in the country. Many months, full-charged with happenings, passed over Tess during her stay in the Froom Valley, and here we see the intimacy between her and Angel Clare passing from mere acquaintance to friendship, and from friendship to marriage.

West Stafford Church would seem to represent the place at which Tess and Clare were married. They had decided to spend the early days of their union at one of the ancestral homes of the d'Urbervilles. The way there is now, as then, along a level road that follows the river more or less closely until it nears the village of Wool. Then, turning to the left and passing 'over the great Elizabethan bridge', we come upon *Wellbridge House* (Wool-Bridge House), clearly seen from the train as it enters the station of Wool. It is probable that of all the scenes which occur throughout the Wessex Novels, no place is so near to reality or so familiar to my readers as this house. Inside it may

be found the old mural portraits which had such an effect on
Tess's imagination. Up to the time at which the novel was published they were quite distinct, but since then injudicious
washing with soap to make them clearer has resulted in their
being nearly obliterated altogether, though we can still trace
the gruesomeness attributed to them.

Now comes before us the gloomy scenery of the second
great tragedy in the life of Tess – the result of her confession
of her past. This background is the Abbey of Bindon. The empty
stone coffin of the abbot, close to the north wall, in which
Clare laid Tess is still there, and may be readily discovered,
tourists sometimes giving themselves the grim pleasure of
lying in it as Tess was made to do.

We now come to the places connected with the exit from
Wellbridge and the separation of Clare and Tess. After calling on
the Cricks at *Talbothays*, they drove together through *Weather-
bury* and *Stagfoot Lane* (Hartfoot Lane) until they reached the
village of *Nuzzlebury*, or *Nuttlebury* (suggestive of Hazelbury
Bryan), on the outskirts of the Blackmoor Vale. Some miles
beyond this village they came to a crossroad, and here they
parted. In all likelihood this was just outside the little town of
Sturminster Newton. Leaving Clare for the present, we will
follow Tess as she drives onwards through the familiar Blackmoor Vale until she reaches the entrance to *Marlott*. Thence on
foot she approaches her father's house by a back lane.

Meanwhile, Clare is pursuing his way westwards towards
Emminster (Beaminster). There is a curious custom still in vogue
at Beaminster: on Sundays it is usual for many of the inhabitants to lock their doors when going to church and to leave the
keys in the locks outside. The origin of this proceeding is
obscure, but it may have arisen from the fact that some of the
keys were ponderously heavy. Clare did not stay here long, but
soon left the country for Brazil.

The next place to notice is a dairy near *Port-Bredy*

(approximately Bridport). This is where Tess lives after her new departure from *Marlott*, but when work becomes difficult to obtain she decides to join Marian at *Flintcomb-Ash*.

The actual position of *Flintcomb-Ash* has always been a debatable point with explorers in the Hardy country. To begin with, the farmhouse cannot be pointed out, though such farmhouses do exist in the vicinity. But the actual site which served our author for his description is discoverable. If we will ascend the steep hillside by a track leading out of Alton Pancras village to the eastward we shall soon reach a flat plateau. It is known locally as Barcombe Down. If we now follow along the crest of the hill we shall in due course light upon the ridged turf which marks the site of what was once a British village. For what reason the ancient people of Britain should have selected so bleak and unproductive a spot as this it is hard to determine. Marian described it as a 'starve-acre' place – a title which is truthfully descriptive today. Vast numbers of flints lie uncovered on the chalky surface, making walking no easy matter, while the wind which sweeps over the plain greets the traveller with an unsympathetic touch. There is a sardonic aspect in the landscape, and the scene which stretches before us is all in harmony with the sufferings that Tess endured here.

It was after she had been at *Flintcomb-Ash* some little while that she determined to call at *Emminster* parsonage for tidings of Clare. The road she took was a rugged one, but quite practicable; a glance at the ordnance map will enable us to trace it exactly. From near the British village a trackway descends by Church Hill to the high road; here we shall see a serpentine lane – Barn Lane – ascending the steep hill due westward. At its junction with the Sherborne–Dorchester road we must turn northwards for a little way, when we shall find another lane leading to the left. If we follow its windings and cross the Sherborne–Cerne road at the point called Lyon's Gate, still making westward, we shall pass over High Stoy and come in due course to the stone pillar Cross-in-Hand, or Crossy Hand as it is called locally. This is a walk which many people have taken since the publication of the story, and it will reward the pedestrian with a beautiful and varied prospect, the woodland that lies below to the northward including practically the whole of the background which serves for the novel entitled *The Woodlanders*. The diversity of landscape from right hand to left hand is truly amazing; the utter loneliness, the almost oppressive silence of Nature, add a weird touch which is intensified by coming suddenly upon this solitary landmark, Cross-in-Hand, springing up from the grassy down like the stem of a giant mushroom. It stands before us as being the stone whereon Tess placed her hand when, at Alec d'Urberville's demand, she swore never to tempt him. The occurrence, it will be remembered, took place on her return walk, d'Urberville coming thus far with her, and, after the oath had been registered, leaving her side to plunge into the valley in the direction of *Abbot's-Cernel* (Cerne Abbas). 'Of all bleak spots on the bleak and desolate upland this was the most forlorn,' says our author – an estimate which I can endorse from personal observation; and I can also corroborate his finding 'something sinister, or solemn, according to mood, in the scene amid which it stands'.

Continuing her journey towards Clare's home, she would come in the course of three miles to another high road, called Long Ash Lane; crossing this, she would soon reach the village of *Evershead* (apparently Evershot). The 'cottage by the church' at which she halted and breakfasted is obvious enough to the passer-by today.

After the disasters that succeed one another we follow her with all her family on a migration to *Kingsbere* (Bere Regis). The loading of the waggon with their household goods and their journey along the road describes a scene which can be witnessed in Dorset any year on the 6th of April, when the work-people move from farm to farm, often forming veritable processions along the lanes.

Clare's return to England, his short sojourn at *Emminster* vicarage, and his search for Tess in the last phase of her life-history, gives us another lead through the landscapes. We may follow him as he leaves his father's house and proceeds along Benvill Lane, passes the *King's Hintock* (Melbury Osmund) estates, and the solitary pillar Cross-in-Hand. We track him to *Shaston*, and to the little village in which he was informed that the Durbeyfield family had settled, where he learns that Tess is at *Sandbourne* (Bournemouth).

The description of this watering-place, with 'its piers, groves of pines, its promenades, and its covered gardens . . . like a fairy place suddenly created by the stroke of a wand, and allowed to get a little dusty' is well known, and is almost literal.

It is difficult to trace their flight – there being, of course, no tangible track of a pair avoiding high-roads, and following obscure paths tending more or less northward . . . into the depths of the New Forest.' They are said to have reached the empty house known as *Bramhurst Manor House*. There are many such houses in the environs of Ringwood, but a careful examination persuades me that the mansion bears a strong resemblance, both in construction, furniture and surroundings, to Moyle's Court – once the residence of Dame Alice Lisle, from which she was taken by the myrmidons of Jeffreys to her execution at Winchester. The house, by the way, is said to be still haunted by her spirit.

Their course northwards from here merges into clearness as they approach *Melchester* (approximately Salisbury). They are now close to Stonehenge, the mysterious pagan temple, the greatest sight of its kind in the country. Here they are imagined to have waited till the morning dawned and Tess's pursuers came upon them and led her away towards *Wintonces-*

ter (Winchester). This favoured city, which preserves much of its old-time historic interest, and over which the hand of the vandal has passed lightly, forms the last background we have to inspect. We can go today to the top of the West Hill and find the milestone beside which Angel Clare stood with Liza-Lu, waiting 'in paralysed suspense' for the final signal. But trees have grown up in later years, and it is not possible to obtain from that point now the view that was obtainable at the time of the novel – except in portions.

For the same reason one cannot behold from the milestone – at least, one could not when the present writer was there – the 'large red-brick building, with level grey roofs, and rows of short, barred windows bespeaking captivity' in which 'Justice was done, and the President of the Immortals, in Aeschylean phrase, had ended his sport with Tess.' Perhaps Nature's screening is well.

35

WILTSHIRE

Edward Hutton, 1939 (Second Edition)

Stonehenge

Amesbury is so fair a place and keeps, though hidden in her heart, so many memories that cannot but be sacred to us, that it would surely be far more famous than it is, but that some two miles away westward, half lost in the vastness of the Plain, there stands what when all is said is, I suppose, the most famous monument in the world – I mean Stonehenge. I call it the most famous monument in the world, and indeed what but the Pyramids of the Pharaohs can compare with it for universal admiration; it stands, and will stand, as famous as the Alps and as enduring, a thing imagination boggles at, and to account for it whole libraries of books have not been enough, nor has all the ingenuity of man succeeded in reading its secret.

Of its universal fame, its interest for all mankind, the curiosity of all Europe about it, let this instance suffice. Langtoft* in his *Chronicle* tells us of

> a wander wit of Wiltshire rambling to Rome to gaze at antiquities, and there skrewing himself into the company of antiquarians; they entreated him to illustrate unto them that famous monument in his country called Stonage. His answer was that he had never seen, scarce ever heard of it, whereupon they kicked him out of doors and bid him go home

---

* Piers Langtoft (d. 1307), Augustinian monk and historian.

and see Stonage. And I wish that all such Aesopical cocks as slight these admired stones and scrape for barleycorns of vanity out of foreign dunghills might be handled or rather footed as he was.

If Stonehenge be then, as it is, a universal curiosity, for us Englishmen it is one of the three things in our island – the other two are Land's End and Hadrian's Wall – which each of us must see once in his life; it is a place of pilgrimage very sympathetic to this age, for Stonehenge is the shrine of an unknown God. We go to Land's End half in curiosity, since there we like to think Europe ends westward, half in love and admiration of a place where Nature is so tragically sombre. We got to see the Wall in admiration of great Rome who redeemed us from the brute and began our history. But Stonehenge is beyond such memories and such sentiments as these, it stands wholly within the shadow, over the horizon not only of history, but of legend, an aloof and inexplicable thing rising from the plain between the sky and the grass, the thin grass of the Downs there, over which the wind whistles so dolefully. It stands there we know not why, as the hills do, these low Downs of which indeed it might seem to be the tragic expression and which certainly holds its secret, since they are so populous with our oldest dead. But they keep that secret, and all the wit of man has been too little to resolve it. Perhaps in all our literature there is but one work which seems to give it any sort of utterance – I mean *King Lear*. The heath in the night of the storm which saw Lear's rage and madness can surely have been none other than this enormous downland so subject to the wind and the rage of the sky; nor can any other stones but these have heard the bitterness of the broken heart of England.

Such is the majesty of this sanctuary; and yet it is most often said that at first sight – and especially now that it is fenced with wire – no great spectacle is more disappointing. It is true that the vastness of the Plain, the immense expanse of the sky, dwarfs any work of man, piled though it be by giant hands; but I confess that I have never been able to conceive of the mind which, coming upon this ruin suddenly on that down-side, should not be immediately overawed by its tragic majesty.

But now it has suffered the indignity of being enclosed within a wire fence, with a booth at one side at which one pays to enter the enchanted precincts. Near at hand is a car park, which yet does not prevent numerous motors from ranging themselves all too close to the monument on most days of summer. Motor coaches bring crowds of visitors ostensibly to see the wonders, but certainly not to show any realisation that this is other than a picnic ground. In 1927 it was learnt that there was imminent danger of private building enterprise within sight of the monument, and an appeal was made for funds to purchase as much of the land round it as possible, indeed to preserve what may be described as the skyline of Stonehenge itself. Some £32,000 was raised, and upwards of 1,444 acres were bought and placed under the care of the National Trust, to be kept free from of any kind of building. Within a few hundred yards of the stones there are still the ugly vestiges of the aerodromes placed there during the war; nevertheless the place has not wholly lost its glamour, its sombre air of remoteness and mystery, its ancient dignity.

The entrance of which I have spoken faces the north-east, and it is in such an approach that even yet one gets the grandest view of the great outline of the ruin. Leading up to this entrance is an avenue some seventy feet in width, formed by two low parallel banks with slight outer ditches, running across the down in a north-easterly direction for about six hundred yards. Without the encircling earthwork, but within the long embanked entrance, the vast block of stone known as the Hele Stone or Friar's Heel, some seventeen feet high and now leaning far out of the perpendicular, stands on the line of sunrise.

Just within the earthwork is another large stone, now prostrate, known as the Slaughter Stone. There are two low mounds and two small sarsens on the outer bank, symmetrically placed opposite each other, so that lines drawn across the area from stone to stone and from mound to mound intersect at the centre of the monument at an angle of forty-five degrees. This symmetry is very remarkable, and it is thought that these Four Stations must have had some definite purpose in the whole great design.

The outer circle consisted of thirty huge upright sarsen stones embedded in the ground some three and a half feet apart. Nine feet or thereabout within this huge outer stone circle, which was more than thirty yards in diameter, was an inner circle. Within this inner circle was the great ellipse; within the great ellipse was the inner ellipse; finally, within the inner ellipse stood the co-called Altar Stone, a vast block of micaceous sandstone. (It was upon this stone, I need hardly remind the reader, that Tess slept her last sleep of freedom.)

Of this magnificent monument only the ruins remain, a confusing heap of tumbled stones that local tradition asserts no man can truly number. Of the great outer circle but sixteen uprights and six imposts are standing; of the inner circle but seven remain in position; of the great ellipse there are but two perfect trilithons and two uprights; of the inner ellipse six monoliths remain in position, within which the Altar Stone still lies. Of course some of the stones have disappeared, and anyone may see today a row of holes drilled across the Slaughter Stone preparatory to splitting it up, which was the usual method of breaking. Happily in this case the fell purpose was not carried out.

That Stonehenge has excited the curiosity of historians and archaeologists these many hundred years goes without saying. It is curious, however, that we find no mention of it at all in any history until the middle of the twelfth century. The first

chronicler to speak of the stones is Henry of Huntingdon
(d. 1154), who tells us that 'the second wonder (of England) is
at Stanenges where stones of wonderful size have been erected
after the manner of doorways, so that doorway appears to have
been raised upon doorway, nor can anyone conceive by what
art such great stones have been raised so aloft, or why they
were there constructed.'

Inigo Jones is the first writer to attribute the stones to the
Romans, as Aubrey is the first to give them to the Druids. Perhaps after all Pepys does best, for he tells us he found the stones
'as prodigious as any tales I ever heard of them and worth this
journey to see'. And adds: 'God knows what their use was!'

It is with Stukeley I think that we begin the speculations
of the modern world.[†] Writing about 1740 he asserts that
Stonehenge was a work of the Druids who founded it in 460
BC. Then in 1747 comes John Wood[‡] of Bath. He asserts that
Stonehenge was 'a temple erected by the British Druids about
a hundred years before the commencement of the Christian
era'. In 1783 Dr Johnson visited Stonehenge, and writes to Mrs
Thrale: 'It is in my opinion to be referred to the earliest habitations of the island as a druidical monument of, at least, two
thousand years, probably the most ancient work of man upon
the island.'

How much further than that have we got? Very little. We
seem to be able to assert definitely that Stonehenge is not earlier than the earliest Bronze Age, because we have discovered
a stain of copper oxide upon the root of one of the stones, and
though it is still believed, on similar grounds, that they were
all hewn with the flint, because of that tell-tale stain they could
not, it is thought, have been set up before bronze was known

[†] The Revd Dr William Stukeley (1687–1765), pioneer of field archaeology at
Stonehenge and elsewhere.
[‡] The famous architect – see Chapter 28, 'Somerset'.

in this island, that is to say, not before 2000 BC. On the other hand, as I say, it is still confidently asserted that these stones were hewn with flint axes; and if that is so we have perhaps established a date after which they could not or were not likely to have been thus hewn, that is to say, we must not consider them later than 1800 BC.

Another, and as I cannot but think it, a less satisfactory method of finding the age of Stonehenge, was first suggested in 1770 to Dr Smith, the author of *Choir Gaur: The Grand Orrery of the Druids*. It is founded upon a theory that the stones are the ruins of a temple for the worship of the sun, and that, therefore, it may be expected that they are built with reference to some particular point in the compass, probably with regard to the point at which the sun rises over the horizon at the summer solstice. It is a fact that cannot be denied that, whether it was intentional on the part of the builders or not, a line drawn between the two uprights of the central and tallest of the trilithons, to the centre of the circles, cuts across the Altar Stone at right angles to its length as it lies on the ground, passes between two uprights of the lintel circle, runs parallel to, and nearly centrally down the avenue, intercepting the Friar's Heel standing in the avenue, and when prolonged cuts the horizon on Lark Hill at the point where the sun is seen to rise on Midsummer Day.

Others again not less distinguished consider that Stonehenge was a temple of the cult of the dead. There is no reason to believe that Stonehenge was itself a burial place, but few visitors can fail to notice the many burial places in the form of barrows congregated within sight of it. With a few exceptions these are round mounds of Bronze Age date, and it seems reasonable to suppose that these numerous barrows were made in its near neighbourhood because of the reverence in which Stonehenge was held. However, it is certainly not impossible to take the other view, that the monument was placed here because, for some reason unknown to us, this area had long been a favourite burial ground.

All such theories are interesting and exciting, but they seem to be incapable of any demonstration. We know nothing of Stonehenge. Its age is uncertain. Its purpose is inscrutable. We salute the stones as we shall salute death, not without dread, and we may as soon say what death is as what these are. Darkly they stand, all broken and clean smitten with age, and worn by the wind and the rain of unrecognised millenniums. What ice has striven to break them? What primeval winds have been wrapt about them like endless banners? What rains have beaten upon them in vain? What centuries of summers have covered them with untold glory?

36
YORKSHIRE

Arthur H. Norway, 1899

Rievaulx Abbey; Swaledale

As the road drops down towards this broken country, a small gate upon the left admits me to a little wood. I pull the bell, and there comes to meet me one who takes a shilling, and leads me through the trees out on what I conceive to be the noblest stretch of turf in England. In full view of the valley curving round beneath the hill in the direction whence I came, far, broad and level, this glorious green sward extends along the hillside, winding as the valley does, soft and springy to the tread like the turf of a sea cliff, and sweet as that is with wild thyme and vetches, and numberless small creeping flowers. This green mead is bathed in the softest golden sunshine up to the very borders of the heavy woods that bound it on the left, while on the right a scrub of bushes falls with a swift descent into the deep valley.

Over this fringe of coppice one looks down upon the narrow meadows of the bottom, drowsing green and gold in the shadow of the trees and hills, and, set among these sweet pastures like a lovely jewel, stand the grey ruins of the ancient abbey. It is late afternoon, and the valley brims up with golden light, the old broken vaults and arches gleam, and over the hill-top one or two sharp crumpled peaks thrust themselves up against the sky, the broken summits of the Hambledons.

I doubt if all the hills and vales of England can show another scene of such wild and solitary beauty. One may sit all day upon the hillside even now, seeing no sight but the changing of the shadows or the trooping of the deer over the wide hill pastures; hearing no sound but the murmurs of the wind and water just as the monks heard them long ago. And if one sits and ponders thus, suddenly it becomes clear how vast a courage and how strong a faith must have been needed to set the first walls of the monastery in this lovely hollow, in an age when the gaunt moors all around were haunted by outlaws, and lay open to the raiding Scots, and when the bonds of society in this northern land, shattered by successive invasions of the Danes, had been torn up root and branch by the ruthless vengeance of the Conqueror. There was worse than solitude among these mountains then, and the perils which the monks came out to face were exactly those which beset a colonist today, in a wild, unsettled land.

Well, they faced these perils – a poor handful of Cistercian monks, coming with the blessing of St Bernard to live the new life of stern and abstinent labour among the lax monasticism of the English Benedictines. They came to testify, and did it nobly, in this lonely valley.

Day by day they saw the sun break over the black moors or heard the storm wind singing over the rough snow, while their buildings rose fair and stately in the wilderness, till at length the valley was no longer dark or silent; and the lost traveller who came stumbling over the highlands to the brow of the Rye Vales looked down on the white-robed monks toiling actively upon their fields, or saw the darkness of the evening pierced by beams of warm light from the windows of the church, heard the sound of chanting on the still air, and pressed forward with renewed strength till he knocked at the fair gateway and was admitted by a brother, who fell on his knees, as was the rule with the Cistercians, and thanked God for sending a weary stranger to rest within the gates.

Come, let us go into the valley. A broken, winding path descends through the steep woods into a lane which ends in a tiny hamlet, built on the abbey precinct. Just beyond it are the ruins, the nave no better than a string of mounds which no one has cared to dig out; the transepts fairly perfect, the lovely choir lacking little but the springing of the roof to restore it to its former state. Apparently there are few who love or care for this exquisite fragment of a noble building. Overgrown with nettles and briars, defiled by cows, the abbey of Rievaulx stands a bitter impeachment of our title to impugn carelessness in other nations towards their ancient monuments.

I would have everyone who visits Rievaulx go down the hill from the little hamlet, and, passing by the pretty rose-clad cottages and the gardens full of stocks and peonies, cross the river by the old stone bridge, just where a mill leat rushes down to join the main channel of the stream. It is the bridle road to Coxwold which runs up the hillside from this bridge; after following it for some distance one may turn off by a gate at a keeper's cottage on the left, and trudge up through a rough lane ending in a wood, where the hillside is gashed with deep valleys of fern and shady coppice. As one mounts upwards by the rugged path, under the scrub of oaks and beeches, one is drawn continually to stop and turn, so exquisite are the gradual unfoldings of the valley depths. One moment it is no more than the mill-house which one sees against the shoulder of the green hill, the next turn brings in sight a corner of the grey ruins gleaming over the fresh grass; and a further climb throws open the whole depth of the valley bottom, a sea of verdure filled with golden light, so still that one can hear the river running over stones below, while the grey ruin stands up solemnly in the middle of the valley.

Just so, one thinks, so perfect and so beautiful, it may have looked on that still evening long ago when a monk who had travelled all day stood upon the hillside and gazed down into the valley. He had wearied of the strict rule of the abbey where he dwelt; had grown restive under the hard labour and the silence and the nightly penance in the church, and had slipped away ere dawn and gone out beyond the abbey bounds, which no monk might do, and sped away into the woods like a bird escaping from its cage. And so he wandered till the sun sank, and the taste of freedom grew bitter in his mouth; and at last, not knowing where he was, he came out on the hillside, and saw a fair abbey glowing in the evening sun, and heard the bell chiming for vespers, and went down and knocked at the gate with a beating heart, and lo! it was his own abbey of Rievaulx to which God had brought him, and his own home which received him back into its peace again.

*

I come at last in sight of the old square-towered church of Grinton, set beside the stream at a spot where dale and river both divide, Swaledale throwing out an arm which takes the name of Arkengarthdale, from the tributary stream that winds among the narrow pastures left below the rugged range of hills. There is an old stone bridge, in the shadow of whose buttresses the trout lurk idly on these summer mornings; and from that spot it is but a little distance to the sloping irregular expanse of green, round which is built, in a somewhat purposeless way, the little town of Reeth.

I am sorry that in this solitary townlet I could find nothing worthy of comment save a pig. Pigs, as Friar Middleton* knew to his cost, are not in all cases beneath the dignity even of

---

* Friar Middleton is a character in 'The Ballad of the Felon Sow', quoted by Sir Walter Scott in his 1813 poem *Rokeby*. Sent from Richmond with two others to fetch the notoriously foul-tempered sow ('the grisliest beast that ere might be'), Friar Middleton attempts to calm her by reading from his Bible; however, 'The sow she would not Latin heare, But rudely rushed at the freare.' Having been forced to shelter up a tree, Friar Middleton and his two comrades eventually flee for their lives back to Richmond to tell the tale of the 'fiend of hell'.

verse; and it would be mere folly to conceive my own poor prose too lofty to concern itself with them. Besides, there may be those who give no credit to the tale of the Felon Sow, but read it with a shrug of wonder at my ready faith in the prowess of a beast which usually frightens only rather small boys. If such there be, I beg them to go to Reeth, where they will find in the piggery of the Buck Inn a beast which will restore their faith in Friar Middleton and me, in addition to curdling their own blood with fear, if it be let out into the yard for their greater admiration, as the too kindly owner did when I beheld it.

I do not mean to dwell on this incident, nor to comment on what occurred when this large and fearsome beast, 'rug and rusty' like her prototype, began to sniff about the yard. I prefer to let the whole matter pass. Life is too short to tell the tale of our defeats, and how I fled from the field of battle is nobody's business but my own.

The road to Buttertubs climbs and climbs with a deadly steepness which one might pardon were it possible to boast of having attained any height when, breathless and exhausted, one lies full length upon the heather at the top. But Great Shunner Fell is little more than a poor two thousand feet, and Lovely Seat, which faces it, is even less. Why, then, can one not get up without all this pother? I am told it is a very ancient byway; and that may be true, for it is certainly decrepit, and is not likely to be restored to health by any such desultory sprinklings of sharp-pointed stones as I found strewn about its surface, unless by persuasion or by force more travellers can be induced to cut their boots upon them than are disposed to use the road at present. In sober truth I met nothing but a sheep, until, coming out upon the very summit, I turned a sudden corner of the rock, and found reclining in the cleft a battered grey old shepherd, musing through the afternoon upon God knows what, while his pipe sent up a blue curl of steady smoke, and his collie stood at bay and snarled at me a few yards further on upon the path. The fellow looked at me with a half-humorous smile. Had he spoken, I should have lit a pipe and sat down beside him, glad to chat with anyone upon that lonely height. But he offered me no greeting; and I went on past the growling collie, while all the thin air of the vast solitude was pierced by the pitiful crying of a lamb somewhere in the valley bottom far below; and, presently, looking backward on my path, I saw the shepherd plunging down the side of the ravine in search of it.

A little way before I reached the summit of the pass — before, that is to say, I had risen high enough to see the wide mountain country which lay beyond the green fells over which I was climbing, I found by the wayside the first of those circular chasms in the limestone which give the pass its name of Buttertubs.† Cool, dark and cavernous, they are deep, black pits, walled by very strangely splintered limestone, standing now in crumpled pillars towering out of the sheer depth, now breaking into fantastic shapes of every kind, with here and there a flowering alder, or a mountain ash growing out of a crevice, or some sweet white flower straying fearlessly down into the abyss. Into the largest of the Buttertubs there trickles down a little stream, sobbing quietly enough as it oozes out of the long grass and struggles through the boggy patch between the slope and the descent; but plunging down the dark chasm with a kind of startled cry which sounds eerie in the great silence of the fells, and so drips out of sight among the shining liverwort, and falls in spray into the bowels of the earth.

Each green ridge attained reveals another, till at length there projects above the grassy slopes something blue and sulphurous and distant which is clearly no part of Shunner Fell; and quick-

---

† Farmers going to market rested here and lowered tubs of butter into the potholes to keep them cool in hot weather.

ening my pace, I find I have reached the top; and standing in the clear air and sunshine underneath the noisy larks which mount and mount even from that high ground as eagerly as from any cornfield in the country, a wilderness of blue ridges and of shadowy summits, basking in the steady light of the afternoon, and stretching infinitely far into the west, with alternation of crumpled hollows and wide open valleys gashing the mountainsides, where my eye loses itself in mazes of green pasture land. There stand the huge flanks of Ingleborough, that flat-topped table mountain on whose plateau old nations in forgotten days kept watch and refuge; and there too is the elongated ridge of Whernside, and the humps of Pen-y-Ghent among a crowd of other summits less well known, but notable and fine. It is a wild and lonely scene.

Index

INDEX